WITHDRAWN

STALIN'S RUSSIA

A volume in the Historical Reconsiderations Series
HERMAN AUSUBEL, *General Editor*

Stalin's Russia

AN HISTORICAL RECONSIDERATION

Francis B. Randall

THE FREE PRESS, New York
COLLIER-MACMILLAN LIMITED, *London*

Copyright © 1965 by The Free Press
A DIVISION OF THE MACMILLAN COMPANY
Printed in the United States of America

All rights reserved. No part of this book may be reproduced or utilized in any form or by any means, electronic or mechanical, including photocopying, recording, or by any information storage and retrieval system, without permission in writing from the Publisher.

Collier-Macmillan Canada, Ltd., Toronto, Ontario

DESIGNED BY FRANK E. COMPARATO

Library of Congress Catalog Card Number: 65-18559

Frontispiece: U. S. Army Signal Corps

TO *Geroid Tanquary Robinson*

AND *Frank Tannenbaum*

CONTENTS

1. The Problems, 1
2. The Man, 14
3. The Rise, 39
4. The World-View, 64
5. The Power, 96
6. The Terror, 121
7. The Villages, 144
8. The Cities, 171
9. The Minorities, 203
10. The Culture, 234
11. The War, 259
12. The End, 286

   Notes, 295

   Bibliography, 311

   Index, 319

I. THE PROBLEMS

*S*TALIN was probably the most important man who ever lived. For thirty years he was master of the dozens of peoples and millions of human beings who live in the Union of Soviet Socialist Republics. He constructed a system of rule as absolute as any in history and far more total in its scope than any save that of his imitators. He transformed the USSR in one generation from a largely agrarian country into the largest industrial state in the Old World. This was probably his most important achievement, for industrialization is the most fundamental revolution in human affairs since the domestication of plants and animals. Stalin presided personally over most of the crucial stages in the industrialization of a major society. No one else, not even Mao Tse-tung, can make quite that claim.

Stalin was the first to industrialize a country by that thoroughly statist means which he and most others called "socialism"—thereby setting a pattern for much of the world.

He fought and had the chief share in winning what we hope will remain the most horrible war in history, and he emerged with the greatest gains. He conquered half of Europe for Communism, provided the inspiration if not the means for the Communist victory in China, and directed formidable Communist movements in dozens of countries. In much of Eurasia he was directly responsible for interrupting the development of the intellectual and cultural life of modern Europe and America, and for constructing instead a very different "socialist" culture. Quite aside from the wars, he killed several million people. Stalin will probably go down in history as one of the two or three worst men who ever lived.

No one could have predicted such a career. His achievements were staggering, even when overshadowed by the superficially more spectacular career of Hitler. When he died he had for years been officially described as "the genius leader of the peoples of humanity" by all Communists save the Trotskyite and Titoist heretics. From this pedestal he has been literally and figuratively toppled by his successors, notably Khrushchëv. In Stalin's last years many Westerners, especially in America, regarded him as an archfiend morally equivalent to Hitler. We say this less often nowadays, probably because we now know that he was not to start World War III, and that parts of his system *could* be dismantled. In the next few decades he may well fall even lower in the official and unofficial esteem of his countrymen. It is difficult to see how he can rise in the estimation of the West.

Among Communists the evaluation of Stalin is at least as partisan and emotional an issue as it was when he lived. The Soviet government expresses a more balanced view of him now than fifteen years ago, but scarcely a more dispassionate one. In the West, however, he really is receding into the past —very slowly, but very surely. As long as there are men alive who witnessed what Stalin did, his career will remain a touchy subject for historians to venture on. But now, more than a dozen years after his death, when a number of historians *have* ventured there safely, it is clear that they can remain true at once to their craft and humanity, that they can discuss even Stalin's Russia dispassionately but not disengagedly, without prejudice but not without judgment. We have reached the time when we can reconsider Stalin's Russia.

Anyone who writes on Stalin's Russia must tackle a number of knotty historical problems. The first problem must be the justification for yet another book on the subject. Tons of worthless material have been produced but several thousand pounds of good and even excellent books have also appeared. Valuable lives of Stalin and histories of one or another aspect of his Russia have been published in many Western languages since at least 1930. Since the end of World War II the serious presses of the West have given us hundreds of books which in sum tell us more than most of us wish to know about Stalin's Russia. A generation ago Churchill said that Russia was a riddle wrapped in a mystery inside an enigma. But now Harry Schwartz of *The New York Times* can properly correct him by saying that Russia is a land of many secrets but few enigmas.[1] We can hardly desire more thoroughly researched, more comprehensive, and more intelligent books than *How Russia is Ruled* by Professor Merle Fainsod of Harvard University,[2] or *The Communist Party of the Soviet Union* by Professor Leonard Schapiro of the University of London.[3]

"Reconsideration" in the subtitle of this study does not mean the author claims to be opening a new era in Russian studies. It certainly does not mean a "rehabilitation" of Stalin. The author has had no private access to the Kremlin archives, and cannot claim to present a large mass of new and unpublished material. A relatively short book such as this cannot be a full scale biography of Stalin, or a history of his Russia, or an analysis of his system. It is a discussion, in topical rather than chronological order, of a number of problems concerning Stalin and his Russia which the author has found most important and controversial in fifteen years of study, teaching, and writing on the subject. It is not intended to be deliberately provocative, but where the author holds a disputed or a minority position he wishes to state it strongly.

The most important problem, and probably the knottiest, is the question of how much Stalin mattered, personally. The major thesis of this work is that Stalin's Russia really was *Stalin's* Russia. He did not rule all things directly by his will, like Jehovah of old, but it will be maintained here that most of the important events and changes in Russia for thirty years took place because he wanted them to, and in roughly the form that he wanted them. Of course he was limited by outside forces such as Hitler, by his many miscalculations, and by the dead weight of the resistant human material he was manipulating—but less so than any other man in history. To an amazing extent the answer to many historical questions— why was a given army moved? a given factory built? a given novel published?—is that it was the will of Stalin. The real historical question, in surprisingly many cases, is why Stalin came to will it.

Readers may wonder who doubts this thesis, since it is simple enough and is explicitly or tacitly subscribed to by the bulk of the daily press as well as the man in the street. But that is just the point: This emphasis on Stalin's efficacious personal dictatorship is disputed by a majority of the historians and other social scientists of the Western world precisely because it seems too simple.

During the first twenty years of Stalin's rule (and to this day in Europe) the very numerous Marxist and Marxist-influenced observers were reluctant to think that one man could accomplish so much unless he were the expression of "broader" and "deeper" economic "forces." Since World

War II economic interpretations have become less obtrusive, especially in America, but they have been succeeded in some degree by emphases on group politics, lobbies and pressure groups, choices between limited alternatives, dilemmas of leadership, and bureaucratic circumscriptions. In such excellent works as *The Governmental Process* by Professor David Truman of Columbia University, it has been shown that a Western leader like the American President has only a limited chance to make a number of particular choices between alternatives presented and circumscribed by many overlapping pressure groups, and that he cannot really secure the passage of a bill to relieve unemployment, for instance, on his own, much less eliminate that problem.

No one claims that Stalin was as limited as an American President. But analogies are drawn. One scholar or another has referred to Stalin as "a prisoner" of his ideology, or of the Communist Party, or of his bureaucracy, or of his system of terror, or of the process of industrialization, or of geographical conditions. Some scholars see Stalin as the victim of "dilemmas of power" or of "irreversible processes."[4] In contrast to all this, the comparative freedom and broad scope of Stalin's decisions will be emphasized here.

Many important interpretive questions can be subsumed under this overriding point. Did Stalin do what he did because of some paranoid neurosis or psychosis? Clearly he was paranoid to some degree, and it is not unimportant to ask how paranoid he was, even if we cannot tell. Although paranoia is not an outside force like the Russian climate or the Communist bureaucracy, Stalin's alleged victimization by it has analogies to his alleged victimization by other things.

Was Stalin a prisoner of Marxist-Leninist ideology? Clearly he was a "true believer" if ever there was one. Those who dealt with Stalin under the impression that his Communism was meaningless verbiage or a smokescreen for some kind of rational interest often suffered disaster. But there was a great difference between the position of a Communist ideologist living within reach of Stalin's heavy corrective hand, and that of Stalin himself, who claimed and exercised the right to adapt Marx and Lenin to changing circumstances, and who could remember them and interpret their writings as his own psyche required.

Was Stalin merely the bureaucrat-in-chief during an age of inevitable bureaucratization, which must afflict all stable modern states? Was his obsession with Communism merely the delusive ideological covering under which, unrealized by him, a particular party-organized variety of all-encompassing bureaucracy was growing? Was he simply the man who happened to preside over an irreversible process of bureaucratic industrialization, through which every "new country" in the world must pass? Stalin found it beyond his powers to make his bureaucracy honest and efficient. But does this mean that he could not have checked its growth? Or that he could not have brought about a very different kind of industrialization? Perhaps the other new countries that try to industrialize on the bureaucratic Russian pattern do so in conscious imitation of Russian success, not out of deterministic repetition.

Was Stalin's entire rule destined to be a bloody terror in consequence of Lenin's fatal decision to seize and hold power by force and violence in a country that did not support him? This was a favorite judgment of many of the non-Bolshevik Russian revolutionaries, notably Viktor Chernov and Alexander Kerensky.[5] In most forms this theory preserves a moment of freedom for Lenin, although not for Stalin. It is highly possible that the horrors of the Russian Civil War and the Cheka were the results of Lenin's decision to seize power, but it seems difficult to insist that, say, the great purges were the inevitable outcome of what Lenin had done twenty years before.

Did Stalin have to do what any ruler of the Russian land mass would have had to do during the same period, when faced with the same "geopolitical realities"? Doubtless any Tsar or democratic Russian leader would have attempted to keep the country unified, and to build up its economy and military strength. But to such an extent? And would every other Russian leader have done what Stalin did to bring Hitler to power, and to help him launch World War II?

These are all complex questions, and they are often raised with suitable complexity. The oppositions are never absolute. No serious scholar holds that Stalin was completely the tool of deterministic forces any more than the author holds that Stalin was a totally free agent. It is usually a matter of comparative emphasis, and it is often a matter of semantics. But a serious issue remains between those who make such remarks as, "Stalin *had* to engage in a rapid program of industrialization involving heavy human costs," or "Stalin was *compelled* to ally himself with Hitler in 1939," and those who do not. It is fair and meaningful to ask for the identity of those who would have removed Stalin from office in 1929, had he seriously wanted to pursue a slow and mild program of industrialization. And if Stalin had insisted on killing no one during the late 1930's, just who or what would have *forced* him to murder hundreds of thousands of people? And if Stalin had refused to sign a pact with Hitler, just who would have twisted his arm until he motioned Molotov to take up his pen? And if Stalin had desired to adopt a different military strategy during World War II, or even to make a disadvantageous peace, just what cabal of generals or anyone else would have deposed him and fought precisely the war that happened?

Far more rides on these questions than the interpretation of Stalin's rule over Russia. In some ways they raise the old problem of determinism and free will in human history. When those who tend to minimize Stalin's personal role are not determinists, they are often supporters of the view that a multitude of chaotic, contingent, mutually contradictory petty chances and human wills defeat large scale, rational, individual human effort. In most of history the latter is certainly the case. But in *all* of history? It takes only one negative instance to overthrow a general rule. At first glance it seems that Stalin, more than any other man, might have "made history." If scholars can show that he did not, then it will be hard to think that anyone can. In a paradoxical way, the cause of human freedom rides with Stalin: if he was merely a creature of circumstance then in a way it is a defeat for us all. But if Stalin really was the mighty tyrant who murdered millions who might otherwise have survived, and who moved mountains that might otherwise have stood in place, then some day someone else may do as much in a better cause. In this way, at least, Stalin was a triumph of the human spirit.

Another whole set of knotty problems derives from a question that antedates Stalin's Russia: Can socialism work? If one merely asks the question in its original form, then Stalin showed that a government can indeed run an economy and produce goods without grinding to an absolute halt. The more important variation of the question is the one asked in all the new countries of the world: Did Stalin find a faster and better way to industrialize a backward area than the traditional capitalist method? While the elites of the new countries puzzle it out in different ways, Western scholars tend to conclude that Stalin's Russia was in a fundamentally different position from all other backward countries, and therefore provides a very poor model to follow. They tend to say that Stalin did not so much increase the rate of industrialization in the USSR as distort it, forcing a rapid growth in heavy and military industries at the expense of light industry and agriculture. They also say that worldwide catastrophes—the great depression and World War II—made Stalin's reign so special a period that analogies are hard to draw, and that the question can hardly be answered in the spirit in which it is asked.

A related question—although many socialists would deny it—is whether a terrorist dictatorship can work in a modern society. Again, it is clear that Stalin could in fact survive. But did his immense terror help him, or prevent him from accomplishing his other aims? It is now generally agreed on both sides of the Iron Curtain that Stalin often used more terror than was necessary. But that leaves the harder question of whether *some* terror was not necessary to preserve his rule, to build the economy, and to defeat Hitler. This problem is at least as difficult morally as it is historically. If one fails to prove that large scale coercion was unnecessary to build up Russian heavy industry and military strength rapidly in the 1930's, then one comes close to admitting that terror in Russia was necessary for the defeat of Hitler—and that is the core of the case for Stalin and his methods.

The ultimate question about socialism is whether or not it is desirable. Conservatives feel that Stalin answered this question. Many others do not think that Stalin's Russia provided a fair test.

Sooner or later one must come to the knotty problem of sources. There are mountains of material to plough through. Most of it is official Soviet documentation, however, so shot through with systematic deception and self-deception that no statement in it, however true, can be accepted merely because it appears in a Soviet document.

Nevertheless, by carefully sifting Soviet materials, foreign historians have been able to establish most of the important facts. Visitors from outside have provided helpful checks, especially during the 1920's when they were most numerous and most freely spoken to. Those revolutionaries who were exiled from the USSR during the 1920's, from Trotsky down, told many inside stories. Prisoners and slave laborers captured by the Germans during World War II were usually in more humble positions, but their stories about daily life in Soviet factories and farms were just what we needed to hear. On rare occasions uncensored archives have fallen into the hands of foreigners, from the time Herbert Hoover's agents collected the files of the abandoned Russian embassy in Budapest in 1919 to the time the German Army captured the records of the Smolensk provincial government when that city fell in 1941.[6] Survivors of Stalin's Russia, from Khrushchëv to the dissident novelists, have spilled many beans. But the bulk of our information comes from materials published under official censorship in the USSR during Stalin's lifetime.

Even Stalin's government could not manage to publish nothing but lies. The overwhelming bulk of the published information, from weather reports to the texts of laws, was "true." To instruct its own citizens and its own agents, the Soviet state had to turn out a huge quantity of accurate material. But one could never be certain that the weather reports might not be concealing a drought in the Ukraine, or that the legal gazette might not have suppressed an administrative order expanding the powers of the secret police. Unfortunately for historians, Stalin was most thoroughly secretive and deceptive about the two classes of information most vital to history: statistics, and inside political decision-making.

The concealment and distortion of statistics under Stalin was more extreme than in any other regime in history. Millions of figures were kept secret on grounds of military security, starting with the most basic figure of all, the population of the USSR. From the First Five Year Plan the regime had committed its prestige to economic successes; when these successes were not uniformly forthcoming Stalin gave in to the temptation to publish inflated production figures. Eventually the regime was so sucked into this quagmire of deception that it had to issue "percentages of increases of production" rather than hard quantitative statistics.

Western scholars were able, nevertheless, to calculate Soviet statistics with a remarkable degree of accuracy. They employed the time-honored methods of the historian: comparing earlier reports to later reports, national figures to provincial figures, "self-critical" documents to propaganda documents, slips of the press to smooth diplomatic presentations, and so on. A group of scholars headed by Professor Abram Bergson of Columbia University was able, even before Stalin's death, to estimate most of the leading indices of Soviet national income and product from 1928 forward.[7] They were soon gratified to see their remarkable intellectual feat confirmed in almost all details by the long critical speeches of Malenkov and Khrushchëv on Soviet industry and agriculture, delivered in 1953 and 1954. In the long run, Stalin failed to conceal his statistics.

The matter of inside political information is more intractable. We know much of what Stalin did, but we are much less well informed about why and how he reached his decisions. An historian of, say, Franklin Roosevelt's America could read Roosevelt's letters and internal office memos, interview family, friends, and fellow workers, judge the accounts in many personal and political memoirs, and otherwise secure a variety of intimate pictures. None of this was possible in Stalin's Russia. Stalin rarely granted interviews to outsiders, and never took off his mask. His private letters, notes, and memoranda may never have been very intimate to begin with, and if they survive they are safely locked up in Moscow. None of Stalin's associates, if they were still alive, dared say anything significant to an outsider—certainly not after 1934—and none of them dared write the kind of private letter or diary that one looks for in other countries. Trotsky in the 1930's[8] and Khrushchëv in the 1950's[9] partly filled the gap, but a vast empty space remains at the very heart of the historical process in Stalin's Russia.

We are left with Stalin's plentiful official pronouncements, which were parroted by everyone else in the USSR. They were *very* official, impersonal, bureaucratic, patriotic, and ideological. The last is our chief clue. The most sincere, revealing, and serious parts of Stalin's speeches and writings were the ideological expositions. For a long time Westerners were unwilling to believe that Stalin could really have been motivated by the ideological chains of reasoning he exhibited when justifying his various moves. But in the last twenty years a number of Western scholars have found this hypothesis worth investigating (among them Professor Geroid Tanquary Robinson of Columbia University, with whom the author was fortunate enough to study).

The word "ideology" is used in many overlapping senses. Here it is taken to mean a developed, systematic, allegedly rational, total world-view of nature, man, and society, such as the one the mature Stalin spent so much time expounding. Much of his ideology he inherited from Lenin. Some of it he consciously generated on his own authority. Much of it was the product of implanting his own views on diverse subjects, from Arctic explorations through abortions to chess openings, in a "Marxist-Leninist" setting. It is tempting to think that Stalin really took his ideological system seriously, and that he really did formulate many of his practical decisions in ideological terms, as he always said he did. No ideology can be a complete guide to all particular actions a man has to decide upon. Stalin had to interpret ideological texts, to apply general ideological principles to specific situations, and to choose which aspects of his ideology to emphasize in a given decision. But he claimed that he considered everything in the light of Marxism-Leninism, that is to say, in the light of the main body of his ideology as he had already formulated it up to any given moment. If we can believe Stalin in this respect there is a chance that we can learn from the materials he left us what made him tick. If on the other hand we decide that Stalin's ideology was a conscious or unconscious screen for the real decision-making factors which lay elsewhere, the inner Stalin is more likely to remain a mystery.

The following chapters on various aspects of life in Stalin's Russia—the villages, the cities, and so forth—will begin and often end with his ideological views. Ideology is not the key to everything in Stalin's Russia, but it unlocks a great deal. This book is written in the hope of shedding light on Stalin's actions by examining his ideology, and of explaining thereby some of the peculiar history of Stalin's Russia.

2. THE MAN

*T*HE baby who was to become Stalin was born on December 21, 1879, and was baptized Joseph Son-of-Vissarion Dzhugashvili. At that time Alexander II had been Tsar of All the Russias for twenty-four years; he was to be blown to pieces by revolutionaries within fourteen months. Bismarck had been dominating Prussia and Germany for seventeen years. Disraeli was Prime Minister of Great Britain and Ireland, a certain Rutherford B. Hayes was President of the United States. Tolstoy had recently finished *Anna Karenina* and was in the throes of his conversion to religion. Dostoevsky was publishing *The Brothers Karamazov* and would soon die. Darwin, Marx, and Wagner were near the ends of their notable careers. Monet and Cézanne were about forty but not yet world-famous. Freud and Dewey had not yet completed their educations. Lenin was a child of nine. Churchill was five. Trotsky was not quite two months old. Roosevelt, Mussolini, Chiang Kai-shek, and Hitler would all be born within a decade. Queen

Victoria had been reigning for forty-two years. Stalin was to be one of the strangest products of the Victorian Age.

Stalin was born in the town of Gori, in the land of Georgia, in the Russian Empire, in the continent of Asia. The Georgians have always been a small people. There are less than four million of them in the world today, and there were scarcely half that number when Stalin was born. They are known outside the USSR chiefly because Stalin was one of them: They might otherwise be as obscure as the neighboring Azerbaidzhani. The world therefore suffers from few stereotypes of what to expect from a Georgian.

Georgians are usually of medium stature by world-wide standards, and therefore they strike many north Europeans, including Russians, as short. We are not certain how short Stalin was, which is testimony to the fantastic secrecy in which he lived, but to judge from earlier police reports and later guesses he could not have been much more than five-feet-four-inches tall, and he could never have weighed much more than 160 pounds. Such small stature would be a real burden for many American males, but Stalin could hardly have had his youth made miserable by his height in a land where it was about average. When he moved to Russia he entered an area in which he was among the shorter half of the male population, although not by very much.

One should be cautious about engaging in amateur psycho-analysis of Stalin. His enemies have often said that he suffered from a Napoleonic complex—that like Caesar, Napoleon, and Hitler he was a short man in a tall world who compensated for the slur upon his virility by a fanatical drive for political power over tall men. It is true that some of Stalin's most hated opponents, notably Trotsky, were taller than he. But so was Lenin. It is more strikingly true that practically all of Stalin's friends and political associates were as short as he, which cannot have happened simply by chance. Stalin liked to wear military boots, a kind of elevator shoe. He managed to avoid being photographed or seen in public standing next to taller men. If two or three inches off Stalin's height really did change the world, we can probably attribute it to his Georgian ancestry and his Georgian diet.

Georgian babies were usually swaddled, that is to say wrapped tightly in lengths of cloth that covered almost all of them save the face, binding the arms to the body and the legs to each other: an elaborate super-diaper that was not changed very often. So were most Russian babies, and those of many other Christian and Muslim peoples. More than sixty years after Stalin was toilet trained the British sociologist, Geoffrey Gorer,[1] and the American anthropologist, Margaret Mead,[2] suggested that such swaddling must leave its mark on the bodies and souls of millions of Russian babies. A baby that can rarely move his limbs, they argue, may continue in adulthood to move his legs and hold his arms somewhat stiffly—as many Russians do. Since babies express their frequent rages by howling and flailing their limbs, a baby whose limbs are tied may become terribly frustrated. Gorer and Mead speculate that many Russians may have emerged from their swaddling clothes conditioned to obey similarly rigid paternal, political, and ideological authority, but also predisposed toward occasional furiously violent rebellions—magnifications of the baby's kicks and screams when his swaddling clothes are at last unwound for an infrequent change.

Both Communists and non-Communist specialists on Russian society received these theories as the funniest thing they had heard in some time.[3] Anyone who has seen a baby swaddled almost to the nose, however, like an infant Jesus in an icon, finds it difficult to conclude that this procedure has no effect on the child and that the swaddled population will be in no wise different from, say, Americans or Chinese who are more simply diapered. The ancestry of Communism is wonderfully mixed; the practice of swaddling may be part of it. Stalin's case is inconclusive. In maturity he was sometimes described as walking stiffly, but he had been sedentary for decades. He held his arms stiffly, but we know that his left arm was injured in childhood. Georgians and Armenians, unlike Russians, often tied their babies to boards as part of the swaddling process, which usually flattened the back of the baby's head. At one time certain physical anthropologists diagnosed this flatness as the mark of the "Armenoid race." The back of Stalin's head was noticeably flattened, almost certainly by his swaddling board. It is this trait, along with the pleasant pussycat moustache that Stalin adopted from so many other Georgians, that leads foreign visitors to Georgia to wonder if half the older men are not members of the Stalin family. If this Georgian practice of flattening the back of the skull, and possibly the back of the brain inside it, has any effect on intelligence or character (the evidence is inconclusive) the world has felt the force of it.

Georgia is an Asian country because ancient and modern geographers, who lived one and two thousand miles away, drew the boundary between Europe and Asia across the crest of the Caucasus Mountains to the north of it. Asia does not possess any ethnic or cultural unity. The Georgians are a Christian people. They have more in common with European Russians who live a hundred miles north across the mountains than with fellow Asians in Arabia or Japan. Stalin was brought up a Christian. He knew what turning the other cheek meant, and what a mass was, and who had died between two thieves. In these and many other things Stalin had more in common with a Christian in Moscow, Vienna, Paris, and even Chicago, than he had with a Muslim from his native Gori. There are, of course, many people who think the Russians themselves are "Asiatic" and therefore inferior. Russians have indeed had many dealings with certain Asian peoples, and have been powerfully influenced by them—as have the Balkan peoples, the Spanish and Portuguese, the French, the Dutch, and the British. To single out Russia invidiously as "Asiatic" blocks understanding. To explain Stalin's career by pointing to his birth in Asia smacks of racism.

Nevertheless Stalin grew up in an age when European intellectual life was permeated through and through with racist ideas, and these ideas helped form Stalin's mind, chiefly by reaction to them. Throughout his public life he denied the inferiority of Georgians or any other Asian people, with understandable bruised feelings and venom. In maturity, when he came to identify himself with the Russian people, he defended them against slurs from Germany or elsewhere. Lenin had often used the term "Asiatic" to attack backward, brutal, and barbaric people and institutions in Russia and other countries. Stalin did so only once, under Lenin's direct influence, in 1913. Marx had postulated an "Asiatic mode of production"—a vast, brutal, all-encompassing state economic system, such as that of Pharaonic Egypt. Stalin suppressed all mention of this idea of Marx's, partly because it was a slur on Asia, and perhaps partly because he was himself running a somewhat similar economic system.[4]

However, in some ways Stalin accepted the idea of Asia as a cultural entity. Asian Communists and diplomats were often received by Stalin with heavy jovial remarks about their common origins. When he built up the industrial plant of the USSR, he built most of it in Soviet Europe, but he devoted a disproportionate amount of his time, and of his propaganda campaigns, to the buildup of industry in "the East." This meant chiefly the Russian-settled areas of western Siberia rather than his native Caucasus or any other traditionally Asian region. There were good economic and military reasons for this: Western Siberia was rich in mineral resources, and it was expected to be beyond the reach of any German army.

Still, Siberia is in Asia, and one cannot entirely discount Stalin's repeated assertions that by building "socialist" industry in the "heart" of Asia, the peoples of the USSR were giving the lie to arrogant European capitalists. Such a triumph for "Asia" was his triumph. His sense of being an Asian was probably a factor in his decision to allocate scarce economic resources to Soviet Asia.

In his foreign policy Stalin devoted most of his attention to European affairs, as any ruler of the USSR would have had to do in those decades. But when he did turn to Asian problems, his statements rang like those of a man who returns to a favorite hobby. The weight of Lenin's ideology compelled orthodox Communists to look to the advanced industrial countries of Europe for the future of the World Revolution. But Lenin in his last years had often been fascinated by the prospects of revolution in colonial Asia. This atypical side of Lenin was much cultivated under Stalin, whose persistent interest in Asia stood in sharp contrast to his lifelong lack of concern for Africa and Latin America. Yet Stalin devoted far more energy to China than to the Muslim countries adjoining his native Georgia.

In some ways, Stalin's concept of Asia was that of a European racist with the values reversed. One can paraphrase his sentiments as follows: You Europeans now rule; we Asians (including Russians) are backward, oppressed, enslaved. You are industrial and rich; we are poor peasants. But you are soft and decadent, while we are hard and strong by virtue of our terrible life. You are selfish and mutually quarrelsome; but we have true brotherhood, we know how to share and how to sacrifice ourselves. You are few but we are many. In the coming struggle you may deal us terrible blows, but our very primitiveness will help us endure, until, armed with our virtue, we rally, counterattack, and triumph. . . . A most un-Leninist complex of sentiments!

Stalin was born into a poor family. Both his parents had been peasant serfs until the emancipation of the 1860's. Stalin's father knew how to make shoes. At the time of Stalin's birth he was trying to make a living as an independent shoemaker in the town of Gori. He failed, and when Stalin was four, his father had to move to the capital of Georgia, Tbilisi ("Tiflis" in Russian), to work in a small shoe factory. His mother had to do washing to support the family. Her first three babies died. The house in Gori in which Stalin was born still survives. It is a solidly built square brick hut, like thousands of others in Georgia. It contains two brick-floored rooms, one for the family, one for the kitchen. The hut is small and dark. It seems very poor and bare to Europeans and Americans, less so to visitors from the Near or Far East, or from the tropics. In his later years Stalin had his birthplace enclosed in a columned marble pavilion, and placed a highly honorific plaque on the door. Nearby he erected a "Museum of Stalin's Life in the Caucasus." Across the whole length of the ruined twelfth century castle that tops the acropolis of Gori, he placed a huge neon sign with letters eight feet high, which flashed in Georgian, "Glory to the great Stalin!" When he died he had not yet finished the large and elaborate hotel for the thousands of tourists who were to come on pilgrimage.

To what extent did Stalin's early poverty affect him, and hence the world? Many journalists have been quick to attribute Stalin's revolutionary aims and violent methods to the "fact" that a poor man has nothing to lose and holds human life cheap. This won't do. Too many wealthy men have wrought violence—if not quite on Stalin's scale—and many have been revolutionaries. Lenin, after all, was the son of a prosperous, ennobled, bourgeois bureaucrat. Stalin's later character and career were hardly typical of the world's poor. To claim that Stalin defeated Trotsky and Hitler (neither of them rich boys) because of any drive, skill, or tenacity engendered by poverty is absurd.

On the other hand, no one would want to say that the poverty of Stalin's childhood made no difference whatsoever and that he might as well have been born in a palace. We know that his face was pitted by smallpox, and that his left arm was stiffened by typhus or some equivalent infection. Money, in the late nineteenth century, could usually preserve a child from these plagues. It is hard to believe that the mature Stalin's sense of social justice, his resentments, his drive to build a new society, his utter brutality toward human obstacles to his plans, were not also in some part the results of life in the wretched brick huts of Georgia, and the wretched food he ate in them.

The question of Stalin's early poverty is inseparable from the problem of Stalin's family. Stalin never wrote any lengthy autobiography, and we should probably not trust it if he had. The existing memoirs of Stalin's youth, whether written by supporters under Stalin's watchful eye or by enemies in exile, are all biased, and all lack eye-witness accounts of his earliest years. Furthermore, no one who knew Stalin and his family in the 1880's would have looked for the kind of behavior that Western psychologists, transformed by the Freudian approach, would be most interested in.

Stalin's mother, an ignorant and religious peasant girl, married at fifteen and saw her first three babies die. She gave birth to her only surviving child at twenty. She was always described as a devoted mother, and those who described her thus always assumed that they were praising her as highly as they could. She lived into the 1930's, still devoted to her son, and honored by him—though usually from a distance. She impressed strangers, regardless of their political views, as the very type of a primitive peasant woman.

Stalin's father was a poor peasant shoemaker, unsuccessful

even among poor peasant shoemakers. He died when Stalin was eleven, and was rarely mentioned by his son or by his son's stable of official writers. Some friends of Stalin's adolescence, who later wrote about him from the safety of exile, suggest that Stalin's father was a failure and a drunkard who beat his wife and child, arousing fierce and lifelong hatred in the son toward his father and by extension toward much of humanity. There may be something to this. Stalin's father *was* a professional failure, but we cannot be sure whether this was an incurable wound to his neurotic ego or whether he took it as ordinary bad luck. Had Stalin's father never drunk and never beaten his wife and child, he would have been unique in his social group. We cannot be sure whether he drank or beat more or less than was customary, and what effect it had on the child in either case. Stalin once described his father as an example of the Marxist law of the proletarianization of the independent artisan. Little neurosis can be derived from that. Emil Ludwig, a German biographer fresh from the Freudian West, once asked Stalin: "What drove you to become a rebel? Was it perhaps because your parents treated you badly?" Stalin's answer was straightforward on the surface: "No. My parents were uneducated people, but they did not treat me badly by any means."[5] Regardless of the honesty of the answer, Stalin probably thought the question both irrelevant and in bad taste.

Yet Stalin must have been a truly rare figure if family experiences left no mark on his soul. A wretched mother who doted on religion and her only surviving baby, a wretched father who could not earn as much as his wife, who drank, who beat his child and beat his wife before his child's eyes— something must have come of this. Freud and many other psychologists assure us that a child is traumatically affected by witnessing the sexual activities of its parents, or by being rudely pushed out of the room in preparation. We know nothing whatsoever about the sex life of Stalin's parents, save that they must have had one. But where could baby Stalin have gone? Into the kitchen? Into the cold? The thought of Stalin with an Oedipus complex raises snickers from the skeptical, but he may have had one, and millions may have died in part because of it.

We know nothing of these things, in any precise sense of the term "know." We know nothing of Stalin's weaning or toilet training, but we cannot pretend that they never took place. Concerning his father Stalin kept his own counsel, and he almost certainly thought he was thereby doing the decent thing. Did Stalin, like Ivan Karamazov, wish the death of his father? No one knows. Stalin's father died when the child was eleven. No one knows what neurotic wounds Stalin might have suffered on the eve of his adolescence. Those who hold to the Freudian faith, in whole or in part, must make the most of such speculations: There is nothing else to go on, save that young Joseph Dzhugashvili grew up to be Stalin.

It seems clear that no simple deterministic scheme will "explain" Stalin. Marx and Freud are of limited help. Hippolyte Taine's quip about how "the race, the time, the milieu" explain all remains naive in its sophistication, for Stalin obviously transcended his nation, his time, and his social class, as well as his family. The hour and circumstances of his birth are important, but not all-important. To understand how Stalin got beyond the brick huts of Georgia, one must first examine his education.

Stalin was an educated man, in the basic senses of the term. We may conclude that he was badly educated or miseducated, but it is perverse to deny that he was educated. It was not simply that he could read and write in at least two languages. It was not simply that he had ten years of schooling. His formal education was admittedly defective; he criticized it himself with customary savagery. But at some point in his adolescence Stalin acquired a taste for reading—whether Karl Marx or Victor Hugo—and for the wider world that books uncover. Stalin seems to have read all the literature, all the science, social science, and philosophy that he could get hold of in Tbilisi. He thereby became a kind of European intellectual. He became, more specifically, one of the *intelligentsia* of the Russian Empire—one of that extraordinary body of men and women who, regardless of national or class origin, read and treasured a large body of Russian and European writings and felt that the injustices of the Tsarist regime could not be allowed to continue.

As Stalin earned his status as an *intelligent* he grew in the eyes of workers and peasants, in the eyes of his fellow students, and eventually in the eyes of the regime. He ceased to be one of the masses and became a member of the elite, to be sure not the "power" elite, but of what sociologists call a "subordinate" elite. This did not happen at the church school in Gori, to which Stalin was sent from the age of nine to the age of fourteen, and where he apparently did very well. It almost certainly happened at the Theological Seminary of Tbilisi, at that time the highest and most prestigious school in Georgia, which Stalin attended from the time he was fourteen to his expulsion at nineteen.

The stone buildings of the seminary stand to this day near the center of old Tbilisi. They now house the rich and beautiful collections of the Museum of Georgian Art. But Stalin and those of his classmates who wrote memoirs of him remembered the seminary as a terrible school. The curriculum, they said, was religious idiocy badly taught by loathsome Georgian monks who spent their best energies spying on the students for signs of subversive reading, which they would eagerly report to the police in order to curry favor. The result, we are told, was that all the best students became atheists and revolutionaries, whether of the Georgian nationalist or the socialist internationalist variety—or both. No doubt the faculty, curriculum, and discipline were dismal, although one wonders if there were no monks at all who were more Christian than police spy. But a school is more than its formal apparatus. No matter how unworthy the monks, the students seem to have been a lively lot. They seem to have succeeded in reading and partly understanding the subjects that ought to have been in the curriculum. They seem to have given each other an education, albeit lopsided. A school in the Russian Empire in the 1890's that did *not* somehow turn its best students into revolutionary *intelligentsia* was not fulfilling its proper social function.

Stalin's biographers, official or hostile, dispute whether Stalin first became a Marxist in those years (which is probable), whether he first became a Leninist in any sense (highly improbable), and whether he became an important revolutionary in the Caucasus (impossible). They agree in portraying his life as a round of reading forbidden books, discussing forbidden ideas, and attending forbidden meetings, along with consequent clashes with the monks. No doubt such activities were the best and most intense parts of Stalin's adolescent life. But we may reflect that Stalin, if he had anything at all in common with other boys of his age, must have spent a good part of the 1890's thinking about more ordinary topics, such as sex. There are vague hints in the record that Stalin may have had to avoid the advances of homosexual monks. We are completely in the dark as to when and how he lost his virginity. We may safely leave these topics to future third-rate historical novels. But those who think our lack of knowledge about Stalin's private life indicates its lack of significance have not been educated in the main stream of the twentieth century.

To the monks, Stalin must have been quite a disappointment—the Tsar's police often used the phrase "politically disappointing" to describe a subversive. A well-recommended and promising student had turned into a trouble-making rebel against God and Tsar, like so many others, and apparently this one was more open and insolent than most. The list of his offenses grew. We groan or smile at the monks' distress at confiscating one of Stalin's dangerous and forbidden books, a copy of Victor Hugo's novel *Ninety-Three*. Perhaps we should remember that the novel's hero is a grim priest, Cimourdin, who is converted to the French Revolution, and who is sent by Robespierre as a commissar to oversee the revolutionary forces in the ghastly civil war in the Vendée. Cimourdin fulfills his mission effectively, bloodily, maniacally, even executing his beloved nephew for treason to the revolution. A true Christian cannot dismiss such a book as a trifle. Neither did Stalin, whose future career was to have more than a touch of Cimourdin. When Stalin was nineteen he was expelled from the seminary, ostensibly for not attending an examination. His formal education was at an end.

Stalin's upbringing and education had given him an insight into two religions, Christianity and socialism, the only two world-views he was ever to understand well. By the age of nineteen he had chosen socialism as his way of life—because the friends he admired and the authorities he detested had shown him the way, because it suited his temperament, and because he believed that socialism was ethically superior to Christianity. Five years earlier he had entered a Christian seminary, apparently willing at least to consider the sacrifices involved in the life of a Christian priest. Now he became a professional revolutionary, a priestly way of life in its own way, and one that promised to impose even greater sacrifices.

Several months before his expulsion from the seminary Stalin had joined his first revolutionary society, *Messame Dassy* (Georgian for "The Third Group"), a circle of Marxists in Tbilisi who were soon to become the core of the Georgian branch of the Mensheviks. He continued in the group while looking for work and growing a somewhat Lincolnesque beard and sideburns. He eventually found a position as a clerk at the astronomical observatory of Tbilisi, which required little work in return for little pay and a room at the observatory. It may help to understand Stalin's Russia if we remember that Stalin was twenty years old before he ever enjoyed a room of his own, and that he kept it for less than a year and a half.

As a revolutionary, Stalin attended meetings and later managed meetings of other revolutionaries and of workers interested in the cause. He made speeches and wrote pamphlets. He helped stage a modest May Day celebration in Tbilisi in 1900, and he was involved in preparations for a more rousing May Day the next year when the police raided his room to arrest him. At this point Stalin went "underground." He never returned to his room. He gave it up, along with his few possessions, his job at the observatory, his name Dzhugashvili, and his whole legal existence. He hid out with friends and sympathizers, and went on to launch a successful May Day disturbance in which the police were provoked into wounding fifteen people. To live underground, to move about with false papers and disguised appearance, to change sleeping quarters constantly, to fear that any policeman may be about to arrest you, to fear that some "friend" may be a spy about to betray you—but to be certain that the cause for which you suffer is just—these were the daily experiences of the young Stalin at an age at which more fortunate youths are at a university. In some ways Stalin was to live underground for the rest of his life.

He was arrested fairly soon, as usually happened, in April, 1902, when he was twenty-two. He was involved in running an underground press, which was a violation of the censorship law, and he was using it to print revolutionary literature, which violated any number of laws. But the police could not find the press (it was reconstructed late in Stalin's rule, and is still shown to tourists), and they could not produce witnesses to convict him even in the Tsar's own courts. He was never brought to trial. But he was, of course, "guilty," as the police knew full well, so they kept him without trial in one Caucasian prison after another for a year and a half. Then they sent him to serve a three-year term of exile in a village in eastern Siberia.

At the time, the Tsar's prisons and exile in Siberia were regarded by many Russians and by the outside world as revolting horrors that spoiled Russia's claim to be a civilized state. After all that has happened since there is a temptation to look back at the Tsar's penal system almost with nostalgia. One could often read books and play chess in a Tsarist prison. Siberian exiles could sometimes visit each other, and even write revolutionary books.

Such nostalgia should be kept in check. When Stalin went to prison he suffered the discomforts and boredom that afflict even the most favored prisoner, the delays and caprice of the authorities, and the torments and petty sadism of the guards. Stalin was never beaten, tortured, or killed, but he knew many comrades who had suffered these things and he never knew what tomorrow might bring. When he made his first journey out of his native Georgia it was not the broadening adventure that such a trip should be, but a month-long agony in a prison train to a desolate village in eastern Siberia. All this came at the hands of a regime that could not condemn Stalin even according to its own laws, a regime so unjust that it was cheating against itself, it seemed, at Stalin's expense. It is not surprising that Stalin was not "rehabilitated" by his punishment.

A little more than a month after he reached his Siberian village Stalin escaped, and many weeks later reappeared in the Caucasus. We have very few details of what must have been a nerve-wracking adventure. As an escaped prisoner, Stalin had to live even deeper underground. In the disturbed period leading up to the revolution of 1905, he had more opportunity for revolutionary work. Yet this was the period at which Stalin, by all reports, came nearest to leading a happy, contented life.

He married. The courtship must have taken place before he was arrested in 1902. The ceremony may have been performed while he was in prison. He lived with his wife only after his escape from Siberia. The girl, Ekaterina Svanidze, was a religious, tubercular, Georgian peasant woman, whom no one described as either beautiful or revolutionary. The marriage was described as "happy" and in no way unusual. Stalin apparently did not beat his wife more than was customary, and he did not encourage her to adopt the egalitarian manners toward men that characterized so many Russian revolutionary women. She bore him a son in 1905, and died a few months later of tuberculosis. Stalin's friend at that time, Joseph Iremashvili, wrote years later that Stalin pointed to the coffin as the earth was shoveled on and said, "This creature softened my stony heart. She is dead, and with her have died my last warm feelings for all human beings."[6] Stalin might conceivably have said or felt something of the sort. His temper and manners, according to Iremashvili, then took a marked turn for the worse.

At this point a study entitled "Stalin: the Formative Years" would probably come to an end. He was twenty-five years old. He had been to school and held a job. He had been a husband and a father. He had become a member of the revolutionary *intelligentsia* and a revolutionary activist. He had been in prison and escaped. It was the eve of the revolution of 1905. He had not yet adopted the name "Stalin," and what that name would later come to mean was not yet predictable.

It seems clear that mature Stalinism did not follow inevitably from the nature of the young Stalin. Most twenty-five-year-olds in the Russian Empire were not revolutionary Marxists, but to be such was not bizarre. It was not symptomatic of mental illness, and it did not of itself foreshadow the collectivization of argiculture or the Five Year Plans. For several years Stalin had regarded the Tsarist regime as a massive evil conspiracy that had to be struck down by violence before it struck down all good men. He had become used to constant vigilance for suspicious noises in the night, and suspicious actions by possibly traitorous friends. But this was not paranoia; it was the world in which Stalin actually lived. It did not of itself foreshadow the liquidation of the *kulaks* or the great purges. Neither the common experiences of revolutionaries under the Tsars nor the particular experiences of Stalin's youth would force the young man of the Caucasus to become the monster of the Kremlin. To understand what Stalin did in the Kremlin, one must first examine how he got there.

Stalin reached the Kremlin by virtue of his association with Lenin, whom he first met in the revolutionary year 1905. Throughout that year Lenin had been frustrated by his inability to take advantage of the disturbances that reached their height with the general strike in October. In December, when the Tsarist regime was recovering its forces and its nerve, Lenin arranged a national conference of his Bolshevik section of the disunited Russian Social Democratic Labor Party. It was held in Tampere, a lumbering and industrial city in the interior of southern Finland. Tampere (Russians and Communists called the city by its Swedish name, Tammerfors) was selected because it was a proletarian city within the Russian Empire, but also in Finland where the Tsarist police were less all-pervasive, and near enough to the Swedish border for a quick getaway if necessary. Stalin was a delegate from the Caucasian Bolshevik group to this conference, the occasion of his first trip to the heart of European Russia and beyond.

In this slum city buried in a dozen feet of snow in the middle of the north woods, Stalin first met Lenin. Just after Lenin's death he described this first meeting in what is surely the most charming passage he ever wrote:

> I had imagined Lenin to be a stately and imposing giant. My disappointment was keen to find him a very ordinary looking man, of less than average height, in no way, literally in no way, distinguishable from ordinary human beings. . . . Usually a great man comes late to a meeting so that his appearance is anxiously awaited. Then, just before the great man arrives, the warning goes around, "Shhh, quiet, he's coming." This ritual did not seem superfluous to me because it made an impression and inspired respect. My disappointment was keen to find that Lenin had arrived at the conference before the other delegates were there, and had settled himself somewhere in a corner, and was unassumingly carrying on a conversation, a very ordinary conversation, with very ordinary delegates.[7]

But Stalin's disappointments were more than overcome by his admiration for Lenin's ability and determined revolutionary position. Stalin remained a follower of Lenin for the rest of Lenin's life, and for the rest of his own. Although Stalin was then young, he never idolized Lenin in any personal, enthusiastic, youthful manner. He certainly did not cultivate Lenin through flattery. In Lenin's last years the increasingly confident Stalin turned some of his celebrated rudeness on Lenin, and more of it on Lenin's wife. Stalin's discipleship under Lenin gave every exterior sign of being due to sober, mature, intellectual conviction.

What Lenin was attracted to in Stalin is a more puzzling matter. There was certainly no personal warmth on Lenin's side. In his last years he expressed open detestation of Stalin's character. And yet we are faced with the fact that Lenin, in the decade after 1905, deliberately selected Stalin for increasingly important Bolshevik Party tasks, making him one of the ten most important Bolsheviks and therefore, after 1917, one of the ten most important men in Russia.

In the initial period of their association, Stalin's chief value to Lenin lay in the fact that he was a Georgian—even the Bolsheviks felt some need of a balanced ticket. Most of the rather small number of Georgians who became Marxists at all were Menshevik opponents of Lenin by 1905, so that Lenin, in casting about for a Georgian lieutenant, had an unusually small field to pick from.

When the revolution of 1905 was put down, Lenin went into exile in Western and Central Europe for twelve years. Stalin stayed in the Russian Empire, which gave him two advantages: He was able to impress Lenin with the revolutionary agitation he was conducting in the Caucasus, and he was kept from alienating Lenin with his saturnine presence.

Stalin was a major leader in a series of strikes and collective bargaining sessions in the oil fields at Baku on the Caspian Sea (at that time still the largest oil fields in the world) at the end of 1907 and throughout 1908. This seems to have persuaded Lenin to decide on Stalin as his man in Transcaucasia. Before the end of 1908 Stalin was arrested and imprisoned in Baku. Early in 1909 he was exiled to a town in the far north of Russia called Solvychegodsk, from which he escaped in four months. A revolutionary who was martyred by prison and exile, and who was able enough to escape, presented a double claim on the Party. Stalin resumed his revolutionary work while hiding in an oil workers' slum near Baku. The police got him again in March, 1910, while he was preparing for another strike in the oil fields. This led to another spell in prison, and another exile to Solvychegodsk. As Stalin was dragged northward, he could not guess that he would never live or work again for any length of time in his native Caucasus. At the age of thirty, his Caucasian period was over.

When his formal term of exile was up in June, 1911, Stalin was ordered to stay out of the Caucasus and the larger cities of Russia. We are not surprised that he violated these terms and sneaked into St. Petersburg, where he was unlucky enough to be arrested the first day, imprisoned for a few months, and shipped back to northern Russia. At this time, January, 1912, Lenin granted Stalin a decisive promotion for his many past and prospective services to the Bolshevik Party. He had Stalin co-opted onto the Party's Central Committee. The Central Committee was allegedly the ruling body of the Party between its rare congresses, although in fact the Party was personally dominated by Lenin. Still, Stalin was now one of the dozen most important Bolsheviks.

An account of his first year as Central Committeeman reads like a Bolshevik adventure novel. He made quick illegal visits to Transcaucasia, Moscow, and St. Petersburg—where he helped launch the first Bolshevik newspaper to be called *Pravda (Truth)*. The next day the police caught him again; three months in prison and another exile to Siberia. In two months he escaped back to St. Petersburg. In November, 1912, he dashed abroad for a few days to Cracow, then in the Hapsburg Monarchy, for a meeting of the Central Committee. From December, 1912 to February, 1913, he was again in the Dual Monarchy, chiefly Cracow and Vienna, for what turned out to be his longest trip abroad, although not one on which he was able to pick up the fine points of European civilization. He then returned to St. Petersburg, was arrested a week later, and was exiled once more to Siberia, where he was to stay this time for more than four years; until he was released forever from the police and the threat of the police by the Russian Revolution.

The Austrian trip was important to Stalin for at least three reasons. It was then that he first adopted the pseudonym *Stalin*. Joseph Dzhugashvili had used a number of pseudonyms, of which the most important so far had been "Koba," the name of a somewhat Robin Hood-like bandit-hero of a Georgian romance. The selection of pseudonyms is often a clue to the ego of the selector. The choic of "Koba" is thought to hint at Stalin's otherwise rather restrained youthful romanticism. Now in 1913 he chose his lasting pseudonym, "Stalin," the Man of Steel. (The Russian word for steel, *stal*, is a transliteration and mispronunciation of the German word for steel, *Stahl.*) The chosen name was astonishingly prophetic. Stalin was to exemplify the virtues and defects of steel: durability, reliability, efficiency, coldness, hardness.

The Austrian trip was the first occasion on which Stalin had spent as much as several weeks in Lenin's company. Lenin's obsession was the organization of a Party that would be at once a well-organized semi-military machine and a body of disciplined intellectuals. The problem was that those who took theory seriously enough to be attracted to Bolshevism often took their own intellects seriously enough to stand their ground in opposition to Lenin when they chanced to disagree. Lenin preserved his ideological autocracy over his Party by driving all determined people of other minds out of it. This left him with few high-quality minds. For Lenin, Stalin must have seemed a compromise solution to his dilemma. Lenin cannot have rated Stalin's mind very highly, but he recognized that Stalin *had* a mind, a Leninist mind. Stalin did follow Lenin through every turn, not blindly or out of self-interest, but regularly, and, after frequent intervals of puzzlement and reluctance, out of genuine conviction. And Stalin did execute Lenin's orders with a Leninist sense of the value of organizational obedience and efficiency that was rare among Russian revolutionaries.

Lenin seems to have confirmed his opinion of Stalin during the latter's Austrian trip. As a result, Lenin asked Stalin to write a Bolshevik analysis of the problem of national differences, at once a compliment to Stalin's intellectual potential and an intelligent effort to actualize it. Stalin, a native of the Caucasus, had amassed a great deal of information about the fantastically complicated nationalities problem of the region. His self-confidence must have been raised by Lenin's commission to tackle the general problem of nationality in theoretical terms. The resulting long article, later a book, was Stalin's only pre-Revolutionary theoretical work, *Marxism and the National Question*.[8] Stalin's memory of this work was to help shape the fate of all the national minorities in the USSR. In 1913, its publication announced the emergence of Stalin as an ideological leader of the Party in addition to his established position as a practical leader.

The third important result of his Austrian trip was his arrest on his return to Russia—and the reasons for it. He was betrayed. Roman Malinowski, Lenin's favorite associate at the time, a member of the Bolshevik Central Committee, the head of the Bolshevik delegation of six members in the Russian Duma, was a paid agent of the Tsar's secret police. Malinowski had already arranged for the arrest of a number of members of the Party hierarchy so that he himself might rise in it. Now Malinowski told the police of Stalin's return to St. Petersburg, and arranged for Stalin's arrest at a concert a week later. When Lenin wrote Malinowski to help Stalin escape from Siberia, Malinowski saw to it that the escape was frustrated by the police, and that Stalin was removed to a still more distant and icy exile.[9]

Neither Lenin nor Stalin was to learn the full details of Malinowski's treacheries over the years until after the Revolution. But when Stalin, fresh from years in an ice hole on the lower Yenissei River in northeastern Siberia, finally did learn how he had been sent there and kept there, we can be sure that he did not forget his knowledge. No paranoiac could have invented a wilder tale of all-pervasive treason—and yet the facts of Malinowski's activities were set down in Tsarist government documents for their Communist successors to peruse. The lesson certainly burnt its way into Stalin's soul: Traitors can be everywhere; even Lenin can be fatally fooled; treachery may lurk in the heart of the Party; no one can ever be wholly trusted; no measures taken against traitors can be excessive.

While Stalin was in his exile on the lower Yenissei, World War I broke out, the Imperial armies were hopelessly defeated, the Tsar and all his regime collapsed, and old Russia was swept away forever. When Stalin returned to St. Petersburg in March, 1917, the name of the city had been changed along with everything else in the Russian world. Stalin's activities for the rest of his life were to be so important a part of Russian history that no biography could be meaningful apart from public events. Henceforth he would have even less time for what we call his "private life," an expression for which there is no real equivalent in Russian.

We know what Stalin looked like, and how his appearance changed over the thirty-six years left to him, for he was not excessively camera-shy until the end. We know that he kept his health and his faculties to a remarkable degree until the end was near, although he grew more thick-necked, thick-middled, and grey-haired. We know that he ate and drank considerable amounts, but not unto degeneration. He always kept up his game of chess, and developed a liking for volleyball. We have a number of accounts of Stalin off duty in the first decade after the Revolution, but very few in the later years save for those of Djilas[10] and Khrushchëv. Almost all accounts tell us that this god on earth was in private life only a man (which is not surprising), and even a man with faults (which is still not suprising). No one seems to have been favorably impressed with his eating and drinking habits, with his stiffness of demeanor or his bearish attempts at humor, with his petty self-importance of his not always controlled temper. Visitors were often shocked at his language: Stalin's favorite Russian oath was "Fuck your mother!" Bolsheviks ought to have been able to endure that.

We know that in 1919, during the most terrible period of the Civil War, Stalin married a second time. The bride, Nadezhda Allilueva, was the half-Georgian daughter of Stalin's longtime associate in Transcaucasia, Sergei Alliluev, who had married a Georgian woman. At marriage, she was nineteen to Stalin's thirty-nine. They had a son, Vasili, in 1921, and a daughter, Svetlana, in 1925. Communists do not approve of thrusting their families into the public eye, and we hear unusually little about the Stalin household. Late in 1932, at a particularly difficult period of famines and purges during the First Five Year Plan, Nadezhda Stalina was moved, when she and her husband were visiting the Voroshilovs, to lament the horrible times. Stalin, in an unusually unfortunate display of his celebrated rudeness, suggested a number of things she might do to her mother. Nadezhda left the company, went home, and was dead the next morning. Many authorities say that Stalin drove his wife to suicide, but some are suspicious enough to suggest that he murdered her that night. At this late date suicide seems more probable, if only because Khrushchëv, Mikoyan, or some lesser figure of the post-Stalin period would probably have publicized the murder story had there been grounds for it. The death was obviously the climax of a domestic tragedy whose details are still unkown to us.

For Stalin, domestic tragedies would continue. His oldest son, Iakov Dzhugashvili, who had been brought up by relatives in Georgia after his mother's death in 1905, lived an obscure life until he was captured in battle by the Germans in 1941. The Germans made great efforts to convert or coerce their captive to their cause. The efforts must have failed, for he was killed in the Oranienburg concentration camp before the end of the war.

The second son, Vasili, was said to have been absorbed in vodka and girls even before the war. He entered the Red Air Force and was said to have become a daredevil pilot. By 1946 he was a major general, brutal and unpopular with his men and still addicted to girls and vodka. Nonetheless he led a flashy career as commander of the Moscow air garrison and organizer of the air shows on May Days. He dropped from view after his father's death. In 1962 he was reported to have died at the age of forty, of heart trouble aggravated by alcoholism. The tragedy of the great father whose overwhelming presence drives his son to neurotic, ne'er-do-well waste of life goes back at least as far as Pericles, but this knowledge cannot have been much comfort to the aging Stalin. If we have any sympathy for the man whatsoever, we should be glad to hear that his daughter Svetlana behaved herself and stayed close to her father all his life, even after an obscure but apparently happy marriage.

In some ways Stalin was history's outstanding example of a type the Greek moralists were always searching for—the great tyrant who successfully maintained his power until death. The Greek's would not have been surprised to learn that all of Stalin's power failed to make him a very hapy man. When a man has killed millions of people and has transformed a third of the world, it may seem frivolous even to mention his personal fate or to estimate his personal character. However, the details of his private life must have helped determine the fate of millions, and his character shaped much of the world. Stalin was the Man of Steel, the nearly faceless machine-man known for organization, production, energy, coercion, and battle—and not at all for the milk of human kindness. Yet Stalin must have died believing himself a secular saint who had sacrificed his whole life for the future of humanity. Insofar as Stalin failed to build a paradise on earth it was not for lack of good will toward men, but for errors of judgment and a failure of intelligence.

STALIN'S greatest talent was for acquiring and keeping power, probably more than any other human being has ever possessed. He had not had any to speak of until 1917, for high position within a persecuted out-group such as the Bolsheviks is not what one means by the word "power." But his rise thereafter was rapid. In his own lifetime the world could see that his rise to power was one of history's classic examples of that process.

Stalin reached Russia's renamed capital, Petrograd, from Siberia on March 12, 1917, just ten days after the last Tsar had abdicated. He was, by virtue of his membership in the Central Committee since 1912, the senior ranking Bolshevik in the city. He accordingly took over leadership of the Party in Russia (from a twenty-six-year-old named Molotov) for about three weeks, until Lenin returned from exile on April 3. From that point, of course, Lenin directed the Party himself, and his associates held such power as they had by inspiring Lenin's confidence in them.

Lenin's new "line" of policy for the Party was, to Stalin's surprise, implacable opposition to the new provisional government of revolutionary Russia, which was composed of shifting proportions of liberals, Socialist Revolutionaries, and (from May on) Mensheviks. The provisional government would not make peace with Germany, and could not defeat the German Army. At the same time it failed to satisfy the demands of the peasants for land, of the workers for an assured food supply ("bread"), of the national minorities for autonomy or independence, of the upper and middle classes for law and order, and of the more radical revolutionaries for socialism. Lenin, with his program of "peace, land, and bread"—and overthrow of the provisional government—found it easy to expand the membership and following of the Bolsheviks among workers and soldiers. His own path to power, however, was not smooth.

In July, 1917, the Bolsheviks were reluctantly dragged into an abortive rising in Petrograd against the provisional government, launched by an enthusiastic and self-proclaimed "Bolshevik" regiment of machine gunners. When the rising was suppressed, Lenin had to go into hiding in Finland. Stalin was then the leading Bolshevik left in Petrograd, and it was he who conducted the semi-secret Sixth Congress of the Bolshevik Party. However, it was at this congress that Leon Trotsky formally joined the Bolsheviks. Since Trotsky henceforth commanded Lenin's highest esteem, and since he had an independent power base in the masses to whom he orated so movingly, it was he and not Stalin who was clearly the second-ranking Bolshevik and presumptive successor to Lenin for the next five years.

The Bolsheviks were able to recover lost ground in August when the provisional government's own military commander, General Kornilov, rose against it to remove its Prime Minister, Alexander Kerensky. Bolshevik-organized "Red Guards"

THE RISE   41

seem to have played a crucial part in blocking Kornilov's march on Petrograd. Capitalizing on their revived popularity with workers and soldiers, the Bolsheviks in early September won majorities in the Petrograd and Moscow *Soviets*—those celebrated representative bodies of the Russian working classes, which had proved to be the only institutions to emerge from the Russian Revolution in which most workers and soldiers had any confidence.

Lenin then pushed on for a *Putsch* to seize power before this wave of mass enthusiasm dissipated. After furious arguments he succeeded in persuading most of his fellow Bolshevik leaders, including Stalin, to support him. The actual planning and execution of the *Putsch* was placed in the hands of Trotsky and Jacob Sverdlov—not Stalin, although he later claimed that role. On October 10 the Central Committee voted definitively for the *Putsch*, and then elected a seven-man political bureau, including Lenin, Trotsky, and Stalin, "for political guidance in the immediate future." Thus Stalin acquired his seat on the famous *Politburo*, which was to prove of no special importance during the *Putsch* but which was to become the ruling body of the Communist Party and the USSR as Stalin rose to power.

Lenin, Trotsky, and their fellow Bolsheviks seized power in Petrograd by their *Putsch* of October 24-25, 1917. During the following weeks they extended their control, for a brief period, over the rest of the country. They won without any reliance on Stalin, and they would have won without him. But once they had won, Stalin, a high ranking Bolshevik, was bound to hold an important post in the new Bolshevik-dominated government. This was an obvious but crucial step in his rise to total power. On October 26 Lenin announced his new cabinet, and included Stalin as "Chairman of the Commissariat on Nationalities" (a designedly revolutionary title in place of "Minister"). This cabinet post was not to prove very powerful of itself, and Stalin was to spend most of his time in the next few years on military and political missions that had little to do with national minorities.

The Bolsheviks' relatively uncontested control of the former Russian Empire came to an end in June, 1918, when a number of virtually simultaneous but badly co-ordinated risings against Lenin's rule, chiefly in the East and South, initiated the terrible two-and-a-half-year Russian Civil War. Stalin's most famous mission came at the very beginning of the Civil War. In June he was sent down to the city of Tsaritsyn on the Lower Volga to assure the supply of grain to Moscow from the North Caucasian wheat area. He soon became involved in the chaotic military operations of the southern front. He took the side of the local Red military commander, his friend Klim Voroshilov, against Trotsky, the founder and director of the new Red Army. Stalin flatly disobeyed Trotsky's orders to retreat if the pressure became strong, and insisted on defending the city in his own way. By October the White forces had been driven back from the city.

Both Stalin and Trotsky claimed victory. Trotsky was probably right. The victory did not matter—Tsaritsyn was lost to the Whites the next year anyway. Stalin's conviction that he had a flair for the military life and for military command *did* matter. So did his feud with Trotsky, which now began. A name such as "Tsaritsyn" could not long survive the overthrow of the Tsars it honored, so the city was presently renamed *Stalingrad*. It became a major symbol of Stalin's career and, a generation later in World War II, a major triumph.

In May, 1919, Stalin saved Petrograd from attack by the White General Iudenich, as Trotsky was to save it in October from a more dangerous attack by Iudenich. But most of 1919 was taken up with civilian tasks that kept Stalin at the seat of power in Moscow. The *Politburo* was emerging as the committee Lenin used to thrash out really important issues, and Stalin's membership in it became his crucial position of power. Stalin was the only member of the *Politburo* who was also a member of the Organizational Bureau of the Central Committee of the Party *(Orgburo)*, the body that governed membership in the Party and distribution of posts and promotions within it. This enabled Stalin to begin building his personal machine by staffing the Party hierarchies with friends, supporters, and dependents.

Most historians and political scientists point to this Tammany Hall-like activity of Stalin's as the basis of his later triumph. But we must not imagine that Stalin was self-consciously preparing for an intra-Party struggle at this early date. The possibility of Lenin's death was brought home to all Bolsheviks in October, 1918, when a Socialist Revolutionary student, Fania Kaplan, shot him in the neck but missed his spinal cord. But Lenin recovered sufficiently to live thirty years more, for all one could tell at the time, and no amount of crude maneuvering could avail Stalin while Lenin retained his powers.

In 1919 Stalin acquired another post in the field of personnel and patronage. He was made Chairman of the Committee of Workers' and Peasants' Inspection (abbreviated in Russian to *Rabkhrin*), a body set up to weed out fools and self-servers from the rapidly expanding bureaucracy of the Communist state. Stalin must have liked this sort of bureaucratic routine—his enemies charged him with small-mindedness because of this addiction. His work on the *Orgburo* must have been approved by Lenin, who thus expanded Stalin's operations into the whole area of government. Stalin certainly used his new powers to build a network of supporters in the state bureaucracy as well as in the overlapping Party bureaucracy. But here his procedures became—apparently for the first time—arbitrary, sweeping, and brutal enough to arouse widespread protest inside the Party.

By the end of 1919 Trotsky's Red Army had reconquered

most of the parts of the former Russian Empire inhabited by national minorities, and Stalin found a new field open to him: the setting-up of local Communist governments composed of his supporters in these minority areas. But his now openly violent methods, especially in his native Georgia, were to provoke an opposition that almost cut short his rise to power.

In retrospect, this period from 1918 to 1922 was the crucial one in determining Stalin's triumph in the Party. The verdict of Western historians has been that Stalin in these four years built the machine within the Communist Party that was to give him control of it during the three following years. The bulk of Stalin's time was devoted to these organizational tasks. Compared to them, his last military venture of the Civil War period, a mission to the southern front in the war with Poland in the summer of 1920 (a fiasco that helped defeat the Red Army when it seemed on the point of taking Warsaw), as well as his part in the Tenth Congress of the Communist Party in 1921, at which War Communism gave way to Lenin's "New Economic Policy," were minor activities.

In retrospect also, this was the period during which Stalin took crucial steps along his path to becoming, along with Hitler and Mao, one of the bloodiest men in history. Stalin had never objected on principle to killing when the cause was good enough. On the other hand, he does not seem ever to have killed anyone by his own hand. In fact, since he never lived on a farm, he may never have killed an animal larger than an insect. But from the time he became a revolutionary in the late 1890's Stalin believed with Marx that some killing would be necessary to bring about and defend the revolution. From 1900 on he promoted labor disturbances in full knowledge that some workers would be killed by the police. After 1905 he was involved in planning spectacular bank robberies to secure funds for the Party, in full knowledge that revolutionaries might sooner or later kill innocent bystanders. A man's first assent to murder is an important threshold.

But for Stalin all this seemed trivial, in comparison to World War I, in which approximately twelve million people were slaughtered. Once the war began it became the supreme symbol of the evil system the socialists hoped to overthrow. To Stalin, as to so many other revolutionaries, no violence for the sake of the cause could be as extensive or as horrible as the violence that would result if the capitalists were left to continue the mass murder. Yet Stalin had no part in killing anyone in World War I or in the overthrow of the Tsar. He approved of the killing involved in the Bolshevik *Putsch*, but he did not participate in it. He was in a Party and government that carried on the war, albeit feebly and briefly, while the peace of Brest-Litovsk was being arranged with Germany. More important for Stalin's moral development, he approved when his government began to shoot counter-revolutionaries.

But only with the outbreak of the Civil War in June, 1918, did Stalin himself become a killer. On the Lower Volga Stalin became used to ordering men into battle. He acquired the habit of approving the executions of counter-revolutionaries and saboteurs—and of people merely suspected of such actions—as the papers came across his desk. On several occasions he approved the shooting of innocent peasant villagers taken as hostages, on the grounds that war is war. Soon he came to kill fellow revolutionaries—of other parties. In Georgia he first became responsible for the killing of fellow Marxists—Mensheviks, not yet Bolsheviks. During this Civil War he also became hardened to ordering the torture of prisoners for information or for reprisal—for war is war. Stalin's killings in the Civil War did not lead directly to the horrors of collectivization and the great purges; many generals have fought bloodier wars without ending in Stalinism. But Stalin's first habituation to mass murder was a very important threshold.

This period came to a climax for Stalin when he received one more appointment on Lenin's nomination. On April 3, 1922, he was made Secretary General of the Central Committee of the Communist Party. The definition of this post was a mass of bureaucratic verbiage, but Stalin was to make it, for the rest of his long life, the most important post in Russia.

The Secretary General and his secretariat dominated the *Orgburo* and thereby controlled the personnel of the Party and of all Party posts throughout Russia. The Secretary General and his secretariat came increasingly to influence the *Politburo* by preparing the agenda for its sessions and by supplying the written materials on the basis of which it made decisions. This alone effectively manipulated the *Politburo* on minor matters concerning which its members had no strong opinions or independent knowledge. Once the *Politburo* had made a decision of any sort, minor or major, the Secretary General and his secretariat officially transmitted the decision to the relevant branches of the Party, and supervised the implementation of the decision. This power enabled Stalin to emphasize or de-emphasize the *Politburo's* policies on minor matters and influenced its effect even on major issues. The secretariat, of course, was in no sense a rival or a check on the Secretary General, but was entirely composed of his creatures. The chief of these creatures was Viacheslav Molotov, whom the wittiest Bolshevik, Karl Radek, ridiculed as "the best filing clerk in all Russia," a joke which even Lenin repeated. Molotov was to prove the most important filing clerk in history.

By May, 1922, Stalin had accumulated many powers, the bases of his imminent triumph. He did not, however, possess supreme power. It was still Lenin who had that: He could have annihilated all of Stalin's powers, and even his life, by merely opening his mouth. Late in May, 1922, Lenin suffered an incapacitating stroke.

While Lenin was ill no one had supreme power. It was believed that he would recover, but no one knew how soon or how much. Stalin's powers, however, could function for the time being without check from any higher authority in the *Politburo*. Machine-building in the secretariat, the *Orgburo*, *Rabkhrin*, and the Commissariat of Nationalities ground on. But the following two years of opportunity while Lenin lay ill were also the two years of greatest jeopardy in Stalin's career. His blunders and excesses during the preceding four years of machine-building came home to roost. His purges in Party and state (the word "purge" still meant dismissal from office or Party, not from life) now provoked active counterattack by persons as important as Trotsky, who proposed the abolition of Stalin's satrapy in *Rabkhrin*. His purges in the Ukraine, and above all in Georgia, where there had been many imprisonments and some shootings of revolutionaries including Mensheviks and, where Stalin for the first time extended his roughhouse tactics (but not yet his death warrants) to fellow Communist Party members, stirred up a more widespread, alarmed, and determined opposition, which came to include the dying Lenin.

Lenin was improving in the autumn of 1922, but he could not resume his former enormous work load. Information was fed to him by the chosen few who had personal access—including the Secretary General, who managed to explain even the Georgians' complaints away until early December. Then other sources of information got through to Lenin with the truth about Georgia. At this point Lenin's confidence in Stalin, which had remained constant for seventeen years, was broken. A healthy Lenin or even the semi-recovered invalid Lenin of those weeks would soon have reduced Stalin's powers. But Lenin suffered his second stroke in the middle of December, 1922. Radek remarked that "God voted for Stalin."

On Christmas Day, 1922, Lenin was able to dictate the

memorandum known as his "testament," in which he expressed misgivings about concentration of powers in Stalin's hands. On January 4, 1923, he added a codicil to his testament in which he recommended that Stalin be removed from the post of Secretary General. From the end of January to early March he dictated and, after delays, had published articles attacking Stalin's work in *Rabkhrin*. Stalin's measures of defense were not very effective. Once he forgot himself so far as to tell Lenin's wife, Nadezhda Krupskaia, what she could do to her mother. On March 5, therefore, Lenin formally broke off personal relations with Stalin. He made arrangements to have the Georgian case brought up against Stalin at the Twelfth Party Congress, which was scheduled to meet in April. But on March 9 Lenin had his third stroke, from which he never really recovered. God had again voted for Stalin.

Stalin was by now fully aware of his jeopardy and his luck. He was in the next few years to display powers of intra-Party diplomacy that he had not mastered before—and which he was to have no need of once he had triumphed. After Lenin's first stroke, Stalin arranged an informal alliance with two fellow *Politburo* members: Gregory Zinoviev, whose bureaucratic base at this time lay in the Petrograd Party organization and in the Communist International, and Leo Kamenev, whose bureaucratic base lay in the Moscow Party organization.

Since their alliance with Stalin at this time was eventually to cost Zinoviev and Kamenev their lives, their motives have been the subject of much interest. They apparently thought that Stalin was inherently slow and clumsy, and that the powerful posts he held posed no real danger to themselves because he seemed to be on the ropes already, whether or not Lenin recovered. Their real fear seems to have been that Lenin would die and that Trotsky would take the leadership of the Party, to the detriment of the Party's cause and their own positions. This triumvirate was to last about three years, during which Stalin won supreme power.

Stalin cultivated this alliance for all it was worth. With the aid of Zinoviev and Kamenev he was able to beat back the attacks on him at the Twelfth Party Congress and on several other occasions during the middle months of 1923. Lenin remained stricken, absent, and silent. One is tempted to say that Stalin also had the help of Trotsky, for the formidable People's Commissar for War, who had the greatest reputation after Lenin in the Party and in the country, and who was in actual control of the Red Army, blundered away, during the middle half of 1923, a whole series of chances to unseat Stalin and establish his own ascendency. The public and the outside world became far more conscious of the feud between Stalin and Trotsky after Lenin's death, but 1923 was in fact the decisive year. The issue was clearly not determined when Lenin had his third stroke, in March. Apparently it was settled when Lenin died ten months later.[1]

All observers agree that Stalin used his organizational and bureaucratic powers with great skill during the middle of 1923, and that alliance with Zinoviev and Kamenev was essential to him. There is little agreement on why Trotsky played his side of the game with so much less skill. Some have emphasized the inherent defect of his position in Russia: He was a Jew in an anti-Semitic country. Some have stressed the defect of his position in the Party: He was a long-time opponent of the Bolsheviks who had come over as late as the middle of 1917. Some have noted that he was the obvious leading contender for supreme power and was bound to rouse a coalition against him. Some have underlined observed or supposed defects in his character: his alleged impracticality, egotism, and lack of tact. Some point up his psychiatric difficulties.

Trotsky certainly experienced a kind of nervous collapse during the winter of 1923-24, which must have begun earlier in the year. He certainly made important miscalculations, such as depending on Lenin to recover and do his work for him after the third stroke, and promoting a foolish left-revolutionary policy in Germany at that time. He was certainly the victim of bad luck, such as the peculiar rhythm of Lenin's illness, and Zinoviev's political blindness. At the end of 1923 Trotsky was still War Commissar, and the likely heir to Lenin in the eyes of the world. But Stalin had so far survived his jeopardy and was still Secretary General, and, far more than Zinoviev and Kamenev, he was the most important actual day-to-day administrative leader of the USSR.

Lenin died of a fourth stroke on January 21, 1924, at a moment so opportune for the political fortunes of Stalin that some of the latter's more uncharitable enemies have suggested that he was a poisoner. We may assume Stalin felt relieved that there was no longer a chance for Lenin to recover and strip him of his high Party offices. We should also assume that Stalin felt some manner of grief at the end of a twenty-year association with a leader whom he had not, after all, joined out of any mania for power or lust for blood.

No doubt Stalin spent much of his time after Lenin's death "scheming for power," but an immediate time-consuming task was the management of the rite of passage that even a Communist state requires on the death of its leader. It was Stalin who arranged the fantastic, colossal state funeral for Lenin, attended by hundreds of thousands of people. (Accounts differ as to how many wept.) The remains of the funeral—artificial black floral wreaths, funeral coaches, artillery cortege—still fill several rooms of the Lenin Museum in Moscow. It was Stalin who decided such details as the observance of an old Orthodox superstition: He ordered that all the mirrors in the great Kremlin hall where Lenin's body lay in state be crisscrossed with strips of tape, in order to "break" them magically, lest the soul be sucked out of the vulnerable newly-dead corpse and imprisoned forever in the Devil's mirror-land.[2] And it was Stalin who decided to pickle Lenin like a medieval saint and display him in a tomb in Red Square, so that all Russia might venerate him there, and, perhaps, as Stalin's enemies have suggested, so that all Russia might be sure that Lenin was really dead and could not come back to life to threaten Stalin. The magnificence and expense of Lenin's funeral celebrations were attributed by Stalin's supporters to his filial piety, and by his opponents to his vulgar politicking and bad taste.

Clearly the visual impressiveness of Lenin's funeral served Stalin's political purpose by identifying him in the eyes of the Party and public as Lenin's devoted follower and, presumably, heir: the more so as Trotsky was totally out of sight, recovering from his nervous breakdown in the Caucasus. We can only speculate as to Stalin's inner need to appease the dead Lenin with this funeral for all the annoyance and pain he had caused the living Lenin in his last years.

Fully as important as the visual aspects of the funeral was what Stalin said on the occasion. On January 26, five days after Lenin's death, Stalin spoke to a packed but hushed audience, including hundreds of upper- and middle-ranking Party officials, at the Second All-Union Congress of Soviets, in Moscow. Needless to say, the speech was forthwith printed in *Pravda* and thereby reached every significant person in the USSR and every significant Communist abroad.[3] The speech was officially entitled *On the Death of Lenin*, but it is known throughout the Communist world as *Stalin's Vow*. It is certainly Stalin's best known address; millions of school children in the USSR and Eastern Europe used to learn it by heart.

From the start, Stalin's opponents sneered at the thick Georgian accent with which he spoke, and denounced the "crude, catechistic rhetoric" of the speech, while dismissing its content as a combination of maudlin sentimentalities and vile political lies. Nonetheless, few historians have failed to note that *Stalin's Vow*, along with the funeral itself, was a distinct step on Stalin's march to total power. Most Western students of Communist affairs are left with the impression that *Stalin's Vow* was indeed the crudely expressed pack of lies we have since learned to associate with his name. It deserves better than that. It is worth analyzing for a few pages here, since it is at once the most important, most effective, and most illuminating example of Stalin's powers of persuasion—his celebrated "propaganda."

We read that Stalin addressed his audience as "Comrades!" and we remember that in 1924 men could still thrill to such a form of address, which was still—for many—a challenge and an exhilaration, and had not yet sunk—for everyone—to being a routine and an irony.

We, Communists, are people of a special mold.
We are made of a special material.
We are those who form the army of the great proletarian strategist, the army of Comrade Lenin.[4]

Thus at the very beginning Stalin employed the repetitive rhetoric of the Christian Church: not the rhythm of the catechism as is so often alleged (there are no questions and answers here), but one of the verse forms of the Psalms and of the ancient Semitic hymns that lie behind the Psalms. It is a three-line stanza in which each line begins with the same repetitive element while the third rolls on longer than the other two. Likewise at the very beginning Stalin used what had already become the basic metaphor of all Communist rhetoric, the military image: The Communist Party is an army; its leaders are the officer corps; the world is a war.

There is nothing higher than the honor of belonging to this army.

> There is nothing higher than the title of member of the party whose founder and leader was Comrade Lenin.
>
> Not to everyone is it given to be a member of such a party.
> Not to everyone is it given to bear the strains and storms that accompany membership in such a party.
>
> The sons of the working class,
> The sons of want and struggle,
> The sons of incredible privation and heroic effort,
> They, before all others, should be members of such a party.[5]

These couplets and triplets can be duplicated in the Psalms, as can several of the expressions. In the Bible, it is the Lord by whom things and qualities are "given." Stalin, in using the phrase without a subject, retained the reverence of Biblical rhetoric without committing himself to an un-Bolshevik belief. In late Biblical Hebrew and in Aramaic, "the son of X" is often used as a locution for "X" (e.g., "the son of man" for "man"). Stalin, in using the locution, which is substantively meaningless in Russian, retained the respect with which sons are treated in patriarchal societies. Under Lenin, Bolsheviks had considered themselves too skeptical and too positivist to use "higher" in this ancient moral sense. Lenin had scoffed at "honor." Radicals had traditionally scorned "titles" as aristocratic and divorced from content. Stalin's reverent use of these terms was quite un-Bolshevik. Yet Stalin was speaking to men who were not only Communists but males brought up in semi-traditional societies in which fighting, ruling men cherished honor and valued titles. His rhetoric seems to have carried weight.

> Departing from us, comrade Lenin enjoined us to hold high and guard the purity of the great title of Member of the Party.
>
> We vow to you, Comrade Lenin, that we with honor shall fulfill this your behest![6]

Lenin was addressed as a Moses or a Jesus, a spirit that survives, hears, and enforces its will beyond the grave. Vows, after all, had force in early societies because of belief in their enforcement by supernatural agencies, and later because one engaged one's honor, which one did not care to lose, on an oath. One wonders if Lenin cared much about "purity," but one sees that Stalin was conjuring up visions of the things that traditional and Biblical armies did in fact guard and hold high: a banner with religious words and symbols, an image of a totem animal, an Ark of the Covenant. Stalin's rhetoric transformed the Communist Party into a very traditional army indeed.

Such is the first of the six sections of *Stalin's Vow*—one is tempted to call them stanzas. Five more stanzas follow, all constructed in the same way: a paragraph or so of Communist-military-Biblical rhetoric concluded by the "Departing from us, Comrade Lenin . . . We vow to you . . ." formula. The formal similarity of the stanzas masks the progression of Stalin's thought.

"For twenty-five years Comrade Lenin tended our Party . . ."

Twenty-five years before 1924 takes one to 1899, a date of no major significance in the life of Lenin or his as yet unfounded Party. One may dismiss the hypothesis that Stalin had his dates wrong. He sought oratorical power from the round-numbered ring of "twenty-five years," the more so since he was appealing to the less intellectual run of Party officials, for whom accuracy in the matter of dates was no moral cause. Although "scorpions constantly chastised our Party," it "stood firm as a rock," and "forged the unity and solidarity of its ranks."[7] Here was a pastiche of Biblical images to provoke the sarcasm of a sophisticated Trotskyite! For the less sophisticated (the more numerous) the point was well prepared for:

Departing from us, Comrade Lenin enjoined us to guard the unity of our Party as the apple of our eye. We vow . . .⁸

Under the circumstances, guarding the unity of the Party meant refraining from internal Party politics. The politicking that Stalin most feared was an attempt by Trotsky and his supporters to remove him from his commanding position as Secretary General, an act which had been enjoined by Comrade Lenin, departing from them. Stalin's rhetoric raised the unity of the Party from a political tactic to a mystical entity, like the seamless robe of Christ, in which he effectively wrapped himself.

The greatness of Lenin lies above all in this:

That by creating the Republic of Soviets he gave a practical demonstration to the oppressed masses of the whole world
That the hope of deliverance is not lost,
That the rule of the capitalists and landlords is shortlived,
That the kingdom of labor *can* be created by the efforts of the workers themselves,
That the kingdom of labor must be created not in heaven but on *earth*.⁹

Stalin was hardly the first to use the language of the Bible and hence the emotional force of the Bible to deny the religion of the Bible. So fortified, he shifted both language and substance:

Departing from us, Comrade Lenin enjoined us to guard and strengthen the dictatorship of the proletariat. We vow . . .¹⁰

In Stalin's audience the phrase "dictatorship of the proletariat" stirred apprehensions, not that the dictatorship would prove a tyranny, but that the Communists' enemies, "capitalists and landlords," against whom the dictatorship was supposed to be directed, might eventually prove too strong for them. An appeal to guard the dictatorship of the proletariat was an appeal for continued vigilance against the enemies of

Communist rule, the elements of the old regime that the Communists had overcome in the Civil War only a few years before and an opposition that no prudent Communist could help but fear again in the crisis of Lenin's death.

In a relatively straightforward and unpoetic passage, Stalin then lauded Lenin's celebrated "alliance between the workers and the peasants," without which, Stalin alleged (a Communist would probably have said "admitted"), the Party would not have won the Civil War.

> Departing from us, Comrade Lenin enjoined us to strengthen with all our might the alliance between the workers and peasants. We vow . . .[11]

To Stalin's audience, the peasants were a class to which Communists were morally committed since they had been desperately poor, oppressed, toiling masses. At the same time they were a class which Communists distrusted, for Marx, Lenin, and the history of revolutionary France had taught them that a peasantry, once it had secured a modicum of land in the first "bourgeois" stage of a revolution, became conservatively hostile to further revolution and willing to support "Thermidorian" and "Bonapartist" reactions. Stalin and his audience identified themselves with the workers in all sincerity. As for the Russian peasants, who had completed their acquisition of the country's arable land by 1918, Stalin could do no better than to use "alliance" in Lenin's marvelous dual sense: an equal connection between morally elevated groups which is at the same time a skillful, hard-and-soft domination over a giant, ignorant, dangerous mass. Love the peasants, and uplift them, but watch them. All this in rhetoric that conveyed the dual message to the Communist audience, while concealing it from the peasantry and the outside world.

Stalin's audience felt a similar ambivalence about the non-Great Russian nationalities of the USSR. They were to be the objects of Communist solicitude, for they had been fearfully oppressed under the Tsars. But their sufferings had driven them to "petty bourgeois nationalism," and many of the national groups had tried (and might still try) to secede from the USSR altogether—attempts which had been suppressed only during and after a Civil War. The nationalities were less dangerous than the peasants, for they threatened to upset Communist rule only at its peripheries, not at its heart: but such amputations might prove fatal in time. So Stalin intoned:

Russians and Ukrainians,
Bashkirs and Belorussians,
Georgians and Azerbaidzhanians,
Armenians and Daghestanians,
Tatars and Kirghiz,
Uzbeks and Turkmenians,

All are equally interested in strengthening the dictatorship of the proletariat . . .

Departing from us, Comrade Lenin enjoined us to strengthen and extend the union of republics. We vow . . .[12]

The audience would remember that Lenin had entrusted the nationalities problem to Stalin even before the World War. Stalin was known to be working on a new constitution for the USSR, which he was to have promulgated before the end of 1924. After Lenin's alliance with the peasants, Stalin's work with the nationalities!

Next came a paragraph in honor of "our Red Army and our Red Navy," linked together in rhetorical equality, although Stalin's audience regarded the Red Army as a formidable force whereas they all knew the Red Navy was largely a matter for the future. It is a surprisingly brief paragraph, until one remembers that the creator of the Red Army was Trotsky, who was still running it as the People's Commissar for War.

Stalin hurried on to his last point, the Communist International, on which he could dwell more happily, since it was the domain of Stalin's ally, Zinoviev.

> Like a huge rock stands our country
> In an ocean of bourgeois states.
> Wave after wave dashes against it
> Threatening to submerge it and wash it away.
> But the rock stands unshakable.
> Wherein lies its strength?[13]

Not in the Lord, as the language suggests, but in "the hearts of the workers and peasants of the whole world." The workers and peasants of foreign countries, Stalin insisted, had been of indispensable help to the Communists in defeating "capitalist" intervention during the Civil War. And so in gratitude as well as goodness Lenin had founded the Communist International, the sooner to liberate the workers and peasants of the world. In an ecstasy of statistics Stalin celebrated "the pilgrimage of scores and hundreds of thousands of working people to Comrade Lenin's bier," the millions that would soon see his tomb, and the scores and hundreds of millions that would testify to his greatness. This prepared for his conclusion:

> Departing from us, Comrade Lenin enjoined us to remain faithful to the principles of the Communist International. We vow...[14]

Once one credits Stalin with the intelligence to organize an effective speech one can see a simple but effective progression of: (1) He dwelt on the almost mystic rightness of the Communist cause. (2) He exalted the unity of the Party and bound it up with the Party's stability under his own control. (3) He kept up the Party's guard against its traditional enemies, the elements of the old regime. (4, 5) He bridged the contradictions in the Party's relations with its two enemy-allies, the peasantry and the national minorities, the greater problem solved by Lenin, the lesser by Stalin himself. (6) He linked Communists at home and abroad in bonds of practical and moral interdependence.

All six points could be included in Stalin's ultimate concern for unity: that unity of the Communist Party of the Soviet Union which implied Stalin's own personal and political security by binding the living leader to the dead leader; that unity which Stalin in all sincerity believed to be the apex of worldly wisdom and the nearest equivalent to heavenly wisdom; that unity on whose behalf he therefore exhorted his audience in both the language of the Party-army of this world, and the language of that other world which had not yet faded from his hearers' sensibilities. Let us admit that on occasion —and Lenin's death was such an occasion—Stalin could deliver an effective speech, an historic speech, with a degree of poetic power.

Now that Lenin was safely and ringingly placed in his grave, there remained, as barriers to Stalin's assumption of total power, Lenin's testament; Stalin's rival, Trotsky; and Stalin's unreliable allies, Zinoviev and Kamenev. Stalin apparently did not yet know about the testament. He spent his time strengthening the already strong position of his triumvirate against Trotsky, notably by enrolling more that 200,000 new and presumably manageable members in the Communist Party in the course of what he called the "Lenin push." Why Krupskaia and the few others who knew about Lenin's testament did not co-ordinate their plans with Trotsky to oust Stalin immediately after Lenin's death is not entirely fathomable. The move would probably not have worked, but all later efforts were even less likely to succeed.

Just before the Thirteenth Party Congress in May, 1924, Krupskaia did read the testament to the Central Committee, in hopes of having it put on the agenda for the Congress. Stalin has been described as looking "small and miserable" during this ordeal. If Trotsky had then moved to strip Stalin of his high posts in accordance with the wishes of the late Comrade Lenin, and if Zinoviev and Kamenev had seconded him, Stalin might have fallen. But Trotsky was once again fatally inactive; he was seen making faces, but he said nothing. He too had been criticized in the testament. And Zinoviev had no intention of breaking with Stalin at that time. He mouthed some phrases about how Comrade Lenin's fears about the Secretary General had proved groundless, and carried a motion that the testament be suppressed to protect the Party from dissension.

Stalin's course for the rest of the year was one of adept diplomacy. While Zinoviev and Kamenev embroiled themselves with Trotsky, and traded charges with him of past disloyalties to Lenin and the Party, Stalin seemed to be a quiet, hard-working moderate who avoided such unpleasant controversies except when he endeavored to moderate their tone. He gave himself much favorable publicity in the Party by implementing the new Constitution of the USSR in the course of the year: It had formally gone into effect in January. He hoped that this creation of a new state structure for the USSR would balance, in the public eye, Trotsky's creation of the Red Army—a deed now receding into the past.

By the autumn of 1924 Stalin was formulating his celebrated and widely misunderstood doctrine that it was possible to build socialism in one country, the USSR, before Communists seized power throughout the world. This simultaneously increased his not over-heavy reputation as a theorist in the Party, and ingratiated him with the more Russia-centered and complacent Communists. The latter welcomed commendation for a hard collective job well done, and feared to become involved in the foreign revolutionary adventures in Germany and elsewhere that Trotsky seemed to be urging. This doctrine was expressed in Stalin's book published that autumn, *Prob-*

lems of Leninism,¹⁵ which was long regarded as his weightiest contribution.

At the beginning of 1925, Stalin's long campaign against Trotsky proved decisively victorious. In January he decided that the time was ripe to have the triumvirate and its majority in the *Politburo* order Trotsky to "resign" as People's Commissar for War: that is, from actual control of the Red Army. Trotsky had lost his ability to rally the Party against Stalin sometime in the middle of 1923; so long as he remained in command of the Red Army, however, there was always the possibility that he might reverse Stalin's triumph within the Party by a military *Putsch*. Such a procedure was apparently contrary to Trotsky's beliefs and personality, and it is not certain that the Red Army would have followed any such orders. Trotsky obeyed the Party's highest organ of authority in accordance with his conscience, and gave up the People's Commissariat for War. It *is* certain that he lost his last real chance to bring off a *Putsch* when he let himself be driven from military command. To the outside world, the most dramatic episodes of the feud between Stalin and Trotsky were yet to come. To the insider and the historian, the struggle was over.

Relieved of this burden, Stalin had less need of circumspection in treating his allies, Zinoviev and Kamenev. They soon realized that he and not they ruled Russia. Accordingly they broke up the triumvirate that Stalin no longer needed. Neither their withdrawal of support from Stalin nor their alliance later in 1925 with Trotsky against him could now avail them. The last occasion that could conceivably be called a "chance" to stop Stalin passed in November, 1925. The man Stalin had chosen as People's Commissar for War to succeed Trotsky, Mikhail Frunze, was reported by such partisan sources as Trotsky himself to have fallen out with Stalin to some slight degree. Had Frunze thrown his by no means absolute control over the Red Army into a united opposition within the Party (but the opposition was in fact disunited), then a *Putsch* at this late date might still have been successful—an excessively hypothetical speculation.

As it was, Frunze was stricken with an illness whose nature is still debatable. It was debated then in the *Politburo* and under Stalin's direction Frunze was ordered to submit to surgery, although some doctors predicted it would kill him. It did kill him. Years later, Trotsky suggested that Stalin deliberately arranged the death. Natural causes are more likely, but no matter: From that time on Stalin was as secure in his power as human rulers can well be. He had supreme power.

His maneuvers over the next fifteen years whereby he expelled Trotsky, Zinoviev, Kamenev, Bukharin, Rykov, Tomsky, and so many other leading Communists and former associates from the *Politburo,* from the Central Committee, from the Party, and finally from life itself, were cautious, super-cautious, and perhaps paranoid measures for the preservation and strengthening of the supreme power he already possessed.

Russia had been subject to the authoritarian rule of the Tsars for centuries. Lenin had forged the Communist Party into an effective authoritarian machine. In such a country, under such a Party, it is not surprising that Lenin's death was followed by the rise to supreme power of still another man. The alternatives of prolonged "committee rule," much less of genuine democracy, were rather unlikely. That the man should be Stalin was much more surprising—no social evolution or broad political movement required that. Stalin's own organizational abilities throughout his rise to power, and his able political in-fighting during the last stages of it, must be recognized when accounting for it. But so must the multiple and strangely co-ordinated blunders of all his recognized and unrecognized rivals. Finally, one cannot escape mentioning Stalin's extraordinary good luck, most notably in the timing of Lenin's several strokes. No abilities, no blunders, no social forces brought those on. Stalin's rise to supreme power was a classic example of the process, but like most classic examples it had little in common with previous dramatic ascents to the top, and would prove impossible to repeat.

4. THE WORLD-VIEW

WHAT kind of world did Stalin think he was living in? How did he hope to move from the dreadful present to the shining future? One must answer these questions before one can understand what Stalin did in the decades after 1928 to transform the USSR and much of the rest of the world. One must answer these questions before one can judge the success of the revolutionary efforts for which he used the supreme power he had won in the early 1920's. Fortunately, Communist documents provide us with voluminous material on most aspects of Stalin's world-view. In this field these is usually little reason to doubt the honesty of the documents.

In the first place, Stalin did not believe in God. He would have agreed that this must come first. He always divided humanity into the progressive "materialist camp" and the reactionary "idealist camp." The supreme idea of the idealists was God. Stalin was brought up in a family, state, and society that were all allegedly devoted to God. His personal liberation was at once the theoretical culmination and shocking symbol of his alienation from his origins. He demanded much more of a man than mere atheism, but that was the first step. "Nothing," he said, "can be done with a man who continues to believe."[1] But what would you do, Stalin was asked, if you should somehow become convinced that God does exist? "That would change everything," he answered. "I would not know what to believe; the whole of science would then be false. I would resign from the Party. I would become a monk. I would go to Mount Athos."[2]

Two moral-emotional consequences followed from Stalin's atheism. He never felt that a Godless universe was dark, lonely, and hostile; he was never plunged into the existential despair of so many Victorians who lost their faith. He mentioned the joy of no longer fearing hell; he did not mention relief from guilt feelings about his own sinfulness. He emphasized his optimism about the Godless world:

If God exists, He must have ordained slavery, feudalism, and capitalism. He must want humanity to suffer, as the monks were always telling me. Then there would be no hope for the toiling masses to free themselves from their oppressors. But when I learned that there is no God, I knew that humanity could fight its way to freedom.[3]

Stalin had exchanged his faith in God for a faith in the future.

And if there is no God, Stalin realized, there is no Divine Providence. In that case, men—and their organizations such as the Party and the state—have the moral responsibility to arrange their lives and the lives of others as best they know how, with a positive, active effort. A Christian may leave his neighbor to the privacy of his conscience and to heaven, but for Stalin this meant abandoning people to laziness and vice. A Christian ruler may limit the scope of state action for fear of encroaching on the prerogatives of Providence, but for

Stalin this meant leaving things to blind chance, or to conspiring enemies.

> The monks said that it was not my place to worry about such questions [social problems], that I should trust God to arrange all for the best in the end. Trust God! If people trust God, they do nothing for themselves. They then leave everything to the Tsar and the landlords and the police. They were very lazy, the monks.[4]

Stalin was accusing the monks not of hypocrisy but of moral laziness. For Stalin the ethical corollary of atheism was ceaseless public activity for the welfare of humanity. In his sentiments about atheism and its ethical consequences, he was in agreement with most Russian and European revolutionaries.

Stalin believed he was living in a physical, material universe, one huge unified system which had already been adequately described by natural scientists in Marx's day. To the end of his life he held pretty much to the picture of the physical universe that had been presented by the mid-nineteenth century radical materialists, a picture which was increasingly out of date.

As a materialist, Stalin believed that the universe was composed of hard, discrete, tangible bodies moving in different ways through infinite, three-dimensional space. He adamantly rejected all notions about the fourth dimension, space-time continua, the "curvature" of space, and relativity as "anti-materialist." Matter was composed of atoms, which came in ninety-two varieties—and it was a great satisfaction to Stalin that the chemical elements had been shown to fall into an intelligible periodic series by a *Russian* chemist, Dmitry Mendeleev.

Like Marx, Lenin, and many other socialists in Russia and Europe, Stalin resisted the idea that atoms were themselves divisible into smaller entities. Electrons, protons, what have you, were "idealistic, anti-scientific." In the late 1930's, when the physicists of the USSR were making great strides in sub-atomic physics, Stalin reluctantly assented to a simplified version of Niels Bohr's long-since outdated "planetary model" of the atom: the atom as a miniature solar system in which the nucleus is the sun and the electrons are planets. This satisfied Stalin's demand for a simple, visualizable universe of discrete primary particles.[5] Further advances, such as the wave nature of certain sub-atomic phenomena, were also rejected on "materialist" grounds. The "uncertainty principle" was outlawed, because its propounder, Werner Heisenberg, was thought to be a Nazi as well as an idealist. Electron sharing was forbidden in Communist countries because its discoverer, Linus Pauling, was thought to be Trotskyite as well as anti-materialist. All these rigidities came during the period after World War II, when Stalin's own scientists were employing most of these concepts to make him an atomic bomb.[6]

Nor did other challenges to late nineteenth century materialism bother Stalin. He was content to think of electricity as a kind of atomic (and later electronic) motion through wires. He believed that wave phenomena were all simple oscillations of matter, and that radiation consisted entirely of the emission of material particles. Sensations, feelings, and thoughts were some kind of electro-chemical process in nerve and brain tissues. Stalin sometimes expressed the mid-nineteenth century German materialist view that the physical basis of thought is phosphorus in the brain.[7]

Knowledge came by material transmission from the outside world through the organs of sense to the brain, where it was stored. Stalin did not write scientific textbooks. He got all these ideas from Marx, Engels, Chernyshevsky, and Lenin, simplifying all of them. (The simplification was most drastic in the case of Marx.) Stalin left the details of his scientific opinions to Communist scientists and writers, but for twenty-five years they had to work within the limitations imposed by his conception of the physical world.

✳ Stalin was not only a materialist, but a "dialectical materialist." Marx, Engels, and Lenin had written many complicated pages on this knottiest of all problems in Communist ideology. Stalin could quote and paraphrase his masters as the occasion demanded. The core of the doctrine seemed simple enough to him: The universe and everything in it develop through time (and Stalin was not concerned with philosophic arguments about the concept of time). Developments through time constitute an evolution. Individual phenomena come into being and pass away, but the universe as a whole, life as a whole, and human society as a whole constantly progress toward a more complex, higher, better state of affairs. The evolutionary process, whether of a planet or of a political party, involves the fruitful conflict of opposite tendencies and phenomena, and results in successive syntheses of the two opposites in which both are raised to a higher level.

This is the platitudinous skeleton of the famous doctrine of dialectical materialism, and this was as far as Stalin went into the subject unless he felt specifically called on to expound the doctrine at great length. He almost always illustrated the dialectical process by paraphrasing Engels's simplest examples: The union of male and female produces superior offspring; the combination of bourgeois productive capacity with proletarian social solidarity will result in a post-revolutionary society of plenty and justice.[8]

Astronomy did not much interest Stalin, in spite of his year at the Tbilisi observatory. He believed that stars were scattered at random throughout infinite Euclidean space. (Sometime after 1930 he substituted galaxies for individual stars.) He approved of the efforts to work out an evolutionary scheme for stars. He spoke of the universe as if it had always been in existence. He liked to attribute the origin of the earth and the other planets to gravitational disturbances caused by the near approach of another star to the sun—for that would have

THE WORLD-VIEW 69

been dialectical, a fruitful clash of opposites. Unlike many scientists, Stalin was too unromantic to be disturbed by the physical insignificance of man in his stellar setting, and he was in a sense too humanist to enjoy it.[9] Stalin had few unorthodox opinions on geological or biological evolution. He remained all his life an admirer of Darwin, whose theories had been so exciting and controversial in Stalin's youth. As a Georgian he liked mountains; as a man from a semi-arid and badly eroded land, he valued rivers and forests. He developed a keen interest in the Arctic, and he had a ruler's concern for minerals. These interests he backed up with a certain amount of scientific reading. He liked to display his knowledge of ice formations and forestry, and of the natural history of coal and oil. He insisted that life had developed quite materialistically out of chemicals floating in warm seas, and had evolved continuously in response to changing physical conditions.

One of Stalin's ideas about the process of biological evolution *did* wreak havoc in Soviet genetics, and stirred up a world-wide furor. Stalin and the other Old Bolsheviks grew up before modern genetics was known or publicized. As Bolsheviks they took no position on the post-Darwinian controversy about the mechanism of heredity. Yet when Stalin was called upon, after World War II, to decide once and for all whether the modern genetic solution to that controversy should be accepted in Communist countries, he decided against it. The factors in Stalin's decision illustrate much of his scientific world-view.

Stalin and the other Bolsheviks were scientific optimists. They saw nature and man as more plastic, more susceptible to scientific and political manipulation and improvement, than most outsiders would agree to. They wanted to believe that living things could be profoundly changed by changes in their environment, because this gave promise of quick improvement in human nature, life, and society, once scientists and socialists came to control them. Under Stalin, zoologists at the Moscow Zoo went to great lengths to show that, with the proper environment, lions *could* be trained to lie down with lambs.[10] The Russian plant biologists, Kliment Timiriazev and Ivan Michurin, had had great success in improving plants and increasing crop yields through practical experimentation. Their successes, and the apparent successes of their successor, Trofim Lysenko, had helped to expand the agricultural production that Stalin so desperately needed. They were successes of Russians of proper political views, and they fitted in with the warm, generous, life-affirming side of the Leninist ethic.

On the other hand, Mendel was a German and a monk, and Thomas Hunt Morgan was an American with a noted capitalist name at a capitalist university. "Mendel-Morgan genetics" emphasized the hereditary limitations on change in organisms, and thereby, in Stalin's eyes, threatened to make scientific and social progress more difficult. To Stalin, believing in Morgan meant accepting a hostile foreigner's abstract theorizing in place of a good Russian's practical success, and closing the doors to certain immediate improvements in socialist society. Stalin could easily explain the origins of Mendel-Morgan genetics: Priest Mendel and capitalist Morgan approved of and benefited from the hereditary class nature of their society, and wanted to block revolutionary change. Consequently they generated a false, reactionary genetics to suit their preconception—and in Morgan's case to damage the USSR.[11]

With the exceedingly persuasive Lysenko urging these views, which so profoundly coincided with Stalin's deepest ethical-scientific convictions, it is not surprising that the aging Stalin chose Lysenkoism instead of genetics. And so genetics had to go underground for some years in Communist countries, and some geneticists went to their deaths in Siberia.

Stalin's wishful thinking and ethical idealism—integral parts of his ideological makeup—had triumphed over his critical judgment.

In short, Stalin looked on the natural world as intelligible, deterministic, and benign. There were many things that no man knew, but there were no mysteries, and nothing was withheld from us. All things proceeded according to evolutionary natural laws. He was willing to use terms such as "inevitable" without philosophizing about the problem of determinism. A universe of iron evolutionary laws did not discourage Stalin, for he was sure the world had always been progressing. The mutability of all things touched off no *Weltschmerz* in Stalin, for he was certain that they would be replaced by better things. Nature was seen as a rich setting for human life. Man's increasing knowledge of natural laws would enable him, within the framework of those laws, to manipulate nature and to build a better life for himself. For Stalin, life in the natural world was an inevitable struggle and a certain triumph. In these views, again, he was in agreement with most revolutionaries in Europe (although not with the voluntarist thinkers of the Russian *narodnik* and Socialist-Revolutionary tradition).

To Stalin, human beings were an integral part of the natural world, and also its culmination. He treasured all his life the knowledge that had been so bold in his youth—that men have evolved in Darwinian fashion from the primates. He believed to the end that man must have evolved in his own Mother Asia in spite of increasing evidence that our ancestors lived in Africa, a continent in which Stalin had little interest.

He was relatively generous to physical anthropologists and archaeologists, and financed much excellent work on the prehistory of man in the USSR. This made possible the discovery of Neanderthal man in Soviet Central Asia, thousands of miles east of his previously known range, and other triumphs. But this support seems to have been a function of Stalin's patriotism rather than of any special interest in early man. Stalin was essentially concerned with civilized men. When he talked of "primitive men" he would cite the mountaineers of the Caucasus, who were Christians or Muslims with a developed iron-age technology and social organization, not really primitive men. Unlike many Russian and Polish exiles in Siberia, Stalin developed little interest in the Siberian peoples. The lessons about human nature which Western anthropologists have derived from their study of primitive peoples did not penetrate to Stalin.

If one asks what Stalin's view of human nature was, one has to wrestle with many contradictory statements. On the one hand, Stalin subscribed to the Marxist-Leninist conviction that men's characters are the product of their social environment, and that they are therefore different in different societies, and evolve as societies evolve. Hence the USSR was thought to be producing a "New Soviet Man." On the other hand, Stalin usually spoke as if human nature were essentially alike everywhere and at all times, exhibiting the same range, susceptible to the same moral judgments.

On the one hand, Stalin insisted on the worth of the common people everywhere, implying that they and not certain corrupted ruling minorities were the real human species, and that human nature was fundamentally good. On the other hand, Stalin usually acted and often talked as if people of all classes and nations were basically a pack of rascals who were chronically selfish and lazy, and who had always to be watched and often beaten into behaving themselves and getting the necessary work done. The strict Marxist view—that capitalists and other oppressors are not personally immoral, but victims of the logic of their system—was sometimes asserted by Stalin, but was usually ignored in favor of the simpler view that all oppressors are villains. When Stalin thought about oppressors, he was all for the people. When he thought about the people, he was contemptuous, distrustful, or saddened by them.

Of the underlying question, what *is* good, Stalin had little to say. Yet he was a man profoundly concerned with morality, a man who insisted on judging every significant act of every person in moral terms. On the one hand, he agreed with Marx and most European revolutionaries (but again, not with many Russian *narodniks* and Socialist-Revolutionaries) that goodness is ultimately happiness and pleasure, and that poverty, oppression, and war are evil because they inflict suffering. On the other hand, Stalin shared with practically all revolutionaries the conviction that so long as the world is beset by poverty, oppression, and war, the good man must forgo personal and material pleasures, and live an ascetic life of service and sacrifice. Stalin himself, in spite of the banquets and "orgies" of his later Kremlin years, believed he led a life of service and sacrifice.

Many good men are called upon to sacrifice their lives, and a good revolutionary of the Stalinist cast might well impose poverty on his people for a generation in the interest of production for the future, and war for the liberation of humanity. For all human history up through the foreseeable future, the *good*, for Stalin and the other revolutionaries, meant service and sacrifice, as it had for the Christians from whom they were descended.

It is possible to say that there were two types of good man for Stalin. There was the *genius*, conceived in German Romantic terms. He was the great creator in science, politics, or art, the pioneer ahead of his time, who might succeed in imposing the future on his generation, or who might be crushed and yet hand on the torch—in any case his life would be one of lonely struggle. Stalin mentioned a number of such genius-heroes, about evenly divided between revolution, art, and science: Democritus, Newton, Lomonosov, Darwin, Michelangelo, Goethe, Beethoven, Pushkin, Spartacus, Babeuf,

Marx, Lenin[12]—and of course Stalin, who habitually had himself referred to in his last fifteen years as "the genius leader of the peoples of humanity."

And then there was the common man, the peasant who ploughs through the oppression of the ages, the worker at the bench who forges the economic future during his long days at the factory, and above all the soldier in the liberation wars of humanity. The common people act together, suffer together, triumph together and/or die together. Together! The common people were not only to act alike but to *be* alike. The Stalinist ideal was not fraternity between distinct individuals, but solidarity among identical units.

Stalin noted how much he liked the scene from Sergei Eisenstein's film, *Alexander Nevsky*, in which many Russian fishermen pull on long fishing lines together, and the scene from the Vasiliev brothers' film, *Chapaev*, in which the Red partisans hum *Stenka Razin* together—a folk song (binding the singers to the whole people) about a revolutionary genius.[13] When Stalin first saw forty thousand gymnasts going through identical calisthenics in a Moscow studium, he remarked that it was the most impressive thing he had ever seen.[14] His taste in May Day parades—hundreds of thousands of disciplined marchers—determined the nature of the greatest ritual celebration of solidarity, strength, and triumph in the Communist year. For Stalin as for so many Russian revolutionaries, the assertion and development of individual character and difference amounted to selfishness, disruption, and *hubris*. The good man (save for the very rare genius) surrenders his individuality to the organization, merges his identity in the people, and becomes "like the grain in the field, the drops in the sea, and stars in the sky," as Stalin quoted several times from Chernyshevsky.[15]

Stalin was not much concerned with man's personal problems. Children, he thought, should be cared for, and trained to grow up to adulthood, the worthwhile stage of human existence. The material welfare of children was important: socialists build state nurseries for their children, Stalin said, while capitalists send theirs to the mines.[16] And the training of children was all-important, for he conceived of young minds as extremely plastic and malleable. Acting on this assumption, the Party took enormous pains to organize an all-encompassing system of schools and youth organizations, which aimed to mold psyches as well as to train everybody for his slot in society. The children Stalin singled out for public praise were those who acted like adults before their time: ten- and eleven-year-olds who had died fighting the Germans, and that little monster, Pavlik Morozov, who turned in his father and mother to be shot by the police for planning sabotage against their collective farm.[17] But Stalin was no more interested in the private world of childhood—in fact or in fiction—than he was in that of the embryo.

"Adolescence," for Stalin, had few of its current American connotations. He did not think of it as a tormented period of betwixt-and-between existence, but as a crucial phase of life in which one received one's final training and took up one's permanent post. He was well enough aware of the explosive tendencies of youth: Communist parties abroad were ordered to harness youthful rebelliousness through worldwide student and youth organizations for revolutionary purposes. But Stalin believed that such youthful discontents, like all other discontents, were functions of the contradictions of pre-socialist societies, not something inherent in being fifteen or twenty. He played down adolescent tensions arising from family life and sex. If parents are politically progressive, children should obey them. If parents are reactionary, children should reeducate them. If parents are obdurate, children should abandon them or turn against them. Other family conflicts are beside the political point. In any of these cases, the child should feel no great psychic stress.

As a Bolshevik, Stalin was not hostile to sex. Sex was supposed to be a natural function like eating and drinking—very much more like eating and drinking than most Westerners believe. A man and (in a softer voice) a woman need some sex to stay healthy, and of course the species needs children. Christian ethics of monastic abstinence and sexual guilt feelings were judged obsolete superstition. But Stalin thought a person who spent any great amount of time on sex was like a person who spent his life on food—a self-indulgent, sensual egotist, who was neglecting his duty to serve humanity.[18]

Stalin and his followers spoke as if they regarded sex, like eating, as the activity of one person, not two. They did not accept the idea so dear to so many of their Western contemporaries that sex and the other elements of mutual love can or should be the most intense and highest experiences of human life. They might be indulgent to young lovers lost to the world—for a spell, until the next work period, when the lovers should be recalled to more important things. But any effort—in life or in literature—to make love the permanently central experience of life was chastised. A man must work and fight, not enjoy himself loving, and women should model themselves on men in these respects. When something serious is afoot, such as a military or industrial campaign, people must cut down on sex, as on food, until the emergency is over. And for Stalin the emergency was never over, for poverty and oppression, wars and threats of wars, prevailed throughout his life. A human being's real emotional bond, Stalin felt, should be not with his mate but with his class and nation.[19]

Stalin's low valuation of sex led him to exclude from the USSR any psychology based on Freud's family- and sex-centered system. This determined the study and treatment of the mentally ill in Stalin's Russia. Stalin did not share the modern world's interest in neurotics. He retained the pre-modern view that the mentally ill are small in number, out of the main stream of life, and unimportant. But during the great purges he came to accept the view that stomach ulcers can be caused by worry: He added his own opinion that in the socialist USSR such extreme worry can no longer come from the contradictions of capitalist society and must therefore be caused by the sufferer's fears that his plots against the state will be found out. Stomach ulcers went underground in the USSR for the rest of Stalin's life, for any bureaucrat who admitted to them was suspected of embezzlement or treason, and was often arrested.

Westerners have often called Stalin a "puritan" in his attitude toward sex. He was in fact rather less Victorian than most of his contemporaries, even if kissing in films offended him. But he had derived from his upbringing and from Lenin views that were very old fashioned by the end of his life. He cherished one of Lenin's few jokes: When Alexandra Kollontai, the leading Bolshevik propagandist and practitioner of free love, proclaimed, "Sex is like a glass of water; when I feel thirsty, I drink," Lenin had quipped, "But who wants to drink a glass of dirty water?"—a genuinely Victorian wisecrack.[20]

Yet Stalin's justifications for tightening up the rather relaxed sexual and family laws and mores that had prevailed in Lenin's Russia were phrased in functional terms. The state needed children for the work force and for coming wars. Family instability was a component of labor instability, during the First Five Year Plan. Therefore Stalin made divorce so difficult and expensive as to approach impossibility for ordinary citizens. Abortions were restricted to the most compelling medical cases. Contraceptives were among the consumer goods produced in least quantity in proportion to demand. Prostitution and dalliance were curbed by the police. Mothers of five and ten children received showy medals and public praise.[21] For the good of socialism the Stalinist family was supposed to be a permanent, solid, and fertile family.

Stalin was equally insensitive about the problems of old age, even when he himself was in his seventies, and ill. Old folks in their dotage were supposed to be cared for with socialist humanitarianism, but until their final decline they were seen as older, healthy adults. Stalin prized the Russian informal title of respect, *"starik,"* which means "old man," but with connotations on the order of "person held in respect and affection by virtue of long, wise, and effective leadership." In most cases, old age meant to Stalin a movement up a status ladder, not a tragic diminution of powers.

It is easy to accuse Stalin of colossal insensitivity to the complexities of human nature, but he himself believed that he was well aware that man is full of unpredictable personal peculiarities. When Milovan Djilas, after World War II, complained to Stalin that Russian soldiers had raped any number of Yugoslav women, Stalin burst out with a remarkable response: Djilas should remember that these Russian soldiers had fought the fascists fifteen hundred miles from Stalingrad, and weren't they entitled to a little relaxation? Djilas should remember that human nature is a complex affair; he should read the novels of Dostoevsky.[22] Stalin *had* read Dostoevsky, and thought he *had* absorbed the lesson of man's complexity. What it meant to him was that human beings are apt to be impossible at times, and that in recognition of this, soldiers, for instance, should be allowed a little rape.

Stalin thus scanted the experience and problems of man's personal life, which are so prominent in Western psychology, social science, and literature, because he had an alternative theory of what makes human beings tick. This was his endlessly asserted Marxist-Leninist conviction that an individual's development and nature are fundamentally determined by society as a whole, and that the most important parts of society in molding an individual are its economy and class structure. His professed ideology told him that the largest groupings into which man can be divided are over-all economic systems, of which there have been and can be only five: primitive communism, ancient slaveholding, medieval feudalism, modern capitalism, and the socialism-communism of the present and future. (He quashed Marx's sixth type of economy, "Asiatic" statism.) The Russian Revolution had shattered the world-wide unity of the capitalist system, leaving a fatally mutilated "capitalist camp" facing the socialist "sixth of the earth"—which grew, after Mao's triumph in China, to "one third of the world's people."

Within an economic grouping, the most important subdivision is the economic class. Marx had defined a class as "a group with a special relationship to the means of production, distribution, and exchange." The landlord owned the land, the peasant worked it for the landlord, and so on. In Marxist-Leninist theory, the workers of all countries live essentially similar lives in similar factories and similar slums, while the bourgeoisie of all countries live similar tasteless, ostentatious lives on the proceeds of similar economic exploitation. Therefore the German worker, say, is thought to have far more in common with the French worker than either has with the bourgeoisie of his own country. The nature of a person's life, the rhythm of his daily work, his food and housing, his education, politics, cultural life, and religion, are all determined— Stalin's ideology dictated—by his economic relations to the means of production that had been developed in that society.

Nothing in Marxism-Leninism is better known than this famous complex of assertions, and nothing appeared more repetitiously in Stalin's prose. The alternative view, held by most modern non-Marxists from Harvard to Java, is that economic classes are indeed exceedingly important divisions of mankind, but usually not quite so important as ethnic-linguistic-religious divisions, especially when the latter coincide with political boundaries to form a modern nation-state.

The lesson of the first half of the twentieth century seems to have been that on many important occasions, such as the outbreak of two world wars, the workers and factory owners of any given nation are very apt to see more common interests with each other than with either of their class counterparts across a national frontier.

Stalin of the Caucasus was as committed as any Marxist-Leninist ever has been to recognizing the importance of the "national question." He emphasized language, territory, historical experience, and possession of a state as the important elements of a nation, and played down religion and race. He often repeated Lenin's dictum that the "national question" ought to be subordinated to the "class question." But he was aware that he was in control of a nation-state (albeit one with an unusually complicated minorities problem) and not an international class. He was aware that most of his fellow citizens and most foreigners acted as if nation were more important than class, and that this Marxist class thesis had always been one of the most controversial, paradoxical, and unconvincing parts of Communist ideology.

Stalin's procedure, when the ideology he received from Lenin was in conflict with his own experience and convictions, was to integrate his own beliefs into his received ideological framework in a way that might not seem logical to an outsider, but which did constitute an emotionally consistent whole. Stalin might insist that he was now propounding what Lenin had always taught in less detail, or that he was adapting Lenin's doctrine to changed circumstances. In dealing with the importance of nations, Stalin was able to expand upon Lenin's discussion of Polish nationalism. Lenin had lamented the tendency of the Polish proletariat to fall for Polish bourgeois nationalist appeals, and had admitted that the force of nationalist sentiment might often obscure class solidarity in certain bourgeois and colonial countries. Stalin was able to work up a Leninist-sounding theory according to which the USSR was essentially a working class nation (after the Constitution of 1936, *exclusively* a working class nation), and the sole hope of the workers of the world. This justified Stalin's role as the leader of a nation-state, for it equated that position with leadership of the world's workers. This theory permitted him to manipulate his own population by patriotic appeals, for it defined nationalist propaganda for the USSR as efforts toward working class solidarity.[23]

When Stalin looked out onto the capitalist world and the survivals within it of its "feudal" predecessor, he saw that it was evil. He saw that the overwhelming majority of the world's people were compelled to work backbreakingly hard just to continue to exist in dreadful poverty, starvation, ignorance, humiliation, oppression, and war. Many Westerners are tempted to say that Stalin and the other Communists exaggerated the misery of the toiling masses of the world, but after looking carefully we realize that it is impossible for anyone, even Stalin, to exaggerate the horror of being poor. We take more serious issue with his judgment of the quality of life for that usually tiny minority which is economically well off. Stalin thought their enjoyment of the good things of life was genuine enough, if clouded in recent times by fear of revolution. But he believed that all their pleasures were intrinsically vile because they were made possible only by the exploitation of the poor. The only really good life possible to a member of the upper classes was alienation from his class and going over to the revolution. But such a revolutionary's life would no longer be prosperous or pleasant.

How would mankind be redeemed from ignorance, oppression, and poverty? The first historic step, in Stalin's eyes, was the struggle against ignorance. The slave economy of ancient Greece, Stalin thought, had made possible a civilization in which a few individuals, such as Democritus and

Epicurus, could break through the prevailing polytheistic primitivism and perceive that there are no gods (always the first point for Stalin), and that the universe is composed of matter only. But then, he thought, the slaveholders generated a reactionary ideological counterattack, first in the form of "idealistic" philosophy such as Plato's, later in the form of mystery religions such as Christianity. Medieval feudalism did not provide the economic base for even a few atheist materialists. With the dawn of modern capitalism in the Renaissance, however, a small but growing trickle of scientists (Leonardo da Vinci, Copernicus—who was even a Slav) began to erect a secular, mathematical, and materialist science. By the eighteenth century, when capitalism was on the eve of its tremendous push for world-wide supremacy, bourgeois science had achieved staggering triumphs, including explicit realization of atheist materialism by such men as the Baron d'Holbach. Stalin regarded these as the most penetrating minds of the day.[24]

There followed the world-wide triumph of capitalism and the construction of the industrial base for future mass plenty, accompanied by bourgeois revolutions such as the French. Stalin, like Marx, commended capitalism in this phase as a progressive force, to be supported where it had not yet triumphed. Yet all the time the capitalists were creating the material conditions for their own destruction and the next phase of human evolution: the mass proletariat and socialism. Certain French *philosophes* (Morelly), revolutionaries (Babeuf), and utopian thinkers (Fourier) reflected the rise of the proletariat and the necessity of socialist forms of social organization. Meanwhile the peculiar, uneven, mixed capitalist and feudal economic development of Germany enabled some German philosophers, notably Hegel, to perceive the dialectical movement of history, without shaking themselves free of idealism.[25]

Then in the 1840's, when capitalism had developed to the point of provoking the first proletarian rising (in Paris, the June Days of 1848), material conditions were ripe for two individuals, Karl Marx and Friedrich Engels, to discover and lay down the main lines of philosophy and science (dialectical materialism) and of history and economics (historical materialism and the Marxist analysis of the capitalist system). Because Marx and Engels, the first human beings to perceive the true nature of the world, possessed this correct ideology, they were the first to know what actions to take in consonance with the inevitable development of the historical process. They published the newfound truth in *The Communist Manifesto*, *Das Kapital*, and other writings. They corrected the ideology of various proletarian movements, and set up a Workers' International organization to co-ordinate those movements and bring on the revolution.

Marx and Engels, Stalin thought, were the first men completely emancipated from ignorance. They provided revolutionary humanity with a world-view, a total ideology, that was both complete and accurate. It made no mistakes and left nothing out. However, social conditions were to change somewhat after Engels's death in 1895, providing some scope for ideological originality among his successors. Stalin, for practical purposes, thought that only two men had made any true additions to Marxism, Lenin and himself. All other modifications of Marx's teachings were false "revisionism" or "deviations" from the truth.

Once socialist ideology had been evolved by Marx and Engels, Stalin thought, only a believer in it could make any true progress toward revolution. He insisted, following Lenin, that one can know what correct actions to take in any given situation only by deducing them from correct ideology. Those whose ideology varied in the slightest from true Marxism would always find their actions turning sour, unsuccessful, and vicious. The revolutionary movements in the advanced industrial countries of Europe had all failed, Stalin thought, for lack of ideologically correct leadership in the generation after Marx's death.

Only in Russia did a man arise who comprehended the slightly changed conditions and took advantage of them. Lenin's contributions, as Stalin saw them, were first of all ideological. Lenin perceived the shift from "industrial" to "finance" capitalism (e.g., Andrew Carnegie gave way to J. P. Morgan in the American steel industry), and he understood that the rivalries among imperialist combinations of finance capitalists had caused World War I. Secondly, Lenin perceived the peculiar nature of the Russian economy, with its mixture of a surviving "feudal" (i.e., Tsarist and aristocratic) state, a state-dominated industrial plant, a weak bourgeoisie, a modern proletariat concentrated in relatively few large cities and factories, and millions of disaffected peasants. Lenin's deduction from all this was that a social revolution might come about in Russia before any other country, although by strict Marxist standards Russia was a backward country with a long way to go. Stalin regarded this conclusion of Lenin's as a piece of brilliant original Marxist analysis applied to Russia. Western scholars sometimes see it as Lenin's youthful agrarian *narodnik* doctrine bursting through a veneer of Marxist theory.

Thirdly, Stalin credited Lenin with perceiving the true theory of how to form and guide a revolutionary party, and of doing so. This was the theory set forth in *What Is To Be Done?* and Lenin's other writings of the first decade of this century, which display so heavy a component of Russian revolutionary doctrines derived from Bakunin, Nechaev, Lavrov, and Tkachev. Progress, Lenin wrote and Stalin agreed, cannot be left to the bourgeois reformers or to the workers and peasants themselves. Progress must come through the agency of critically thinking individuals, intellectuals of upper or middle class origins who theoretically understand the world and the revolution it is heading toward, and who alone are capable of guiding the toiling masses rightly to and through the revolution.

The agency of revolution, Lenin wrote and Stalin agreed, was the party. For them a party was not an organization to contest elections and pass bills in legislatures. Before the revolution, a party was supposed to be an illegal group dedicated to overthrowing the Tsarist (or some other oppressive) system and all its works by means of lawless agitation, and eventually by violent revolution. The proper way to run such a party, Lenin taught and Stalin agreed, was to keep its ruling committee abroad, where the Tsar's police torturers couldn't get at it. The party center abroad would organize units of the party within Russia as "cells"—a famous metaphor taken from physiology—in which members would know only each other, and only the head of the cell would be in touch with the next highest level of the party. At intervals delegates from the various cells would go abroad and hold a congress of the party, at which decisions would be arrived at democratically, under the tight guidance of the ideologically correct leaders. But otherwise the party would be the union of hierarchical, authoritarian organization with hierarchical, authoritarian theory. The party's tasks would fall under two headings: managing the revolutionary effort day by day, and preserving the ideological purity of the movement by ruthlessly purging deviationists.

Aside from the image of the cell, almost every metaphor in Communist ideology comes from military life. The world is at "war"—open or covert class warfare as the case may be—interrupted by "truces." The war is fought by two "armies" dwelling in "camps." Before the revolution, and sometimes after it, the Communist party is the "army" and its leaders are the "officer corps." At other times after the revolution, the whole population of a Communist country is the "army" and the party as a whole is its "officer corps." The party fights on various "fronts"—industrial, agricultural, educational—as well as military. Its history is a succession of "victories" and "defeats"—mostly the former. It proceeds according to an over-all "strategy" drawn up by the leadership, but each over-all strategic plan allows for differing "tactics" in different "sectors" (industries, organizations, countries).

This military language put to revolutionary use goes back to a number of sources: the Jacobins who *were* engaged in wars; many of the Romantics who were absorbed in ideas of universal struggle, including Marx himself; a number of Western Marxist socialists, notably Rosa Luxemburg whose rhetoric much influenced Lenin. This strand of Bolshevik metaphor was much strengthened and added to during World War I, and of course during the Civil War, which the Bolsheviks were running themselves.

Military imagery was very suitable to the Bolsheviks' purposes. It really did express much of their world-view, which was based more on war than on peace. It summoned powerful strains of idealism: the heroism, fraternity, discipline, all-out effort, and self-sacrifice of soldiers, the trained intelligence, *esprit de corps*, and sleepless responsibility of officers, the instantly effective hierarchical chain of command that a good army is supposed to be. For Russians sick at heart at the material grabbiness of so much of society during the last decades of the Tsardom, the military ideal might be an attractive alternative. For Russians agonized at the sloppy, backward, Oblomov-like inefficiency of Tsarist Russia, an army (although hardly the Russian Army) might seem to be the proper institution to introduce progress and technological efficiency into a backward society. (This appeal of a revolutionary army was to prove even stronger in colonial and semicolonial areas, such as China.) It was not for nothing that so many Bolsheviks including Stalin (but not Lenin) emerged from the Civil War thinking of themselves as soldiers. Stalin was long given to wearing a simple military tunic. Eventually he degenerated into a display of self-awarded medals, and granted himself higher and higher military ranks, until he became the only "Generalissimo" in Europe, except for Franco.

As Stalin saw it, Lenin had carried Marxist theory forward, set up and guided the right-thinking and correctly organized Party-army, and in consequence had been able to seize and maintain power in Russia. Lenin had shown how the Party should organize hierarchical, authoritarian institutions of government—the new bureaucracy, the new economy in its various sectors and phases, the new army, and the new terroristic police—to protect, increase, and spread the Party's revolutionary power. Then Lenin was stricken and passed the torch, Stalin was certain, to himself. From then on it was not only Stalin's world-view of nature and history that was relevant, but also his picture of the future, which he was to have so great a part in making.

Under the original Marxist scheme, workers would seize power only after the industrial revolution had run its course in any given country. For most of his life, Lenin had believed that revolution would spread rapidly throughout the world once it had succeeded in any one country. As Stalin took over Russia, it was apparent that these two errors of Marxist-Leninist theory were the two major problems confronting his Party and government: the pre-industrial and war-ravaged poverty of Russia, and relations with the wholly capitalist outside world.

The great debate that raged within the Communist Party in the 1920's centered on these two problems. Stalin developed a complicated set of answers that was known collectively as the doctrine of "socialism in one country." In its relations with the capitalist world Stalin proposed that the USSR adopt a moderate position: The optimists who looked for a speedy World Revolution were ignoring the temporary post-war stabilization of capitalism, and the pessimists who feared another capitalist attack on the USSR were disregarding the manifest war-weariness of the European capitalist powers. Consequently the USSR would enjoy a breathing spell in which it could recover from war damage, provided that it was ceaselessly vigilant against counter-revolutionary plots from within, and provided that foreign Communist parties were cleverly used to keep the capitalist powers disunited and off balance.

But Stalin always insisted that the stabilization and war-weariness of the capitalist camp were temporary. He dated the end of stabilization to the onset of the great depression in 1929. The inevitable crisis of capitalism would once again provide conditions in which the World Revolution (the spread of Communism to lands beyond Russia) would be possible. But at the same time, the crisis of capitalism would inevitably stimulate the desperate capitalists to a renewed attack on the USSR. Stalin later believed that Hitler's attack on the USSR was the fulfillment of this prediction.

The chief defense of the USSR against the inevitable renewed capitalist attack, Stalin argued, would have to be the military machine that Communists could build on Russian soil in the decade or so before the attack would come. Therefore the primary effort of the Party would have to be the construction in a poor and largely agrarian land of a giant industrial economy—first to supply the matériel for an invincible defensive army, secondly to support the World Revolution after the capitalist attack is repulsed, and only thirdly to provide the basis for the future mass prosperity of the Soviet peoples. That is to say, the task for the Party from the late 1920's on would be above all the building of "socialist" (i.e., Communist Party-controlled) agriculture, industry, and armed forces within the USSR. Hence "socialism in one country."[26]

Thus at the beginning of his rule, Stalin had already arrived at the viewpoint that set the pattern for his own regime and for the first decade or so of all Communist regimes in other countries: They spend massive amounts of their energies on internal security, and they push gigantic and intensive programs of co-ordinated economic and military growth. If the Communist regimes are great powers (Russia, China) or think themselves in exposed positions (e.g., North Vietnam, Cuba) they often devote a substantial part of their energies to subverting their neighbors near and far.

At this point one must discuss Stalin's methods. The Western world recites that Communists believe the end justifies the means, and that this is immoral. The dictum, "the end justifies the means," is not, however, used by Communists. When Stalin was bearded with it, he replied that Communists do not employ loathesome means such as torture and assassination.[27] He believed this in a sense. Bolsheviks had eschewed the kind of public assassination that a few of the Socialist-Revolutionaries had committed before the Revolution and during it—Lenin had thought it bad tactics. And while Stalin maintained that "harsh measures" were necessary in wartime, he was sure that Communists neither enjoyed torture as the White forces (and later the Nazis) did, nor had engaged in anywhere near so much of it.

Yet Stalin and his fellow Communists did, in effect, believe that the end justified the means. By an "end" Stalin meant an intelligently calculated result, not just any foolishly pursued purpose. Part of the intelligent calculation was the question of whether the means tend to corrupt or defeat the end. For an end that was good enough and certain enough in their own minds, Stalin and his fellow Communists were willing to employ confiscation, imprisonment, slavery, torture, murder, mass murder, and war. This did not distinguish Stalin from many other men. Churchill, Roosevelt, and Eisenhower, along with all their fellow countrymen save for a few pacifists, were willing to wage World War II at the cost of killing, starving, and inflicting injuries as painful as torture on tens of millions of people, because they believed that the good to be derived from overthrowing Hitler, Mussolini, and the Japanese leaders would more than compensate for the dreadful cost.

Yet Roosevelt and Eisenhower were not morally equivalent to Hitler and Stalin. Unlike Stalin, they never used such murderous methods in peacetime, and they never used them against their own people. They did not hold to an ideology, as Stalin did, that sharply emphasized the desperate conflict in daily existence and politics, that guaranteed "inevitable" results from "necessary" actions. And undeniably they were simply softer by training than Stalin, more reluctant to conclude that harsh measures were necessary, and less resolute in pursuing them to their logical conclusions. Stalin did indeed act more harshly than the Western democratic leaders, but Roosevelt and Churchill killed their millions too. The difference was there, but it was not so great as most Westerners like to think. It was a difference in judging the degree of emergency in the political and international scenes: Stalin saw emergencies constantly and everywhere, Roosevelt only sometimes and only at the theatres of war. But when an emergency was recognized, all the world leaders of Stalin's day acted as if the end justified the means.[28]

Stalin saw the future as consisting of two stages in the emancipation of man. The first stage would last during the lives of his generation and perhaps the next—he was never precise. For these generations life would be grim in material terms, a constant struggle against external and internal enemies, a ceaseless effort to build up the economy and the army. These generations would have to sacrifice themselves, and to be forced to sacrifice themselves, in order to undo the horrors of the past and to build the foundations of the future. For twenty years Stalin was sure that a world war would be the climax of these ordeals. After it came and went, he often spoke as if another inevitable world war would have to be fought before the dark forces of capitalism could be destroyed. Outside the USSR most peoples would have to endure even longer agonies, for they had started later on the revolutionary road. There is no mystery about the precise nature of the trials, for Stalin administered them for thirty years.

What confuses the picture is the flood of Communist propaganda claiming that in an increasing number of aspects of life the trials had already been overcome. Stalin adopted the position that the Soviet peoples had lived in complete freedom and justice from the Revolution on. After World War II he sometimes claimed that they enjoyed the world's highest standard of living as well. A large component of all this was simple propaganda lying, especially about the standard of living. Yet Stalin's professed ideology stated that "freedom" meant perfect and comprehending obedience to perfect laws:[29] In which case Stalin might in good conscience have thought that the USSR was a free society. The ornery individualism so prized in some Western circles has rarely been well thought of in Russia, while the mass collectivism so repellent to most of the West is genuinely valued by many Russians. Since Stalin *had* ended *capitalist* exploitation in the USSR, and since he did not recognize what he himself was doing as exploitation, he might well have believed that he had ended injustice.

In some ways, the most important victim of Stalin's propaganda was Stalin. From 1928 on, according to Khrushchëv's denunciations, Stalin was increasingly cut off from the realities of Soviet life, increasingly unwilling to accept or even to hear information contrary to his own propaganda and wishful thinking. He seems to have had different moods. Sometimes he seems to have believed an astonishing amount of his own rosy propaganda. At other times he deliberately inflicted terrible punishments on individuals and groups for betraying him, falling down on the job, or otherwise proving unable to put his high ideals into effect.

When one comes to look for Stalin's ultimate vision of the Communist paradise to come, the ultimate stage in the emancipation of man, it is surprising how little specific detail can be found in all his many volumes.[30] By the end of the terrible struggle, Stalin was sure, capitalism would be destroyed, even in its American retreats. In the first half of his reign, Stalin sometimes predicted that the whole world would become unified in "World Union of Soviet Socialist Republics," as the revolution swept over various countries and they voluntarily joined the existing USSR. ("Voluntary" was the word frequently used by Stalin to describe the process of forming the existing USSR through conquests by the Red Army.) The "capitalist environment" would be liquidated and replaced by a "socialist environment."[31] But after World War II Stalin occasionally spoke of "socialist countries"—in the plural—as existing in the indefinite future. This was no real change from the idea of a worldwide USSR, for Stalin seems to have anticipated that all future socialist countries would be as docile in their tutelage to the USSR as his East European satellites were in his last years.

Class oppression and other injustices would vanish on the morrow of the revolutions in different countries. With no remaining capitalist enemies in the far future, and not even a remnant of the bourgeois mentality among the working class populations, one might expect the state and its coercive machinery to "wither away." So Stalin said on several occasions, but with peculiar qualifications. The state would die out, not by being weakened, but by being strengthened to the utmost. Factories, collective farms, and other existing institutions of coercive state control would be further strengthened. A single world-wide socialist economy would survive the state, apparently under the control of a "central directing economic organ." In effect, Stalin stood by the words he had inherited from Marx, Engels, and Lenin about the end of the state, while in fact he pushed for an endless, overpoweringly strong, world-wide, centralized, coercive authority that would be the extension and perfection of his existing system in the USSR.

Public education would become really universal, and its prime function would be to teach true doctrine in all the various sciences. The entire world would become heavily industrialized. Goods of all sorts would become abundant for everyone (but Stalin never listed the goods that he thought humanity really needed). The transition to the ultimate economic and social stage of human development—"communism" with a small "c"—could then be completed. "Communism" in this sense was sometimes defined as "the socialization of consumption," a condition in which public authorities distribute free goods to each person. Men would produce the various goods and services they were trained for, and receive in turn the various sorts and quantities of goods that they required: "From each according to his ability; to each according to his need." Not the individual but the central directing economic organ would presumably decide what he needed. The model for such "communism" was perhaps one of the communes of the early Revolutionary period, or an army barracks. But these were Spartan communes in times of poverty, and gave no real picture of the ideal life to be led in the "communist" future with material abundance.[32]

With the advance of socialist science all over the planet, a large number of human problems would disappear, such as deformity, ill health, mental retardation and disease, and (according to some hints) death itself.[33] A moral revolution would inevitably follow the political and economic revolution.

Not only would the bourgeoisie have disappeared, but also the last traces of their mentality: selfishness, individualism, the sense of private property. The New Soviet Men (or New Communist Men) who were beginning to emerge in Stalin's day would spread over the earth. They would be molded from infancy, under the guidance of the theoretically correct central authority, into hard-working, disciplined, scientifically educated (including knowledge of the only true scientific socialism), affirmative men, whose every act would be in accordance with correct ideology for the good of humanity. Machines would do all onerous work, and men would have much leisure to cultivate the arts and sciences.

Each man, Stalin predicted, would be developed under socialism to a point at which he and all his fellows would surpass the giants of the pre-socialist past, such as Michelangelo or Goethe.[34] Yet nothing sounds less like Michelangelo or Goethe than these hints of Stalin's about the ideal future condition of man. The men of the future were in fact intended by Stalin to resemble the New Soviet Men of his day—hard-working, utterly devoted, utterly self-effacing, utterly submissive Stakhanovite workers and other heroes. The world was to be transformed into what the Communist ideology of Stalin's day said it ought to be. And that was essentially Stalin's Russia, writ large, spread over the whole world, made prosperous at last, and rid of all save those who obeyed voluntarily and perfectly the perfect laws of Communism.

It is not surprising that Stalin was so infrequent and vague in his references to the ideal future. For the masses, dwelling on the future in which all goods would be abundant would be a subversive distraction from the toil and sacrifice of the present. For Stalin himself, life after the complete triumph of Stalinism would have lacked the exhilarating total struggle that so fascinated him. Stalin would have been most unhappy in his own Utopia, for it was a static, Apollonian goal, while Stalin was as dynamic and Faustian as any man on earth.

Such were the outlines of Stalin's world-view, which Stalin called "Communist ideology." The bulk of it was taken over from Lenin, and the bulk of that had been common to hundreds of thousands of socialists before Lenin made Bolshevism a doctrine to conjure with. The Marxist-Leninist core of Stalin's ideology was supposed to be logical, systematic, complete, and true. Most of what Stalin added to his inheritance from Lenin was shared by many other men, and all of it was grafted onto Leninist doctrine in the belief that the additions were consistent with what was already there. Ultimately, Communist ideology during Stalin's reign was whatever beliefs and sentiments he happened to hold at any given moment, and Communist ideology changed whenever Stalin happened to change his mind. But Stalin and his fellow Communists thought of their beliefs as a system, not as a collection of impulses. Stalin judged all significant information and decided all significant actions in the light of what he believed to be a systematic ideology. He changed his mind relatively rarely, and added to his system relatively rarely over thirty years of rule.

In all these things, Stalin was meaningfully different in his procedures from the usually non-ideological Western leaders, such as Franklin Roosevelt. He was significantly different from all others who shared some or all of his ideology, in that he had very much more power than the others, including the power to change the ideology. He was so implacably resolute about acting on his ideology that he eventually provoked world-wide accusations of insanity. The study of any aspect of Stalin's Russia must begin with the relevant part of Stalin's ideology.

5. THE POWER

*A*LTHOUGH Stalin did not philosophize about the meaning of the term "power," he subscribed to a detailed Marxist-Leninist explanation of the nature of power in human societies. Power, he thought, resided with the social class that controlled the means of production, distribution, and exchange in any given society. Power could not be held by individuals, even by an ostensibly absolute monarch. The monarch or other leader was "merely" the instrument through which the ruling class expressed its will. When a leader attempted to thwart the ruling class that had thrust him forward it would remove him, as the landed aristocrats of eighteenth-century Russia had removed several Tsars.

Marxist-Leninists have always had to argue with two more widespread views of the question, the belief that leaders really do lead masses of lesser men, and the position so memorably expressed by Machiavelli—that power goes not to the masters of wealth, but to the masters of armies. Stalin, like Marx, dismissed the theory that history is dominated by great men as naive Romanticism, and had his historians maintain that the independent actions of most great men of history—even Hitler —have been grossly exaggerated. Theoretically Communists were to believe the same thing of Stalin's own heroes, including Lenin and himself. In fact, Stalin's gigantic program of self-glorification, the "cult of personality" that Khrushchëv was to denounce, elevated the Man of Steel far above any iron laws of history or economics. Yet Stalin denied any inconsistency, and probably did not perceive any.

As for the armies, Stalin asserted that under relatively stable conditions economic and military power are in the same hands. The landowners of eighteenth-century Russia were also its military officers. But in time of rapid economic change such as the last hundred and fifty years, which most interested Stalin, there was often a shift of economic power to some new class while military power often seemed to remain with the old ruling class. The result, Stalin asserted, was revolution. The French bourgeoisie who gained economic power in the eighteenth century were able to seize political power in 1789 from the aristocrats in spite of their army. The Russian bourgeoisie and working classes were able to overthrow the Tsarist regime in 1917, in spite of the ostensible control of the Imperial Army by aristocratic officers, because the old upper class had lost the landed base of its power after the emancipation of the serfs in 1861.

If the possession of economic power guaranteed the acquisition of military power, as Stalin believed, he was facing a serious threat as he began to rule in the 1920's. Political and military power, as he saw it, were wielded by the proletariat and poor peasantry through the Communist Party—the most advanced stratum of the working class. But economic power in the countryside, under Lenin's New Economic Policy in the years after 1921, was thought to reside chiefly with the richer peasants, the *kulaks*, who controlled the farms that produced most of the agricultural surplus. And much economic power in the cities was supposedly held by the small private manufacturers and traders, called NEP-men, after Lenin's relaxed policy that had called them into being. To non-Marxists, Communist power seemed quite secure after the Civil War was won. But Stalin had ideological reasons for believing that he faced a deadly threat of counterrevolution by *kulaks* and NEP-men.

The Communists' position would have been hopeless, Stalin alleged, if Lenin had not wisely reserved the "commanding heights" of the economy to the working classes in 1921, that is, if he had not maintained the regime's direct ownership and control of heavy industry, transportation, communications, and financial credit. From this economic base, Stalin argued, the Communists might still shatter the forces of counterrevolution if they struck first. The Communist task was to "liquidate the *kulaks* as a class" by seizing the lands that were their power base and putting them into Party-controlled socialist farms; and to eliminate the power of the NEP-men by building up a huge socialist industrial plant. These two of Stalin's most important enterprises will be dealt with in subsequent chapters. But it should not be forgotten that Stalin's first and most immediate purpose in collectivizing agriculture and going through with the First Five Year Plan was defensive: to preserve Communist power against ideologically postulated counterattack.

By 1936, when most of the villages of the USSR were in collective farms, and when the Second Five Year Plan was more than half completed, Stalin was confident that the farms and factories of the country were firmly in Communist hands. There was no remaining economic base, he judged, for the overthrow of Soviet power from *within*. He proclaimed in the new Soviet Constitution of that year that the population of the USSR was and would henceforth be composed exclusively of the working classes—the proletariat and the working peasantry. Therefore the restrictions in the Constitutions of 1918 and 1924 against the bourgeoisie and the other former exploiting classes were now unnecessary, and were repealed. (E.g., every person born in the USSR was now a citizen, and could serve in the Red Army, vote in elections, and hold public office, regardless of his own or his parents' former social class.)

This ideologically certified security of Soviet power should have been followed by a period of benign relaxation of the regime's controls. There was in fact a let-up in police activity —by Stalinist standards—during the early months of 1936. But from the middle of the year this relaxation gave way to the climax of the great purges, an apparently contradictory turn of events.

It is hazardous to speculate about Stalin's psyche, but it is neither novel nor extreme to speculate that Stalin suffered from feelings of insecurity in the 1930's (and thereafter), feelings that continued to afflict him whether or not there was much reason for them. And no matter what Stalin had just said about the class nature of Soviet society, there were reports of plots at home and news of Hitler's progress abroad that seemed to justify his fears. He explained these to himself in ideological terms, and justified his consequent security measures to the world in ideological terms. The result was an interesting extension of the Communist ideology of power.

There was no longer a capitalist or a *kulak* class in the USSR, Stalin now decided, but there were many former capitalists and *kulaks* who were not psychologically adjusted to their new position among the toiling masses, and who were still bourgeois-minded and *kulak*-minded. They desired the restoration of capitalism ever more intensely, Stalin surmised, as the chance of it faded. Since there was no longer an economic base in their possession from which they could launch a counterrevolution, they turned to acts of wrecking, sabotage, economic slowdown, defeatist propaganda, and betrayal. The "harshest measures" were justified to put down acts of violence against the Soviet economy, but these acts could never overthrow Communist power. The real threat from the ex-bourgeoisie and the ex-*kulaks* was that they might succeed in betraying the USSR into the hands of foreign capitalist powers. The economic base for counterrevolution (i.e., attack on the USSR) certainly existed in Germany and among the Western powers.[1]

The two worst categories of treachery were spying for Germany and the others before the coming inevitable war, and preparation for collaboration with the Germans or whomever during the forthcoming invasion. For Stalin as for his Tsarist predecessors, "spying" meant not only the divulgence of the kind of military information that would be secret in any country, but also the transmission abroad of any information about the country that the regime had not itself publicized. This included any estimate of how the Soviet population or any part of it felt or behaved politically, and any economic information such as the location and equipment of plants, or production statistics. Stalin really believed that knowledge was power, and that the exposure of his secrets would leave him naked to his enemies.[2]

Preparation for future sabotage of the Soviet war effort was thought to include any failure (real or imagined) in one's daily job, any responsibility for accidents or failures to meet production quotas, any remark or sometimes even a facial expression that might possibly be interpreted as criticism of Stalin's regime. The prevention of such threatened damage to and betrayal of the USSR was Stalin's ideological justification for the great purges.

After the great purges had run their course—which sated

even Stalin's suspicions for the time being—Hitler invaded the USSR. Stalin had little difficulty persuading himself to maintain the utmost and most murderous vigilance throughout a war in which millions of Soviet citizens did in fact surrender, desert, and/or collaborate with the enemy. After victory in 1945 there was no real threat to Stalin from any source save possibly an assassin, but his feelings of insecurity did not end with the external threats since the sources of those feelings were not entirely external. He justified his continued police terror in the USSR, and its extension into Eastern Europe, by reference to the stop-at-nothing desperation of the tiny remnant of anti-Soviet individuals in the USSR, and the much larger group in Eastern Europe, who now spied and betrayed for the new chief foreign foe, America. None of these later threats required any real development of Stalin's ideological innovation of 1936.

Such were the threats to Communist rule against which Stalin believed he needed to maintain his vast coercive machine. The essential instrument of his rule was, of course, the Communist Party of the Soviet Union. As Stalin rose to power, Lenin's small, elite, revolutionary Party had long since been swamped by hundreds of thousands of new Communists who had been allowed or persuaded to join during the Revolution and Civil War, when Lenin relaxed his standards for the sake of broadening his support. The Party numbered almost six hundred thousand men by the end of the Civil War. Stalin was ordered to remove incompetents and opportunists when the emergency had passed. He had purged over a quarter of a million members from the Party rolls by Lenin's death.

Thereafter he packed unprecedented numbers of presumably reliable supporters into his Party. It passed the million mark in 1926, and reached three and a half million by 1933. There followed a drastic cutting-down during the great purges, which reduced the Party to less than two million. Since then the Party's expansion has been continuous. It boasted 5,760,-000 members by 1945, and almost eight million by Stalin's death.[3]

Here was material enough for Stalin to work with. Originally most Communists had joined the Party when already adult. Applicants from different social classes and levels of education needed different recommendations and apprentice training. They were all given courses of study in Party ideology and history, and tasks on behalf of their Party cell during their probationary periods, which were proportional to their apparent merits or to the Party's need of them. The severest tests were set for applicants who had formerly been members of other political parties, especially Mensheviks. For a long time they had to secure the recommendation of at least two Bolsheviks who had joined the Party before 1917.

From the early 1920's on, Stalin organized the system of Party recruitment that still obtains in the USSR, although he was able to make it universal only after World War II. Children of kindergarten age, unless they were retarded or of suspect families, were herded into the Communist children's organization called the Little Octobrists, for indoctrination and junior Party-style activities such as the singing of patriotic songs. At about the age of nine they graduated into the next Party youth group, called the Pioneers, in which their Party-style training continued until the age of fifteen. At fourteen an adolescent was eligible to join the Communist Union of Youth (abbreviated in Russian to *Komsomol*). This was a more strictly Party organization, which had begun as an elite corps of proletarian adolescents. In 1936 it was opened formally to all qualified persons in the age group, and by Stalin's death it included over sixteen million members, well over half the Soviet youth. A far higher proportion of the elite youth in universities and elsewhere were in the *Komsomol*. Members were supposed to master Marxism-Leninism, do a great deal of Party leg work and clerical work, propagandize, and (to some extent) police all youth and many elders—a very time-consuming program.

The Party members who ran the youth organizations thus had years in which to observe potential Party recruits, and to train them. When a *Komsomol* reached his majority, he might be invited to join the Party, or he might apply on his own. Under Stalin, such invitations were declined at one's peril. The probationary period and tests still lay ahead. After World War II, practically everyone who entered the Party came to it through this hierarchy of organizations for the control and direction of all young people.

Stalin's policy on the admission of Party members was pulled in many contrary directions. He wanted the ablest people and also the most loyal, but often these were not the same. Ideology indicated that the most loyal members would come from the proletariat, but the facts of life taught that the ablest members came from the former bourgeoisie and the new Soviet middle class. There was a serious effort during the 1920's to "proletarianize" the Party, and by 1929 over 60 per cent of the Party was announced to be of proletarian origin—although many had ceased to be workers at the bench. During the Second Five Year Plan, and again after the great purges, and ever since World War II, there have been special efforts to bring the "technological *intelligentsia*" (the educated members of the new Soviet middle class) into the Party. They almost certainly outnumbered the proletarians in it by Stalin's death, although such calculations are difficult, since the Party had long since ceased to give out detailed sociological statistics about its membership.

Ideology suggested that it would be both moral and politic to recruit peasants into the Party—to strengthen the Communists' hold on the countryside. There was never much hope that many peasants would shine in the ranks. It has never even been boasted that the Party ever contained more than 28 per cent persons of peasant origin, and many of the "peasant" members were longtime residents of the cities, or urban Party men on mission to the countryside. Women were urged into the Party on purely ideological grounds, for Communists have never feared women as they feared the peasants. Stalin took over a Party with scarcely 5 per cent women—including a handful of real distinction, such as Nadezhda Krupskaia and Alexandra Kollontai. He left the Party with over 21 per cent women, all of them politically faceless. As with the peasants, the proportion of women shrank as one went up the scale of Party offices.

The nationalities presented Stalin with special membership problems. Great Russians were most likely to be loyal, and in effect he relied on them. But enlarged membership among the smaller nationalities was desirable to increase support and control in their territories—if they could be trusted. Georgians and Armenians had been relatively numerous and powerful in the Party since Stalin's earliest machine-building days. Ukrainians were always much fewer and weaker than their population would have indicated: a telling reflection of their dangerous disaffection. Jews had been enormously important in Lenin's Party, although they never constituted more than 6 per cent of the Party under Stalin's rule. Stalin seems to have subscribed to some extent to the prevailing Russian prejudices about Jews. He stated in the 1920's that as a group the Jews were the best educated and most efficient members of the Party,[4] but at the same time (and thereafter) he acted as if he shared the concomitant prejudice: that Jews were apt to use their abilities for their own advantage. Stalin's many anti-Trotskyite and anti-Semitic campaigns steadily reduced the proportion of Jews in the Party. In his last years it was virtually impossible for a Jew to join the Party or to get anywhere in its ranks.[5]

THE POWER

By the end of Stalin's reign, there were more than 350,000 primary Party organizations in the USSR—still informally called "cells." They were based on geographical or occupational divisions, such as a village or factory, and they averaged fewer than twenty members each. The cell was the lowest of four or five levels of Party organization, which culminated in the Party divisions for the various Union Republics (usually eight for the huge Russian Republic) and in the Party Center in Moscow.

Theoretically, the members of the cells elected—in a complicated and highly indirect electoral procedure—delegates to the All-Union Congresses of the Party, which were supposedly sovereign annual parliaments of the Party with power to decide all issues and appointments. This was said to be the democratic part of the Leninist doctrine of "democratic centralism," according to which the Party was supposed to be organized. After the Party Congresses had taken their decisions minorities would obey the majority, and lower bodies would obey this highest of Communist organs. This was said to be the centralist part of the doctrine.

In fact, delegates to the Party Congresses, like all other Party officers and members, were chosen by Stalin's Party bureaucracy. Congresses under Stalin decided nothing for themselves, but merely ratified and propagandized decisions already taken by Stalin. He came to postpone the supposedly annual Congresses for two, three, four, and five years, and (after 1939) for thirteen years. This virtual abolition of the Party's ostensibly central ruling body amounted to an open proclamation that Stalin thought it best to rule the Party by himself, and not to bother with the rules of its constitution or the will of its members.

Stalin ruled the Party through its *apparat* ("apparatus" or Party bureaucracy) of full-time, professional Party men engaged in the management of the Party itself. These were the famous faceless men in Moscow and the provinces who actually admitted and expelled Party members, appointed them to their various tasks, appointed Party officials of all sorts, and saw to it that the decisions of Stalin and his immediate associates were ratified immediately and unanimously by all relevant Party organs. The very number of the apparatus was a secret. The regime hinted at a number less than two hundred thousand, while its enemies accused Stalin of having built the apparatus up to two or three times that number.[6]

The Party apparatus under Stalin was a staggeringly important hierarchy, certainly the most powerful in the USSR. Soviet citizens and exiles (notably Trotsky) often had the impression that the apparatus ruled, and that Stalin's power derived from his leadership of the apparatus. Certainly Stalin's rise to power came about through his control of the apparatus, and his expansion and use of it. But in his years of power, Stalin built up at least three alternative hierarchies through which he also ruled: the state-economic establishment, the army, and the police. The extent to which these four hierarchies were separate, and the relations among them, were the subjects of intense debate among Western analysts until Khrushchëv rendered the whole controversy academic after Stalin's death by reasserting the primacy of the Party apparatus.[7] Most of the army officers and police spent their entire careers in their own fields, as did many of their leaders, such as Voroshilov and Beria. On the other hand, the personnel of the apparatus and the state-economic machine were often interchanged, while many of the top leaders, such as Mikoyan, Malenkov, and Khrushchëv, worked in two, three, and even four of these hierarchies.

Anyone important in any of the hierarchies was a Party member, and as such was to some extent under the control of the apparatus. Yet the police were employed to purge the apparatus when Stalin desired it. After the great purges, Stalin developed what was known as his "personal secretariat" into a large group through which he interfered in the workings of all the hierarchies, including the apparatus. Stalin never claimed to be balancing the hierarchies in any such way, and would have denied it vigorously if he had been asked, but in effect he did so. He certainly blurred the distinctions among them in many ways, and took care to remain above them all.

Everything of importance that was done in Stalin's Russia, except for some of the creative work in the arts and sciences, was done by Party members acting on orders from above. The most gigantic tasks of the Party were safeguarding Stalin's rule, building up the Soviet economy, and fighting World War II. The last two enterprises will be discussed in later chapters. Here and in the next chapter we shall be concerned with the activities of the various branches of Stalin's Party-state machine in defense of his power against internal enemies.

Stalin took no stock in man's alleged unconscious mind, but believed that men act in accordance with stimuli from their environment. Since he saw men's minds as rather plastic and manipulable, he placed great faith in the ability of his propaganda machine to influence the Soviet population on his behalf, and he simultaneously had great fear of the potency of hostile propaganda. He never took the common Western position on propaganda—that its effects are usually limited, and that overmuch exposure stops up the ears of the hearers, inducing skepticism and apathy. Therefore Stalin went to enormous lengths to see to it that the environment of the Soviet population was suffused with stimuli toward loyalty to the Communist cause, and utterly sterilized against contrary stimuli. Propaganda and censorship were never more intensely employed than in Stalin's hands.

Censorship operated against two supposed sources of hostile, "negative" opinion and information: the capitalists abroad, and the capitalist or capitalist-minded remnant at home. Only a few trusted citizens were permitted to go outside Stalin's empire even on official missions. Even his own occupation troops in East Germany and other newly acquired parts of his post-war empire attracted his active distrust. Very few foreigners, even foreign Communists, were allowed into the USSR, and they of course were restricted to a few cities and showcase collective farms, herded about in guided groups, and followed if they took a walk on their own. Foreign publications (and eventually even most foreign Communist publications) were barred from the USSR, save for a few copies kept classified in government offices and libraries. Foreign broadcasts were systematically jammed at great expense, and by the end of Stalin's rule no private citizen was allowed the kind of shortwave radio set that could pick them up.

Goebbels and later Churchill described this enforced isolation of the USSR and its dependencies as the "Iron Curtain." It was astonishingly effective. Foreign visitors to the USSR were always amazed at the utter ignorance of Soviet citizens about the outside world, even where political questions were not directly at stake. A poignant example will suffice: After Stalin's death an American historian visited the poetess Anna Akhmatova, who had long since fallen into official disfavor, in her dingy Moscow room. He spotted a youthful portrait of her on the wall, in a style he could not fail to recognize. But from her explanations it became clear that she had never had the chance to become informed of the great fame that had come, in the decades since Stalin rose to power, to the portraitist, an Italian acquaintance of her parents named Modigliani.[8]

A dissident inside the USSR could not form a political party or other organization to criticize the regime, since all organizations were authorized and indeed run by the regime.

He could not publish his views, since all presses belonged to the state. So did all radio stations. He could not make public speeches, for they had to be supervised by the police. These were the standard precautions of a number of modern dictatorships, but they were unusually difficult to circumvent in the socialist economy of the USSR, where there was no private source of the materials for dissent, right down to a simple piece of paper. And the success of revolutionaries under the Tsars in evading censorship through the use of obscure references and private "Aesopian" languages could not be duplicated under the eyes of Communist censors, trained above all to detect and chastise just such tricks.

While we shudder at the awesome effectiveness of Stalin's police state in which a type-setter was once sent to his death in Siberia for accidentally misprinting the name Stalin (Man of Steel) as "Salin" (Man of Lard),[9] we should remember another side of the situation. In Stalin's Russia gangs of black marketeers were able to organize on a large enough scale to steal whole locomotives and trains loaded with goods, and deliver them a thousand miles away. On one occasion a gang in Gorky stole eight printing presses and untold tons of paper. These they used to print not Menshevik pamphlets, but paper bags with the labels of various ministries on them, including the Interior Ministry, which they proceeded to sell at great profit to government enterprises, including the police forces of fourteen cities.[10] There is a persisting paradox about a regime that can censor the slightest expression of dissent, but cannot suppress the theft of billions of rubles worth of goods. It suggests not only that Stalin feared minuscule dissent more than wholesale crime, but also that there was a better market in Stalin's Russia for illegal goods than for illegal ideas.

The complement to Stalin's all-pervasive censorship was Stalin's all-pervasive propaganda. The word "propaganda" in Russian is used to denote ostensibly high-level argumentation directed toward the educated elite, such as appeared in the Party's theoretical magazine *Bolshevik* (later *Kommunist*). High-pressure pep talks, mass sloganeering, and the like, are referred to as "agitation." The whole vast enterprise that foreigners call "Communist propaganda" is abbreviated in Russian to *agit-prop*. Government newspapers were stuck up on every wall, surrounded by even cruder posters. The state radio blared into every ear with no possibility of turning it off. All communications, from a lecture on tractor repair to a book on chess openings, included frequent praises of Communism and of Stalin.

It was these forms of *agit-prop*, directed publicly toward the entire population of the USSR, that were most frequently encountered by foreigners. It was this saturating use of mass communications and this omnipresent verbal obeisance to Stalin that first came to mind when outsiders thought of Stalin's internal propaganda. Yet most of this was preaching to the converted, the continued stimulation of loyalties that had already been inculcated. For the regime, the most important parts of the process of molding New Soviet Men came earlier in life. From the nursery on, the Soviet educational system was directed toward producing new generations who would be Communist from infancy. The central institution of Communist persuasion was the Soviet school.

Stalin rose to power in a country where the majority of the population was illiterate. He boasted that one of his finest achievements was putting everyone to school. His Constitution of 1936 stated "Citizens of the USSR have a right to education." The first step in education is literacy itself. To embody his ideal, Stalin allocated the material and personal resources to build a network of schools in every city, and at least one school in practically every village. The first schoolhouse in a district might be a requisitioned shack, the first teacher might be barely literate himself, but by 1940 there was a school for almost all Soviet children.

The school population, which had stood at 7,900,000 in 1914, rose to almost 35,000,000 by 1940, in roughly the same total population. (World War II and a declining birth rate were to send the figure down to about 28,000,000 by Stalin's death.) In 1940 and thereafter Stalin claimed the literacy rate in the USSR was over 99 per cent, the most literate country in the world. This was incredible, but there is no reason to doubt that Stalin pushed the Soviet literacy rate to some point around 95 per cent, which compared favorably with most advanced countries.[11] Considering the immensity of the USSR, its 175 languages in which instruction was given, the primitiveness of much of the population, and the desperate shortage of buildings, educational materials, and teachers, Stalin's alphabetization of his many peoples was a great and staggering achievement, and one that cannot be argued away by pointing to the shortcomings of the rest of his school system. Making the USSR a literate nation was Stalin's greatest contribution to the liberation of man.

Stalin's laws guaranteed more than literacy. They provided for eight years of free compulsory schooling for everyone. This was more than Stalin was willing to deliver. When he died, most children in Soviet cities were actually receiving seven years of education, but in many villages the school fell even further short of the law. Lenin had instituted coeducation in all schools as a progressive reform, but Stalin decreed the separation again of girls from boys in 1943. Since this involved doubling the classrooms and teachers, it could not always be implemented.

The Soviet school system had been the scene of much progressive and libertarian experimentation in the 1920's. Stalin, as he expanded the school system enormously in the early

1930's, more than re-established the Tsarist centralization and uniformity of the schools. The freedom of the teacher in the system and the freedom of the child in the classroom were both eliminated. Once again the child was to work hard at the standard academic subjects, although the emphasis in Stalin's schools was on school work in the classroom rather than homework that might have interfered with the child's efforts to help his parents at their jobs, especially on the farms. Once again the teacher was to discipline the child rigidly.

Rigid discipline in the Communist school was definitely not supposed to mean harsh, loud-voiced management of the classroom or physical punishments, although the latter were kept in reserve. The teacher was told to win the confidence of his charges (most Soviet teachers were men) by friendly, helpful behavior, and to persuade them to follow the right path by exhortations, by shaming them, and by enlisting the other pupils to help reclaim a recalcitrant. Teachers were to instill obedience, unselfishness, and collective-mindedness, Individual competitiveness was to be suppressed and group spirit cultivated.

Communist educational theory suggested many effective methods of instilling a collective identity. All the boys came to school in military-style school uniforms (when the cloth was available), and girls wore equally uniform jumpers. (One limit to Communist collectivism is indicated by the fact that Stalin did not clothe boys and girls the same way.) Children in a given row of desks were made into an academic team, which was judged by the swiftness and accuracy with which the entire team learned assignments. This induced stronger students to help weaker ones learn, so as to raise the collective average. Choral singing in unison was preferred to solos, and team sports were encouraged over individual sports.

Recitation in unison, marching in unison, and even sleeping in identical postures on precisely parallel cots, were the rule.¹²

Thus the purpose of the early grades in the Soviet school system was to teach the basic educational skills without which the citizen would be of little use to the regime in an increasingly modern, industrial society, and to inculcate and internalize the habits of obedience and collectivism that made the citizen readily usable by the regime. Some openly political indoctrination was carried on in the early grades, either in the schools themselves or in the youth groups that were usually organized around schools and usually met in school buildings. But most explicit political training came later.

Every Soviet city and many privileged villages did have schools that offered the full ten years of preparation for higher education. Soviet schools, compared to their American counterparts (although not to their European equivalents) taught an impressive amount of mathematics, physics, chemistry, geology, and biology. Students were supposed to choose a foreign language and study it from the fifth grade on (usually German before 1941, usually English after 1945). The course in Russian language and literature all over the USSR, and the courses in the languages and literatures of the smaller Union Republics (which were compulsory within those Union Republics) carried a heavy freight of Communist morality, of Soviet patriotism, and of the desirability of national unity under Moscow's leadership. The history, social science, and philosophy courses amounted to straightforward political indoctrination. In these upper grades the supposed natural combativeness of boys was directed toward preparation for Communist wars and industrial struggles, while the alleged nurturing propensities of girls were channeled toward preparation to stand behind and aid Communist men.

Practically all students who reached the seventh grade

would already have joined the Pioneers, and practically all students who completed ten years of schooling would be members of the *Komsomol*. Communist schools and Communist youth organizations worked hand in hand to inculcate the desired views and to produce the desired personality. The schools urged their students to join the youth organizations, and helped them fulfill the youth organizations' assignments. The youth organizations urged their members to work harder in school, and helped them with their school work.

Beyond the ten years of regular schooling was the realm of Communist higher education, for the future elites of the USSR. Least prestigious were the trade schools, which fed trained workers into the skilled branches of industry and agriculture. More valued were the technical institutes for the training of practical agronomists, geologists, and so on. The schools of performing arts were worlds of their own, of which the most sought after were the musical conservatories. Most prestigious were the universities, from whose various faculties came the scientists and engineers, doctors and lawyers, and professionals in the social sciences and humanities. By Stalin's death there were a million full-time students in the universities alone, the largest number in the world after America.

Soviet higher education had been free on Leninist principle until 1940, when Stalin changed the principle and exacted tuition payments. These were modest enough by American standards, but they would have kept most Soviet youth out if Stalin had not simultaneously instituted a comprehensive system of scholarships that covered almost all places in higher education. This tuition and scholarship system was not simply equivalent to free higher education, however. It was a double-pronged instrument of control: Scholarships were revocable if the student failed to keep his grades up, and if he showed any signs of disloyalty. Almost every student in Soviet higher education was a member of the *Komsomol* throughout his student life, even if he joined the Party itself in his twenties. All students were required to take certain courses with high ideological content, notably the university courses in dialectical materialism, which provoked noticeable apathy and restlessness even under Stalin.

Stalin made no distinction between indoctrination and substantive education. For him there were no value-neutral technological subjects. A science such as biology could not be correctly taught without showing its dialectical materialist nature, and its place in the Party's plan for Soviet society. Foreign critics of Soviet education, however, can and do distinguish between political tendentiousness and genuine education in the Soviet school system. They also try to estimate what parts of the Soviet educational program "took" and what parts were not mastered by the students, or were rejected by them.

In the earlier grades reading, writing, and arithmetic were taught to everyone and absorbed by all save the feebleminded. It is far more difficult to guess how many students became obedient and collective-minded, although virtually all acted that way when paraded before foreign visitors to the schools. The upper grades of the regular school system produced millions of people competent to labor in modern factories and on mechanized farms. If they did not work very hard or very well, it was more often due to lack of incentive than to lack of proper training.

The system of higher education produced hundreds of thousands of trained personnel to fill the top levels of every branch of Soviet life. Neither Stalin nor anyone else was wholly satisfied with the results. In spite of Stalin's insistence that all fields were equally impregnated with Communist ideology, foreign critics and his own successors have agreed that Soviet education produced the best graduates who went on to the most fruitful careers in the technological fields that were furthest from the heavy hand of political indoctrination—and did worst in the most political fields such as modern history, economics, and philosophy. The real geniuses to emerge from the Soviet educational system have been in mathematics, the natural sciences, and the performing arts.

Stalin usually recognized a great scientist or performer, and he was perennially annoyed at the mediocrity of most graduates in the politically most sensitive fields. But in sum, he was satisfied with the schools as a system of political persuasions and controls. Almost everything the Soviet youth learned about nature, man, ethics, and politics was learned either at home or at school. The family might instill different behavior patterns from the school, and it might contradict the school's teachings about local political and economic matters, and about religion, although open contradiction proved dangerous to many parents from the great purges on. But the youth would almost certainly take the school's word about the rest of the universe: about science, about the outside world, and about the systematic expression of ethics and politics.

The youth might want the good things of life for himself, but he would probably accept the school's ethical teaching that such anti-collective individualism was wrong and selfish. He might feel very bitter toward the regime after some blow to himself or his family, but he would never have learned any coherent expression of dissent, and he would certainly have learned that prudence dictated the smothering of every manifestation of dissatisfaction. By the standards of most countries, Stalin did not have a youth problem; he had taken care of it in his schools. When young Soviet citizens emerged from the various schools at various ages, they had been broken into the rules and procedures of Stalinist society very effectively. Practically all of them had been trained to assent to much of its ethic and rationale in the abstract, even if they had little desire to become Communist saints. In his later years Stalin's major problem with the youth of the USSR was not dissidence but apathy, which is a measure of the success of the Soviet school as the central instrument of Communist persuasion.

In later youth and maturity, all categories of Soviet citizens were involved in one or more of the Party's "transmission belts to the masses"—youth organizations, trade unions, women's leagues, and the like. These inflicted lengthy public meetings and other sessions of propaganda on their members, as well as extracting great amounts of Party-style activities, such as circulating government-sponsored petitions. The military and its associated organizations for veterans and civil defense (which Stalin took with deadly seriousness before World War II[13]) were caught up in the same net. No citizen could get away with mere passive attendance. From kindergarten on, each person had to take part in many rituals of celebration of Communism. Each person had to show his loyalty and enthusiasm out of his own mouth (if not always in his own words) and with his own gestures.

It was this all-pervasive regimentation, along with the vast police terror, that was the core of what hostile foreigners meant when they called Stalin's Russia a "totalitarian" society. The regime touched everyone in all his activities. Everyone was made an active accomplice of the regime. Everyone had to vote for Stalin's men, and millions had to serve in petty offices under him. That was what "democracy" meant in Stalin's Russia: the active participation of all the people in every activity of government save the making of decisions. Everyone was supposed to report on his brother. Everyone who had committed an offense—or was accused of it—had to confess his own error, breast-beatingly, before a "self-criticism" meeting, or before a police or judicial body.

No area of privacy, conscience, or personal inviolability was supposed to be left to a Soviet citizen. No two or three could gather together save in the name of the Party—as exemplified by the intensive pre-war use of the clenched-fist salute to greet friends. Husband and wife, parent and child, were all supposed to trust and to feel closer to the Party and to Stalin than to each other.

Could such a system really have had its intended effect? Judgments have varied over the whole possible range. Stalin did succeed in crushing all revolt and all organized opposition, and in preventing any new organized opposition from forming. But this is very different from saying that Stalin really did raise two generations of "New Soviet Men" or that all Soviet citizens loved Big Brother. The tens of millions of people in prisons and labor camps, on the more coercive collective farms and in the more hard-pressed factories and among the more persecuted national minorities, must have had their own opinions, even if they kept quiet. Now that Stalin is deep in his grave, the evidence is coming out that people did not always keep so quiet. To judge by many present day accounts of interviews with Russians, practically everyone hated Stalin and held him accountable for the miseries of daily life. An admitted former supporter of Stalin is now as hard to find in the USSR as an admitted former Nazi in Germany.

The pendulum has swung too far. Stalin cannot have enjoyed as little support during his lifetime as Soviet testimony now indicates. Children will believe almost anything. It is difficult to think that most of the millions of Little Octobrists and Pioneers who sang such rousing ditties as *Glory to the Great Name of Stalin* in massed unison with such apparent happiness did not in fact enjoy the fun. Adolescents are apt to rebel, and millions rebelled, if only for a time, against family and traditional life toward the bright future promised by the Party. The First Five Year Plan and World War II clearly did enlist the idealism of millions, even if not permanently. Not everyone in Stalin's Russia lived wretchedly by his own standards. Millions in the new Soviet middle class, and in many government organizations from the secret police to a soccer team, had never had it so good.

Nor did all of those who suffered blame it all on Stalin. The most illiterate peasant knew that life is suffering and always had been. The sun and rain, the inherent evil in men and governments, the Jews and the foreigners, "them"—any and all of these received as much or more blame from many people than did Stalin. Millions were skeptical when Stalin justified the hardships of the First Five Year Plan by the threat of foreign invasion, but no one was skeptical after the invasion came. Millions seem to have articulated a hatred for Stalin, after such hatred became officially approved, who concealed it even from themselves while he lived because they could not accept the realization that they were themselves in the despised and threatened category of the disloyal.

It is not strange that Stalin's super-saturating propaganda machine failed to convert millions of people. It is not strange that it came to have for millions the deadening effect of too many television commercials. But it is frighteningly strange that the propaganda did persuade thousands of children, parents, husbands, and wives to turn their nearest and supposedly dearest in to the police. It is astonishing that dozens of Russians report that they could not trust their wives enough to talk politics with them, since they had only been married ten years or so.[14] It is disturbing to find that hundreds of thousands of eyes shone with true belief as they strained to catch a glimpse of the great man at a mass ceremony.

One cannot estimate the spread of Soviet public opinion of Stalin during his lifetime even with gross approximations. Probably no majority of Soviet citizens ever loved Stalin in any positive sense. But at one time or another, millions, maybe tens of millions, did. Both facts are enormously important for our understanding of the nature of man. Certainly most Soviet citizens assented to most of the things that Stalin told them, even if they withheld assent in some matters that most concerned their own lives. Stalin proved that what we call "totalitarianism" can work—not so well as Stalin hoped, and perhaps not so well as some alternatives, but well enough to preserve a regime and to build up a country to the point of victory in the greatest war in history. And totalitarianism can go on working until the tyrant himself—or his successor— wills a change.

6. THE TERROR

S*TALIN* did not rely solely on manipulation of the environment of the Soviet populace by censorship and propaganda. If these defenses failed, and disloyalty or outright hostility to Communist power developed in the USSR, Stalin had many more lines of defense: the coercive bulwarks of the regime. Eternal vigilance was the price of Stalinism.

The most elementary part of security is making sure that one is not killed. Within limits, Stalin was willing to trust a number of close associates not to kill him. *Politburo* members were not frisked anew every time they entered a room Stalin was in, although guards often eyed them for suspicious bulges in their clothing. Guards did not usually cover members of the *Politburo* with submachine guns during meetings, but they were always within call. So far as we know, no serious effort was made by any of Stalin's associates to kill him in a meeting room, such as the effort of some German generals to blow up Hitler in June, 1944. Many of Stalin's henchmen must honestly have supported many of his policies throughout his reign, The dogged loyalty with which Molotov stuck to Stalin's principles and memory after Stalin's death (although his own wife had once been jailed by Stalin) shows that Stalin retained the genuine loyalty of this most faithful of his servants to the end, and beyond the end.

For a long time some of Stalin's close associates in office were also his close personal friends, notably some of the Georgians, such as Sergo Ordzhonikidze. Apparently Stalin spent a late evening in 1938 with his old Georgian friend, Avel Yenukidze, playing cards, drinking, and telling dirty jokes; shortly after Stalin went home to his own apartment, the secret police came for Yenukidze and shot him.[1] Clearly Stalin had come to mistrust his friend, yet he had the confidence to risk his very life in Yenukidze's presence all through the fatal evening. Khrushchëv reported in his "secret speech" that Stalin sometimes glared at him in the course of meetings, demanding to know why he shifted his eyes so, and why he was afraid to look at Stalin. Since Stalin permitted Khrushchëv and others to live for years after such encounters, he must have calculated, correctly, that he was in no personal danger at their hands.

Stalin had a large establishment of personal guards who were carefully selected for blind obedience, and who were rigidly instructed to avenge any foul play to Stalin from his high officials. That was a restraining factor against conspiracy, but not a paralyzing one. Stalin's guards gave the impression of being faceless automata rather than personally devoted young men, such as Hitler and many traditional kings gathered around them. What they would have done when faced with the murdered body of Stalin—whether they would have machine-gunned the murderers down or saluted them—cannot be known.

Stalin's precautions against assassination by outsiders were far more thorough. He lived in well-guarded, well-armored apartments in the Kremlin and in suburban villas. He traveled unannounced in armored limousines, but along thoroughly guarded routes. He saw relatively few people outside his inner administration, traveled little, and made few public appearances. Khrushchëv accused him of never having met the Soviet people after a trip to Siberia in 1928. That was an exaggeration: Stalin appeared at a few factories, collective farms, and honorary societies throughout the 1930's, but very rarely during the war and thereafter. There were some ceremonial appearances at the Supreme Soviet, at Party congresses, and in Red Square on November 7 and May 1—but after 1940 he often skipped these too.

Fantastic precautions were taken during his most exposed public appearances, those in Red Square. Stalin would sit in a box on a grandstand built on or near Lenin's tomb. Every spot for blocks around from which anyone might conceivably shoot him with a rifle was occupied by secret police troops with frequently-executed orders to shoot all unauthorized persons on sight. Over a million soldiers and civilians used to march past the reviewing stand even if Stalin did not always wait to see the whole show. Every single one was frisked at least twice by different security guards (in case any one policeman was a traitor) blocks from Red Square. None of the rifles or heavier weapons marched past Stalin was loaded. Police fighter planes had orders to shoot down any unauthorized planes that might be able to bomb him: They shot down three blundering army transports for this reason on May Day, 1949.[2]

The extent of these precautions impressed many observers as a sign of paranoia. Yet when Stalin consented to go abroad to Teheran and Potsdam during World War II to meet the allied leaders, he did not seem to be strained or fearful or concerned about assassination, although the massive enough security measures taken there were far less than he was used to at home. To Roosevelt and Churchill Stalin never behaved liked a paranoiac. To Khrushchëv and Mikoyan he sometimes did. Certainly Stalin could adopt different modes of behavior when he wanted to impress different people. But Khrushchëv and Mikoyan knew him better.

After taking precautions to avoid assassination, a ruler must be concerned with avoiding a military coup. However fit or unfit the Red Army was to defend the frontiers, it clearly had the preponderance of military power within the USSR throughout Stalin's reign. Stalin's problem was to make the Red Army militarily powerful while rendering it politically null, a problem he shared with most other governments. As a Marxist-Leninist, Stalin believed that the political role of the army depended on its class nature. Ideally, the Red Army should have been composed of Communist proletarians. There were rarely enough of these to fill the army, and most of them could not be spared for that purpose anyway. Millions of non-Party proletarians were in the army for their service periods, but even in World War II the regime needed millions in the factories for production purposes.

The bulk of the Red Army and especially the overwhelming bulk of the infantry were always of peasant origin. Theoretically the "poor peasantry" was a progressive, pro-Communist class. In fact Stalin recognized that the peasantry was often "petty-bourgeois minded": at best unreliable and often hostile to his regime, especially if it came from the national minorities. As in most countries, the majority of the weapons were in the hands of people who could not be trusted.

The infantry was the most lightly-armed combat branch of the Red Army. Until the emergency of World War II, the proportions of the peasantry in the artillery, tanks corps, air force, and other branches were kept down by quotas. The peasant soldiers were kept in check, as they are in most armies, by an oppressive system of military discipline. Any American would have found discipline in Stalin's army intolerably severe. A German would probably have found the discipline bearable and in some ways slack, but he would have been shocked to find how much of it was designed to enforce his dubious loyalty rather than to make him a more perfect military machine. Yet Stalin did not go to real extremes. Frederick the Great, for instance, would rarely let his soldiers pursue a defeated enemy, for fear that most of them would desert. Stalin was more trusting than that, justifiably.

The extensive system of spies in the ranks to test the soldiers' willingness to desert, steal, shirk duties, soldier on the job, and listen to subversive talk probably exceeded that of any other army. The endless efforts and hours devoted to propaganda among the men doubtless exceeded those of any other army. The hundreds of thousands of jailings and executions of soldiers during World War II for suspected disloyalty, especially of trapped soldiers who found their way back to their own lines, and of recaptured prisoners, had no parallel.

These efforts to ensure the loyalty of the soldiers were excessive, but Stalin judged them to be necessary and effective in the test. In spite of all his precautions, millions of Red Army men surrendered rather easily to the Germans early in World War II, and almost a quarter of a million eventually served the Nazis in military units. But the real menace, rebellion by the peasant soldiery such as had overthrown the Tsar in 1917, never materialized in Stalin's Russia.

The other great security task in dealing with an army is the control of its officers. The Red Army that Stalin seized control of from Trotsky in 1925 possessed an officer corps divided between former Tsarist officers lured or coerced into defending Red Russia against invasion, and Communists of varying origins who had been drawn into Trotsky's war machine. Stalin distrusted both groups. He purged all overt Trotskyites from the Red Army by 1928. Most of the Civil War officers had been retired by the great purges, save at the top ranks. Then, anyone who might possibly be suspected of Tsarist or Trotskyite leanings found himself among the more than 3,400 Red Army officers who were shot—including the former Tsarist officer who had become the most eminent of Red soldiers, Marshal Mikhail Tukhachevsky.[3] Thenceforth the officers of the Red Army, like all other important individuals in Stalin's Russia, were all Stalin's men.

In the case of the Red Army officers, that was not enough for Stalin. The wielders of such great power had to be carefully pampered and rewarded for their loyalty. Trotsky's Red Army, which was as egalitarian as a working army can well be—no fancy uniforms, high pay, deference, or privileges for officers (although their orders had to be obeyed)—suffered a progressive normalization. Pay, uniforms, privileges, orderlies, clubs, sport teams, public commendations and deference: All came back slowly to the officer corps during the 1920's and much more rapidly from the mid-1930's on. After World War II the haughty Russian general with a chestful of garish medals could feel at home in these respects with his fellows all over the world, except when faced with the silent reproach of the plain-living and plain-coated Chinese Communist generals whose revolutionary purism disturbingly reminded him of Russia's vanished revolutionary past.

If such incentives did not suffice to attach the Red Army officer to the regime, Stalin had other methods of keeping him in check. Trotsky's Red Army had been co-commanded by political commissars, Communists attached to military units, who were to watch the regular officers for signs of treason, and to conduct political work among the troops. Stalin replaced this crude and highly resented system in gradual stages with a much more comprehensive set of controls. The Main Political Administration of the Red Army, as eventually set up, was separate from the purely military command of the armed forces, and independently responsible to the People's Commissariat for Defense and to the Party. It governed thousands of members of the Red Army directly, guiding their often full-time efforts to indoctrinate both officers and men—in propaganda meetings, in special schools for the political education of the military. It was largely responsible for the Party careers of Red Army officers, and few officers reached the higher ranks without having joined the Party. It provided for elaborate observation of all officers' devotion and loyalty, obtrusively or unobtrusively as the situation demanded.

In addition, the police ran its own organization within the armed forces, partly openly—every unit down to the battalion level had a dreaded "special section" of policemen attached to it—and partly secretly—no officer knew which of his fellows and subordinates might be police spies. On top of all this, Stalin would not trust his own Red Army to garrison his own capital. There were many units of the Red Army stationed in the Moscow area, but in peacetime the city was effectively occupied by police regiments armed with artillery, tanks, and fighter planes, who could physically protect Stalin against any military coup. In Merle Fainsod's brilliant epigram, "The political insecurity of the military command is the guarantee of the military security of the political command."[4] These were the reasons why Stalin's Russia did not break down into a land of military coups, as did many revolutionary governments in Asia and Latin America.

With the actual wielders of armed force neutralized by these means, it was customary, but misleading, to say that power lay with the Communist Party. Stalin protected himself against removal by the Party with pulverizing precautions. If his fellow *Politburo* members had actually gotten as far as voting him out—which was their constitutional privilege, and which was actually tried against Khrushchëv in 1957—Stalin would perhaps have had his guards mow them down on the spot. Or he might have done what Khrushchëv later did: had himself voted back in by the full Central Committee packed with his henchmen, since it constitutionally had the power to appoint and remove *Politburo* members. If the Central Committee, under the leadership of Stalin's opponents in the *Politburo*, had voted Stalin out—as it voted Khrushchëv out in 1964—Stalin would have been in serious trouble, for a Communist leader who loses control of his own Central Committee must already have lost his grip on the coercive reins of power.

In Stalin's day, the mere speculation would have been fantastic. Stalin prevented anyone on any level of the Party from even speaking about a motion to replace him, save for a maudlin moment in the collectivization crisis, when he offered to resign and was urged not to by the rest of the *Politburo*. If some foolhardy member of the *Politburo* or the Central Committee had broached the subject, he would have been silenced by his colleagues in a fulsome show of loyalty. A lower official or common member of the Party would have been howled down by the outraged or frightened members of his apparatus-packed Party unit. The apparatus would have been instantly informed, and would have ended his Party career with ever-increasing swiftness from the mid-1920's on. From the beginning of the great purges any such madman would have disappeared into the police dungeons within the hour.

The apparatus, backed up by the police, protected Stalin from the Party as a whole and from any dissenting section of it. If the apparatus had conspired, the police would have had the armed force to crush it. The apparatus was gone over thoroughly during the great purges. From that period on, Stalin greatly expanded his personal secretariat as a kind of inner apparatus to control the Party apparatus and other hierarchies. Even such hardened members of the apparatus and the police as Malenkov and Beria came to hate this personal secretariat, which they seem to have regarded as illegitimate even in Stalinist terms. It was not controlled even by the bureaucrats whose job was secret control. Its funds were covertly procured without the knowledge even of the bureaucrats who were in charge of allocating secret funds. Insofar as it was not run by Stalin personally, its head was a shadowy character named Alexander Poskrebyshëv, who was apparently detested by Stalin's inner circle. He disappeared without mention the day Stalin died.[5] Had there ever been a problem of protecting Stalin from his personal secretariat, the police would have been eager to move in.

Hence all threads led to the police. Even before the Revolution Lenin had insisted that a police force with secret and terrorist powers would be necessary in the early stages of the new regime to suppress counterrevolution. He thereby horrified many Russian and foreign socialists, but not Stalin. True to his ideology, Lenin set up the first Communist secret police force within six weeks of seizing power. It was called the Extraordinary Commission for the Suppression of Counterrevolution, Sabotage, and Speculation. The name indicated Lenin's intended victims, and his view of the body as a temporary emergency organization. Five years and many thousands of victims later, the Extraordinary Commission (known shudderingly throughout the world in its Russian abbreviation, *Cheka*) was reconstituted into what Lenin apparently hoped would be a regular political police administration: smaller, less active, more open, and more normal in its operations, for the Civil War had been won.

It was this ostensibly cut-down and regularized police

administration that Stalin took over as he rose to power: the State Political Administration (known by its Russian initials, *G.P.U.*). The *G.P.U.* continued the *Cheka's* exaggerated vigilance against real and hypothetical counterrevolutionaries, and against NEP-men who interpreted Lenin's partial restoration of capitalism to mean the resumption of such widespread old Russian business practices as cheating the public and defrauding the state. But as Stalin tightened his grip, the *G.P.U.* became chiefly famous for its terror against Communist Party members, whom Lenin's *Cheka* had let alone. Tens of thousands of Trotskyites, Right Deviationists, and those suspected of such tendencies passed into the prisons of the *G.P.U.*, where most of them were rather roughly persuaded to "capitulate": to sign confessions of their alleged crimes and political errors, and statements of their repentance. The capitulation was followed by a term in prison or at labor, or by release; but the victim was usually rearrested and, during the great purges, finally disposed of.

These activities of Stalin's *G.P.U.* in the second half of the 1920's gained him his first international reputation for being a monster—chiefly among leftists, for center and right wing circles abroad at that time still regarded Stalin as a comparative moderate under whom the excesses of the early Revolutionary years would not be repeated. They were not shocked at the sight of a Communist government jailing Communists. Capitulations were wrung from Zinoviev, Kamenev, Radek, and many other former top leaders of the Party. Although no major Bolsheviks were executed in this period, the process of compelling a groveling and breast-beating confession of errors and repentance struck many Communists and other leftists in the USSR and abroad as something sick, Christian, and even more vile than execution.[6] It now became apparent that Stalin sought to subdue the souls of men as well as their bodies. His agents, notably Henryk Yagoda, the effective head of the *G.P.U.*, seemed to express the satanic nature of the enterprise. Yagoda was a short, shriveled, lame, jaundiced man, who was described as looking like a bat or a devil.

Yet the real expansion of Stalin's police came only in the following decade. When Stalin collectivized agriculture he had not expected to kill and enslave millions of peasants, but, as will be seen in the chapter following, he allowed himself to proceed to such extremes. It was the expanding *G.P.U.* troop units that were called upon to surround villages and force them into forming collective farms. It was the *G.P.U.* that was given the responsibility for arranging famines in recalcitrant regions, and for arresting and disposing of millions of *"kulaks."* The *G.P.U.* found itself with several million political prisoners of peasant origin on its hands, most of them sentenced to terms at hard labor. In this First Five Year Plan period of furious economic construction, it was natural for the *G.P.U.* to set its prisoners to work as unskilled laborers in basic extractive industries and construction projects in remote and unpleasant parts of the country where free labor was almost absent and almost impossible to import.

Thus without any ideological prevision (a rare thing in Stalin's Russia) and without any long term planning of any kind, the *G.P.U.* expanded by degrees from the political police of a dictator to a giant, mass-murdering economic empire. It controlled the timber and pulpwood industries of the far north of European Russia, railroad repair and canal building in most of the country, and—most famously—mining all across the Russian and Siberian arctic as well as in other parts of Soviet Asia. The *G.P.U.* and its successors came to be the real government of large areas of the north and of Siberia, with towns of tens of thousands of people directly under its administration. There were not only workers serving penal sentences, but those who had completed their terms and who were usually compelled to live in conditions of semi-servitude in police-controlled or nearby areas of Soviet Asia.

And thus without any ideological prevision, and without any long term planning of any kind, Stalin finally in the early 1930's became what he will always be remembered as: the enslaver and murderer of millions of people. Of all Stalin's great enterprises, the killing of millions was the one that had least place in his ideology as he rose to power, and the one that is least explainable in terms of ideology alone. The collectivization of agriculture was Stalin's point of no return. When he had killed his first million people, he could take the killing of further millions in his stride. He would no longer think twice about anything so comparatively minor, say, as the murder of a few thousand Polish officers in the Katyn forest in 1940. As was Stalin's custom, he fitted the non-ideologically dictated things he came to do into his ideological framework. He proceeded to justify the "liquidation of the *kulaks*" and other "harshest measures" on ideological grounds, and used them as ideological precedents for his many later mass murders. And so mass murder came to be a standard part of Communist ideology for a generation, to be employed from the start by all other Communist regimes (save that of San Marino[7]) during his lifetime in their efforts to follow the Stalinist path.

This huge expansion of the *G.P.U.* during the collectivization of agriculture required a reorganization, which culminated in 1934, when the whole vast system was renamed the People's Commissariat for Internal Affairs *(N.K.V.D.)*. This enlarged administration was responsible for all police activities, both ordinary and political, for all prisons and work camps, for security guard duty from the Kremlin to the frontiers, for highways and much of the other modes of transport, for the collection and transmission of vital statistics and information (it was the *N.K.V.D.* that took censuses and compiled maps), and various other enterprises such as the fire departments of the USSR. All the ordinary police were now placed under the political police. Heavy armored divisions with tanks and airplanes were strengthened to make the *N.K.V.D.* independent of the Red Army in dealing with peasant risings and restive national groups. This was the empire of terror, slavery, and death that was to endure for the rest of Stalin's reign.

This reorganization of the police was followed almost immediately by the climax of Stalinism, the period of almost five years known as the "great purges." It began in December 1934 with the assassination of Sergei Kirov, who was often spoken of as Stalin's most important subordinate and likely successor. It used to be thought that the killing frightened Stalin into gigantic reprisals to save his own neck. It now seems more likely that Stalin arranged the killing of Kirov to get rid of a possible rival, and to provide an excuse for going ahead with the purges. If so, Stalin had taken one further step in his moral evolution; Kirov was the first important Communist, the first member of the *Politburo* itself, to be killed by Stalin. This was the point in Stalin's career at which Khrushchëv, twenty-two years later, began to condemn his actions. First, Stalin had more than a hundred people shot who had been in jail at the time Kirov was assassinated. Thousands of persons from Leningrad—Kirov's satrapy and the scene of the crime—were sent to Siberia. Zinoviev, Kamenev, and other members of the former Left Opposition were secretly tried and convicted of plotting to kill Stalin. The Party membership was re-examined for loyalty, and almost 800,000 seem to have been purged from its ranks.[8]

After a pause associated with the optimistic proclamation of a new age in the Soviet Constitution of 1936, the mass horrors began. The public and the outside world were treated to the famous series of three show trials in which Zinoviev,

Kamenev, Radek, Bukharin, and other surviving Old Bolsheviks confessed in astonishing detail all their supposed plots to kill Stalin in collaboration with Trotsky and the capitalist powers (chiefly Germany), and to establish their own dictatorship in the USSR, which was to restore capitalism and serve foreign enemies. Practically all the leading Communists who had opposed Stalin at any time during the 1920's or even earlier were shot or died in labor camps. Meanwhile, Stalin's agents abroad were killing off Trotsky's friends and family. One of them was to kill Trotsky himself with an ice axe in 1940, making him the last victim of the great purges.

Stalin also purged many of his own most important partisans from the struggle of the 1920's, although they were still bulwarks of his regime. Three members of the *Politburo* (four if one includes Kirov) and three candidate members disappeared—without show trials or publicity. In his "secret speech" Khrushchëv was to recall that the USSR learned of the fall of Stanislav Kossior, a member of the *Politburo* and boss of the Ukraine, when the Kiev radio station stopped calling itself "Radio Kossior." When Stalin disposed of one of his henchmen he purged all of the immediate associates of the doomed man as well, and many of the numerous persons who might have been given jobs by the doomed man, or benefited in any other way from his career. Stalin could be quite thorough; when he purged Kossior, he also deported to Siberia most of the inhabitants of the three peasant villages that Kossior had named after himself and to some degree favored.[9]

As 1937 and 1938 ground on, the purges were extended throughout the Party and, with lesser incidence, throughout the country at large. The number of victims has always been disputed. Nine hundred thousand men may have been shot— roughly the number that later died at Auschwitz. Six million people may have passed through the prisons of the *N.K.V.D.*

—to their deaths, to labor camps, to assignments in remote parts of the USSR, or, with shattered souls, back to their homes if not to their former jobs. These figures are taken from the lower range of the relatively non-partisan estimates, but mere caution does not ensure accuracy.[10]

It is even harder to estimate statistics about the fate of the millions sent to labor camps. Many died on the way, many succumbed to brutality, exhaustion, starvation, disease, and cold in the camps themselves. The camps were not supposed to be death camps, like the later Auschwitz and Treblinka, but labor camps, yet we cannot be sure whether more or less than half the deportees survived their sentences. The greatest torture and the biggest killer may well have been the sheer cold of the Soviet north and east—for which Stalin was only partly responsible. He did not create the cold, but he did little to protect his prisoners from it. Perhaps the most awful statement to come out of the camps was made by the prisoner-hero of Alexander Solzhenitsyn's post-Stalin novel, *One Day in the Life of Ivan Denisovich:* "A man who is warm cannot understand a man who is cold."

The terror was of such magnitude as to defy any straightforward rational explanation. The outside world's initial puzzlement centered on the confessions of the defendants in the show trials. The gigantic plot alleged in their testimony was incredible. Why had figures of striking intellect such as Radek and Bukharin confessed in open court? Some suggested they were soul-sick Russians with a compulsion to confess, and cited the novels of Dostoevsky as relevant parallels. Some believed that Communists were people of a special psychic makeup, holding loyalty to self, truth, or whatever, below loyalty to the Party; this group was much impressed with Arthur Koestler's *Darkness at Noon.* Some suggested that the victims had been drugged or broken down by months of subtle psychological tortures, derived from fiendish Communist extensions of Pavlov's experiments in manipulating laboratory animals.

Now that so many of the purge victims have survived to tell or write their experiences, there is less mystery. An arrested man was utterly helpless in the hands of the police. No reprieve, no escape, no justification by friends outside or by outraged posterity seemed possible. Endless interrogation, anxiety, and sleeplessness could break most wills. Tortures, from compelling a victim to stand up for days on end to more fiendish horrors, could be applied as needed. Psychological pressures, from promises of light sentences to threats against one's family to appeals to Party loyalty *in extremis*, played their part. Any holdouts could be secretly shot. Only a few thousand victims were ever brought to public trial at any level. Radek and Bukharin were thought to be sufficiently tamed to be trusted in show trials, but their banter and doubletalk in court, and their confessions of conspiratorial details that foreign newsmen could easily prove impossible (e.g., the alleged meeting in a hotel in Copenhagen known to have burned down years before) were clear signals to those with the intelligence to hear.

More puzzling to this day is the question of Stalin's motivation. He certainly believed that there were plots against him, yet he clearly had many of the plots fabricated. Since he believed that people's actions are determined by their social groups he seems to have found it easy to believe that all members of a group—say the entourage of an arrested People's Commissar—were in on the plot, or likely to join it at a proximate stage, or likely to form one in revenge when their principal was caught. There were probably a few real conspiracies whose exposure by the police made Stalin think he had proof of the gigantic conspiracy he feared. To him, the fabrication of plots was justifiable if the regime could secure some gain from removing the victims or from the attendant propaganda.

As the great purges proceeded, tens of thousands of bureaucrats with blots on their records were arrested. Stalin's apparatus had picked these men, so he thought they must have been competent to some degree. If they had failed in some enterprise, it must have been sabotage, Stalin thought, not foolishness—and to Stalin, genuine foolishness deserved scarcely less severe punishment. Where a harvest failed, or a train was wrecked, or a code was broken, traitors must have been responsible. In the case of Marshal Tukhachevsky and his fellow generals, Stalin's suspicious nature seems to have been exploited by Nazi intelligence agents, who planted faked incriminating documents in Czechoslovakia, where they would be sure to be transmitted to the Soviet government.

Almost certainly Stalin did not go on with the great purges self-consciously in order to bring the new Soviet middle class, dependent on him alone, into lower and middle power positions, although that was a major result. It is very doubtful if Stalin planned to kill a million people in 1934 or even in 1937, but it is more doubtful that the high fatalities came about because the whole process got out of control. Certainly police officials exceeded their orders in many places out of anxiety or ambition, but nowhere near enough to account for the great difference between normal dictatorial precautions and the great purges.

Although the great purges as a whole did serve some of Stalin's purposes, they were also a crushing disability. Thousands of his hitherto most loyal, effective, and experienced servants were butchered. Their loss was felt most strongly in the top military command during the disastrous opening months of World War II. The survivors and the beneficiaries through promotions to vacant positions were terrorized out of any thought of active disloyalty, to be sure, but also in most cases out of any but the safest and most routine of initiatives. Never again would anyone, even Molotov, dare to tell Stalin a plain truth without the most elaborate precautions, if at all.

These disadvantages of the great purges, even when considered from a hypothetical "rational Stalinist" point of view, have led many Western observers (at length backed up by Khrushchëv and Mikoyan) to cite them as the clearest and most horrifying example of Stalin's "insane suspiciousness," "paranoia," or some less psychiatric but equivalent phrase. The full-fledged paranoiac is a person who believes that he possesses some extraordinary power or virtue, often granted to him by some higher authority, often to be used for the benefit of some "good" group. Furthermore, the paranoiac believes, many evil people and groups are conspiring against him to deprive him and his good group of their treasure, often on behalf of some remote higher evil authority. Since the evil conspirators are everywhere and will stop at nothing, he must take extreme violent measures to forestall them.

It is easy to see why many psychiatrists have found Stalin to be a paranoiac. Communist ideology, like Nazi ideology, has the structure of a systematized paranoiac delusion. Marx and Engels handed down the priceless truth of socialism through Lenin to Stalin for the benefit of the workers of the world, but the evil capitalists, headed by remote foreign powers, conspire everywhere to kill Stalin and overthrow the USSR, and so the harshest measures must always be taken to forestall them. Of course Christian ideology, with its God and Christendom, its evil pagans, heretics, and Devil, its crusades and inquisitions, can be seen in the same way. Mere belief in the ideology fails to distinguish Stalin and Torquemada who may have been paranoiac from Sergei Eisenstein and Francis of Assisi who certainly were not.

Many Western psychiatrists have believed that paranoia is a peculiar mental makeup determined before birth by body chemistry, which unfolds regardless of the environment. In this view, Stalin would have developed megalomania, insane suspiciousness, and murderous behavior, even if he had been born into a happy, wealthy, English home. Other psychiatrists (including Freud) believe that environment makes the paranoiac. The non-Communist can see enough in Stalin's career in Tsarist Russia and the Communist Party to make most men paranoid to some degree—but hardly to Stalin's degree. The Communist is embarrassed to reflect that Stalin's experiences under the Tsars were no more paranoia-producing than Lenin's, and that his later environment was Lenin's Party, so that environmental explanations of Stalin's psyche are damning to Communism as a whole.

If psychiatry is a science at all, it cannot operate on the dead Stalin or on the documentation he left us in accordance with professional standards. A precise diagnosis of Stalin's (and Hitler's) mental condition may always be impossible, as it certainly is now. Encouraged by Khrushchëv, Western historians dwell on Stalin's megalomania and super-suspiciousness and wholesale violence, but they often cloud the medical issue by calling him "paran*oid*" (like, or tending toward, paranoia), and often shrink from attributing great historical events to the mental condition of one man. But the issue cannot be avoided. If Stalin was a true paranoiac, and paranoia is set at birth, then historians need not seek *historical* explanations for Stalin's motives: He killed millions of people in his middle age because of his body chemistry. If Stalin was a true paranoiac, and paranoia is the result of developmental misfortunes, the historians must examine Stalin's youth, but not his maturity, to account for his motives. If Stalin was not a true paranoiac, but was pressed toward paranoid behavior by extraordinary circumstances in his maturity, then historians must look at his adult life for his motivations. Historians as such cannot answer the question. They do not have the necessary medical competence. But it is not thereby an unimportant question.

In the great purges, even more than in other periods of Stalin's rule, one can see that Stalin's ultimate tool for protecting himself against enemies by removing them first, and by keeping everyone in a constant state of tension, was the police. But the result of such extraordinary use of the police was their expansion into a state-within-a-state that comprised at least 10 per cent of Soviet society by one measure or another in certain years; an empire that was topped by a large body that served the functions of a Praetorian Guard in Moscow itself. Therefore Stalin's last problem of defending his power was to protect himself against dethronement by the police themselves.

Neither the Party apparatus nor the Red Army nor any other outside body watched the police; it was controlled by constantly-shifting elements within itself. The security officers were constantly put through the severest loyalty screenings. Their privileges were as insolent as any in the Red Army. Moves against Stalin were always inhibited by the thought of how intensely unpopular the police were, and how likely it was that a police coup, more than any other possible political maneuver, would stir up Party and army against it. The high police chiefs were outsiders in Russian society as no other power-wielding group was, not even Stalin's Georgian and Armenian circle.

Stalin inherited and worked fairly well with the founder of the *Cheka*, Felix Dzerzhinsky, a compulsive Pole who had become fanatical even by Bolshevik standards. After his death in 1926, Stalin turned the police over in fact (and eventually in formal title) to Yagoda, who was a Jew and a physical and psychic freak, and for all three of these reasons most unlikely to secure power apart from Stalin. After launching the great purges for Stalin, Yagoda and all his following were themselves purged in 1936 by other police officers whom Stalin had apparently been holding in reserve for this purpose. The new chief of the *N.K.V.D.* was a Great Russian named Nikolai Yezhov, who seems to have been both paranoid and manic-depressive.[11] He was somehow capable of administering the worst phase of the great purges, which has always been named after him—the *Yezhovshchina*—but he was apparently neither attractive enough nor coherent enough to have a chance of plotting successfully against Stalin. There was little difficulty in purging Yezhov and all his followers in 1939.

He was replaced by one of Stalin's Georgian protégés, Lavrenti Beria, a far saner, abler, and milder man, who kept his head and his job for the rest of Stalin's life. If any police chief could have removed Stalin, it would have been Beria— not before the war when he was new to his job, nor during the war when there was other business to attend to, but after the war when Stalin appeared even to many of his close associates to be going into a paranoid decline. Yet Beria never moved, and almost certainly never tried to. Some of Stalin's last actions, notably the concoction of the "doctors' plot," indicated that he planned another major purge that would sweep out the police command first of all, yet Beria did nothing detectable to defend himself. After Stalin's death, Beria's armored garrison held Moscow in its hand, but he did not seize power. His brief post-Stalin career revealed him as a man who courted support by granting liberal concessions, until he was victimized by his colleagues and shot. It seems likely that Stalin's ultimate protection against the last dreaded chief of his terrible police was that he had chosen too mild and unaggressive a man.

Stalin's system of power can be seen as the world's most colossal system of defense-works. Everything was set up in law, in administrative practice, and in deliberately or unconsciously produced psychological effect to check everything else, to watch everyone else, to render everyone too insecure to try to move against Stalin or even to think about it. The world's image of Stalin's rule is that of a driving, aggressive machine, designed to subvert, revolutionize, and transform everything—and there is much to this picture. But on a closer look, Stalin used his power for defensive purposes above all others. He tried to propagandize every citizen from birth on, to enmesh him in a close net of Party and state institutions, to mold his very soul, because every citizen was in Stalin's mind a potential threat. All institutions, all bodies of men, every official had to be pulled in contrary directions because Stalin was never sure where the next threat might come from. Nowhere was the threat greater than from Stalin's own agents. The higher and more successful the agent the greater was the danger from him, and the more intense was the system of scrutiny and restraints.

Stalin had many purposes that could fairly be called aggressive. But he himself regarded his enterprise as an island in a sea of evil. There could be no ultimate security and no one could be trusted forever—until the world was completely changed. The only effective defense was a continuous offense. The innumerable enemies had to be forestalled; the omnipresent traitors had to be unmasked. The mainspring of Stalin's system of power was fear, general free-floating insecurity. Insofar as we do not see the threats that Stalin strove so mightily to forestall, we call him paranoiac. Insofar as we claim we would not engage in Stalin's methods even to save our very lives, we call him a monster. Insofar as the real threats to Stalin's rule were often the reactions called forth by his own excessive measures of defense, we call him the victim of self-fulfilling prophecies. But Stalin died on his throne, and he died old. We may judge his power excessive.

He thought it more relevant that his power did in fact defend him.

This is certainly the most discouraging thing about the history of Stalin's Russia, the apparent success of his totalitarian system. Stalin did not believe the cost was excessive. He did not seem to be paralyzed by the effort. He thought his system was making possible unparalleled economic growth. He was right in thinking it had won the greatest war in history. By the standards of most rulers before our times, Stalin was the most successful ruler in history. The horrible lesson that Stalin may have left to history is that future rulers can adopt Stalin's totalitarian system, modified and improved in a few details, and rule in horror for a generation until they too die on their thrones—old.

7. THE VILLAGES

*A*LTHOUGH Stalin never lived on a farm, he had risen from the peasant class. When he dealt with the peasantry, he was proud to claim that he was dealing with people whom he really understood from within, people like himself. The central fact of peasant life all over the world, for Stalin, was exploitation by landlords, brutal, pitiless, and crushing.[1] Landlords, whether they were great nobles who owned tens of thousands of serfs, or petty *kulaks* who hired one or two of their fellow villagers, condemned the vast bulk of the peasantry to starvation or semi-starvation, filth, disease, physical maltreatment, humiliation, religion, and ignorance. The great landlords were gone from Russia when Stalin took over, but several million *kulaks* remained to be eliminated.

The exploiters, Stalin feared, had done their work only too well. They had succeeded in reducing virtually all peasants to utter backwardness and thoroughgoing degradation. Almost no trace of the Russian *narodnik* tradition of "peasant worship" can be found in Stalin's speeches and writings. When he thought of the peasantry as "the people" he admired their toughness and their folk culture, but when he thought of them as peasants he dwelt on their depressed condition. The lucky peasant who rose from semi-starvation and acquired a paltry landholding became a *kulak*, an even harsher exploiter than a nobleman, for his margin of survival was so much less. The peasant rebel of the past, such as Stenka Razin, and the Bolshevik peasant of the present, such as Chapaev, transcended the ordinary vile condition of the peasantry. But the bulk of the peasantry, although they were toiling masses, and although they had been used by Lenin to bring about the October Revolution, were unreliable allies, always tending toward *kulak*-like petty bourgeois-mindedness, a potential counterrevolutionary threat of the gravest proportions.

The inherent unscientific inefficiency of the landlords and the hopeless backwardness of the peasants had combined, Stalin asserted, to make Russia's fields the scene of wholesale economic idiocy. The peasant planted what was traditional, not what was scientifically sensible. In the eighteenth century, Stalin recalled, thousands of Russian peasants had preferred to die rather than to cultivate the newly-introduced potato, which they regarded as un-Christian and sexually unclean.[2] The peasants divided up their fields into innumerable crisscrosses of vastly inefficient strips, due to their viciously strong sense of private property. They employed priests' charms instead of fertilizer and witchcraft instead of pesticides. Even a good Bolshevik peasant, returned from the Red Army that might have educated him, had no resources with which to set up a model scientific farm. When the Communist regime itself set up such model farms in the 1920's, the spread of progressive techniques from them was painfully slow.

Consequently, Stalin believed that the villages of Russia would have to be radically transformed before anyone could be expected to lead a good life there. The counterrevolutionary threat from the countryside had to be eliminated as soon as possible. Furthermore, the dismally inefficient agriculture of the Russian villages had to feed the cities of the USSR, which it did with very mixed success during the first years of Stalin's power. Beyond that, the farms of Russia would be required to supply the food for the enlarged work force during the anticipated expansion of Soviet industry, and to provide a surplus for shipment abroad to pay for machinery and other imports to make that expansion possible.

Communists were agreed that Soviet agriculture would some day have to be "socialized," but there was no agreement during most of the 1920's as to precisely what that meant, or how or when it should be done. Agricultural policy was the subject of some of the most intense wrangling during the great debate on the Party's future course, which raged in the mid-1920's while Stalin was building up the power to end all debates. No Communist forgot that the Party ruled in the name of the proletariat in a country where at least 85 per cent of the population lived in peasant villages.

The range of policies debated in the Party extended from what Communists call a "right" strategy—in agriculture as in other matters a policy of relative mildness, relative permissiveness, and relative passivity on the part of the regime; to what Communists call a "left" strategy—a hard, active, driving, forward-moving, coercive policy.[3] The Soviet government had been following a "right" strategy in agriculture and industry ever since Lenin adopted his New Economic Policy in 1921, under which the state ceased to requisition food from the peasants by force and collected instead a fixed tax in kind, while allowing the peasants to trade surplus crops freely on the local markets. Lenin insisted this right strategy was necessary to restore Soviet agricultural and industrial production after the disasters of the World War and the Civil War. He fell ill and died before deciding how long his temporary right strategy need be continued.

The leading spokesman for Stalin's government and for the continuation of the right strategy in economic matters was Nikolai Bukharin, a member of the *Politburo*, the editor of *Pravda*, the Party's leading theoretician of the period, and Stalin's right hand man after the break-up of his alliance with Zinoviev and Kamenev. Bukharin was relatively optimistic about the prospects for continuing Lenin's "alliance" (i.e., *modus vivendi*) between the "proletariat" (i.e., the Party) and the peasantry, and relatively less fearful of counterrevolution by the peasants. The Party, he thought, could and should safely allow the peasants and the NEP-men to hire labor, trade privately, and make private profits—as they had been doing since 1921—in order to restore the ecenomy and raise production. These petty capitalists might be motivated by private gain, but in fact they would be building the economy for the service of the socialist state. Bukharin insisted that socialist industry, and indeed any industry in the USSR, could grow only on the basis of a healthy, growing peasant agriculture. The state should positively encourage peasant agriculture by lowering the prices of industrial goods from state factories so that peasants could buy more, by importing cheap foreign goods for peasants to buy, and by treating the peasants in a legal, orderly, fair, and friendly manner to restore their confidence in the state and in the economic future. Bukharin recommended that the Party tell the peasants to "enrich yourselves."[4]

According to Bukharin, the consequent general prosperity of the peasants would reduce the special position and counterrevolutionary potential of the *kulaks*. Lowering prices on agricultural implements would help the peasants buy more and hence produce more crops. Lowering prices on consumer goods would encourage the peasants to sell more food to the cities in return for these goods. Thus the threat of counter-revolution, the low productivity of Soviet agriculture, and the periodic shortages of peasant food deliveries to the cities would all be eliminated.

Stalin's government did in fact lower the prices of state factory goods several times in the mid-1920's, but without greatly increased production the results were periodic "goods famines," during which all goods produced were snapped up at low prices and many would-be peasant buyers could find no industrial goods to buy. The peasants, who had indeed raised production almost every year from 1922 on, often ate more food, lent more to other peasants, and stored more, instead of taking it to the city markets. The apparent influence of the *kulaks* among the peasantry did not diminish. Bukharin remained optimistic. By 1927 he came to believe that the time was ripe for taxing the *kulaks* more heavily, since they were now rich enough to bear it. He came to favor "collectivization," by which he meant state encouragement of the voluntary formation of co-operatives by the more socialist-minded peasants, and state support for these co-operatives through favorable credit and purchasing arrangements. These co-operatives would shine by example and slowly attract more and more peasants into socialist agriculture. Bukharin voted for the collectivization resolution at the Fifteenth Party Congress in 1927. For Bukharin these were slight steps to the left, but he remained at least moderately rightist in the terms of the controversy. He almost always favored longer postponements of the collectivization drive, slower rates, and, in effect, less collectivization than any other major participant in a given debate. One wonders if Soviet agriculture would ever have been collectivized if Bukharin had gained power.

Bukharin's rightist position was widely shared in the Party for much of the 1920's, but unfortunately for him and for the peasants many Communists, including (eventually) Stalin, came to find at least five things wrong with his advice: Soviet agriculture had indeed recovered rapidly after 1922, but by the later 1920's its growth had leveled off at roughly the prewar figures, and it showed signs of continued stagnation. The periodic goods famines and consequent cutbacks by the peasantry on the delivery of food to the cities continued—not only in the fall and winter of 1925 just after Bukharin had formulated his position, but in the fall and winter of 1927 and in the spring of 1928, after his policies had apparently been tested, and therefore found wanting. Many Communists continued to believe in the ideologically postulated threat of counterrevolution by *kulaks,* and thought that the cutbacks in food deliveries were proofs of their fears. Bukharin's policy grossly affronted the sentiments of many Communists about the sinfulness of capitalism and the necessity of socialism. And Bukharin was thought to be too "brilliant," too intellectual, too facile, too inconstant in his policies, and too prone to offensive mockery and wisecracks.[5]

There was a whole packet of opposing left strategies in agriculture and industry. The ablest presentation was made by an economist named Evgenii Preobrazhensky,[6] who supported Trotsky through most of the 1920's. Preobrazhensky was pessimistic about the prospects for Communist power if the New Economic Policy was continued. The peasantry, he said, had been freed from oppression by landlords and Tsarist bureaucrats during the Revolution. It was now in full possession of the agricultural land of the USSR, with more economic, and hence political, power than it had ever had before. It had more surplus food to sell than could be exchanged for the limited industrial consumer goods that came forth from the USSR's war-worn factories—hence the goods famines in the countryside and the consequent cutbacks in food deliveries to the cities. Peasant economic dissatisfaction generated by this surplus and unfulfilled demand might soon be harnessed by *kulaks* in conjunction with foreign capitalist powers to start a counterrevolution. Invasion from abroad might well be imminent. The situation was fraught with danger, Preobrazhensky thought, and required rapid drastic change.

Peasant demand and peasant consumption, Preobrazhensky urged, should be cut down, partly by higher direct taxation, but mostly by raising the prices of industrial goods so that most peasants could no longer afford them, while the richer ones would have to pay far more for them. The Communist state should use this greatly increased revenue in money and kind to undertake a great program of building up Russian industry. The greatest investments and most rapid growth would be secured for heavy, capital goods industries. Unless the Party constructed a giant, industrial, socialist sector of the economy, which would eventually swallow up the private sector, the capitalists, especially the *kulaks*, of the private sector would swallow up the socialist sector—and with it the political power of the Communists.

The investments in this proposed expansion of Soviet industry had to come from some place. The Soviet state had few reserves of capital, due to the World War and Civil War. The existing industrial sector was too small to finance the desired huge rapid expansion. Preobrazhensky favored some borrowing from foreign capitalists, but doubted if they would invest heavily enough to build up the economy and military strength of their deadly socialist enemy. This left only the peasants as a major source of capital for industrialization. The peasants' grain would have to be brought to the cities to feed the hordes of new workers, and sent abroad to pay for shiploads of new machinery.

Preobrazhensky reasoned that the peasants would not sacrifice themselves *en masse* to produce more grain to build socialist industry. The state would have few consumer goods, during the period of rapid buildup of capital industries, with which to bribe the peasants into producing more. This left only coercion as the method for extracting grain from the peasantry. Preobrazhensky's ideas of coercion were laws, taxes, and high prices, not machine guns and labor camps, but he knew that he was proposing a grim period for the Russian peasantry. This process of extracting the capital for industrialization from the peasants he ominously called "primitive socialist accumulation"—echoing Marx's term, "primitive capitalist accumulation," for the savage exploitation of workers, artisans, and peasants during the early Industrial Revolution.[7]

The views of Preobrazhensky were roundly condemned by Bukharin and other spokesmen for Stalin's regime in the mid-1920's. Preobrazhensky was attacked as a Trotskyite. He was accused of denouncing Lenin's policy during the Revolution of alliance with the poor peasantry, and of opposing Lenin's New Economic Policy. He was criticized for proposing a break between Party and peasantry that would precipitate a new counterrevolutionary crisis. He was belabored for favoring an economically unnecessary and immorally un-socialist program of exploiting the toiling peasants. He was dismissed as a pessimist about the revolutionary devotion of the peasantry and the economic potential of the USSR. Along with Trotsky and the rest of his following, Preobrazhensky was expelled from the Communist Party at the Fifteenth Party Congress in 1927. (Two years later he broke with Trotsky, on the grounds that Stalin had in fact adopted the gist of his own views. Soon he was guardedly protesting against the horrors of collectivization. Like his theoretical rival, Bukharin, Preobrazhensky was killed in the great purges.)

Theoretically, the question of whether to squeeze the peasants to extract the capital for industrial buildup could be separated from the question of collectivizing agriculture. A Communist might adopt Preobrazhensky's stern views on the peasants without advocating collective farms. On the other hand a Communist might reject Preobrazhensky and still favor some form of socialist agriculture. If a "socialist farm" meant an agrarian area in which private property had given way to joint, communal, state, or public forms of agriculture, there were a variety of socialist farms already in existence. They could be classified along two sliding scales: the degree to which they were run by the state, and the degree to which they were collective in structure.

The most statist variety of socialist farm was called the *sovetskoe khoziaistvo* (shortened in Russian to *sovkhoz*), which means literally "conciliar economic enterprise," but which is usually (and better) translated as "state farm." A state farm in the 1920's was usually a very large farm including up to several dozen villages, for Lenin had had a Marxist's exaggerated opinion of the economic virtues of large scale production. A state farm was an entirely state-owned enterprise. Its fields and equipment, and even the peasants' houses (in theory) were to be held by the state. The peasants (in theory) were to receive wages and wages only in return for their labor, along with whatever social services the state could provide. These and other parallels to the industrial factory led to the proud designation of the state farm as the "factory in the field." The parallel was ideologically desirable, for the peasants were supposed to become proletarians by virtue of their relationship to the means of production, and therefore (ideology suggested) proletarians in their psychology and politics.

Far less statist in the 1920's were the three leading kinds of *kollektivnoe khoziaistvo* (shortened in Russian to *kolkhoz* and translated as "collective farm"), which were not owned or directly controlled by the state, although they were licensed, blessed, and sometimes subsidized by different government agencies. The loosest and least collective of the three was the "society for joint land cultivation" (known by its Russian initials as the *toz*), in which the peasants retained all save ultimate legal ownership of their houses and fields, but formed a co-operative organization for cultivation, purchase of equipment, marketing, and so on. The middling collective of the three was the *artel*, a word of many meanings in Russian agrarian and revolutionary history, here applied to a co-operative in which the peasants retained virtual ownership of their houses, garden plots, and domestic animals, while the fields, forests, and major equipment were in the hands of the co-operative. The strictest and most collective of the three was the *kommuna* ("commune") in which everything short of tooth-fillings was idealistically held in common, and each peasant received food, clothing, and whatever as he needed it. Ten years of experience after the Revolution with the different forms of socialist farm provided no decisive evidence of the superiority of any one form to another, or to private agriculture.[8]

A Communist might select his preferred form of socialist agriculture, and still debate how rapidly he wanted to spread it throughout the countryside. And he might still debate whether the Party should rely on the example of existing socialist farms to attract the peasants into such institutions, or whether the taxing, pricing, and subsidizing powers of the state should be used to press the peasants in, or whether outright coercion was the surest policy. The Soviet debate on agricultural policy, along with the contemporary arguments in Mexico, were the first thorough thrashings-out of this basic revolutionary dilemma by twentieth century revolutionary governments. Both the arguments and the solutions have been remembered and sometimes imitated in many of the other revolutionary backward countries of the world.

The decision was Stalin's. He did not find it an easy one. His ideology, as he had developed it by the mid-1920's, involved some commitment to socialized agriculture sometime, but left all the argued options open save permanent relaxation, which could not be judged truly Leninist. At the Fourteenth Party Congress in December, 1925, Stalin proclaimed that "We are, and we shall be, for Bukharin," but at the same time he repudiated Bukharin's injunction to the Party to tell the peasants to "enrich yourselves."[9] Over the next two years Stalin continued to work with Bukharin, while he completed the ruin of the "left opposition" in the Party. At the Fifteenth Party Congress in December, 1927, which saw the expulsion of Trotsky and the left leaders from the Party, the regime expressed its concern about the renewed goods famine and cutback of food deliveries to the cities. The Party was made to order the drawing up of a Five Year Plan under which heavy and defense industries would forge ahead rapidly (which had been urged by the expelled leftists) while staying in balance with agriculture (as Bukharin recommended). Taxation of the *kulaks* was to be increased (as the leftists had urged, a policy with which even Bukharin now came to agree). And the Party was made to pass a resolution in favor of collectivizing the agriculture of the USSR. Even Bukharin voted for this resolution, since the form of socialist farm that seemed to be recommended was the mild and loose *toz*—the resolution carefully avoided specific statements about the form, the rate, and the methods of collectivization—and since Stalin had said the process would be both slow and voluntary, at least for the most part. Stalin seemed to be moving left, but slowly, and only as far as the center.

In fact Stalin may already have decided upon drastic and genuinely leftist changes.[10] Rural officials and Party members were told to exert stronger pressures to get the peasants to resume grain deliveries to the cities. Food did come in in larger quantities during the first three months of 1928, but the crisis burst out again in the spring and continued in varying degrees of intensity throughout the year. In April Stalin had the Central Committee pass more "temporary" measures for extracting food from the peasants. Then he introduced, but soon withdrew, a draft of a new land law under which peasants would retain their rights to cultivate land only if they joined socialist farms, and *kulaks* would lose their rights to land altogether. At a Central Committee meeting in July, Stalin clashed openly with Bukharin, and demanded a renewed period of "tribute" from the peasants to industrialize. Outward unity was preserved, and some measures against the *kulaks* were actually repealed, but collectivization was reaffirmed and Stalin no longer insisted that it be voluntary. He had indeed adopted the core of Preobrazhensky's position, and from then on worked for the downfall of Bukharin and his fellow rightists.

The First Five Year Plan was formally launched in October, 1928. In November he insisted to the Central Committee that the USSR had to build up its capital goods and military industries fast, to defend itself against future capitalist attack. He had the Central Committee denounce "rightist deviation." Most rightists hurried to capitulate during the winter, but not Bukharin, who began to be stripped of his many high posts in April, 1929. After the harvest of 1929, Stalin began the all-out drive to collectivize the villages of the USSR.

Thus Stalin came to adopt the leftist position about the necessity to build socialist industry rapidly by squeezing the peasants in order to avoid counterrevolution by *kulaks* in conjunction with foreign capitalists. At the same time, he was considering which form of socialist farm to use for this purpose. He was skeptical about the possibility of extending the full commune over the whole countryside, although after 1925 he helped some of them financially. To him the commune was too far in advance of the historical process to be broadly appealing or practical. He distrusted any kind of socialist farm that was not directly under the control of the regime, as most collective farms, in the 1920's, were not.

During 1927-29, Stalin seemed to prefer the state farm, which was a more advanced socialist institution than the *toz* or the *artel* and yet not so advanced as to provoke his skepticism. And the state farm was a completely state-controlled institution. It was usually larger, and otherwise seemed to have more Marxist-Leninist credentials and precedents.[11] It was the most susceptible to scientific and mechanical agriculture. But the state farms actually set up in those years were seriously hampered by the lack of new machinery and buildings necessary to put the idea into effect. Much more serious, few peasants were readily enlisted. The *kulaks*, who were drawing Stalin's darkest suspicions of counterrevolutionary sabotage upon themselves by their periodic refusal to send food to the city when there was nothing to buy with it, offended again by refusing to join the *sovkhozes* and by urging poorer peasants not to do so.

And so the form of socialist agriculture to which Stalin turned, reluctantly but with increasing certainty from 1929 on, was the *artel*. An *artel* could be formed from an existing peasant village, without any special investment in new buildings or other plant. The peasants in an *artel* could (in theory) keep enough livestock and garden space to feed themselves, without any payments by the state. The very continuity in houses, gardens, and livestock (in theory) would reassure the peasant about his entry into socialist agriculture, and lessen his resistance. In these ways, Stalin came increasingly to believe, the *artel* was a less fully socialist but more practical form of socialist agriculture than the state farm.

Yet all through the collectivization period Stalin proposed that a larger minority of Russian agriculture be organized in *Sovkhozes* (more than 25 per cent) than proved practicable (less than 10 per cent). Until the end of the major collectivization drives in 1936, Stalin often described the *artel* as merely the first step in collectivization, which would soon move on to universal state farms. However, the *artel* came to be the permanent form of organization of the Russian village, rolling back the *sovkhozes* and eliminating the other forms of collective farm altogether. Consequently the word "*artel*" gave way in official and common usage to the previously more general term "collective farm" (*kolkhoz*), which is still universally used in the USSR (and which will henceforth be used in this study) to describe Stalin's final choice of socialist organization in agriculture.

After the harvest of 1929, Stalin shifted from propaganda and financial pressure against peasants to bring about collectivization—to legal coercion and outright military force. Communists from the cities descended upon the tens of thousands of villages in the USSR and made one last attempt at forming collective farms voluntarily. If this failed, the police were summoned to arrest recalcitrants, after which the remaining peasants would vote "freely" to form the collective farms, to which they would then be legally committed.

If these proceedings merely stimulated further resistance, the village would be surrounded by police (and sometimes Red Army troops) armed with machine guns and more, who would make mass arrests and force the rest to form a collective farm. If the peasants tried armed resistance to the troops, they might be shot down, followed by the burning of the village and the deportation of the survivors to Siberia. Skeptical or apprehensive Communist organizers might arrive with police troops to begin with. Since there were neither enough organizers nor enough police troops to collectivize every village at once, and since Stalin said he desired a smooth transition to socialist agriculture, the government put out vague and shifting schedules for collectivization, which supposedly spread the process out over ten years or more. But the local

Communist organizers in fact went ahead far more quickly and disruptively, not because Stalin had given them secret hurry-up orders (as his enemies charged) but because schedules were hopelessly vague, and because both idealism and careerism pressed the Communist organizer ahead as fast as possible.

To Stalin the enemy in the villages was above all the *kulak*, while the poor peasantry and even most of the middle peasantry were merely coerced or misled by the *kulaks*. During the first years of his rule, Stalin had agreed with Bukharin that simple mass expropriation of the *kulaks* was wrong. In April, 1928, he had advanced the severer policy of "liquidation of the *kulaks* as a class." By the middle of 1929 he had definitely adopted this policy, which he began to implement after that year's harvest. This phrase did not at first mean mass murder or deportation to Siberia. It meant the forcible seizure of the *kulaks'* lands, which (in theory) ended their existence as a class separate from the poorer peasants. After this, the former *kulaks* would be compelled to join the *kolkhozes* like any other peasants.

But by the end of 1929 Stalin had hardened his heart still futher in response to widespread peasant resistance to collectivization, which he interpreted as systematic *kulak* sabotage in the interest of counterrevolution. From then on Stalin forbade the former *kulaks* to join the new collective farms lest they continue to disrupt them. The unpublicized corollary of this prohibition was the deportation of all *kulaks* to labor camps. What else, the *G.P.U.* reasoned, could be done with masses of counterrevolutionary peasants banished from their villages?

But who were the *kulaks*? They were defined in various contradictory ways in Communist ideology. The term was supposed to mean richer peasants who "exploited" (i.e., hired) labor. But how many petty possessions made a peasant a *kulak*? And which of the many forms of labor in the villages constituted exploitation? When the Communist organizer reached a village, he had no complete list of the *kulaks* in it, and no workable criteria for identifying them. The modestly wealthy and clearly exploitative peasants (if any) in each village were *kulaks* all right. But any opponent of collectivization might be declared a *kulak*, any saboteur or rebel, anyone suspected of these things, and anyone whose goods, position, or personality excited the greed or malice of the peasants who *did* see fit to work with the Communists. A meaningless census in 1927 had declared that 4-5 per cent of the peasantry were *kulaks* without designating which ones, so that many organizers felt compelled to arrest at least 5 per cent of each village, arbitrarily, to live up to the imagined quota.

By the time the Communist organizers hit most villages, the peasants had heard about the terrors of collectivization from other villages, magnified by rumor. Hysteria prevailed throughout the Soviet countryside. Many villages, especially in national minority areas, prepared pathetically futile armed resistance. Enormous numbers of peasants fled temporarily into the mountains, forests, and swamps. Since it was rapidly known that most of the crops and animals would be seized by the regime for its collective farms, most peasants who had such wealth ate as much as possible before it should vanish. Even a *kulak* can only eat so much, so he often prepared breads from his grain, slaughtered many of his animals, and gave mad, hysterical, gargantuan feasts for family, friends, and often the whole village. These feasts often combined elements of a potlatch, of Nero's banquet while Rome burned, and of an apocalyptic holy communion table. To Stalin's men, however, not only the givers of the feasts but the poorest banqueters were saboteurs, knowing destroyers of the people's food supply.

There was an enormous amount of intentional sabotage as

well, especially after the collective farms had actually been formed. Collective fields were fired, collective animals were murdered wholesale by enraged, vengeful, self-destructive peasants. In many villages more than half the grain crops from 1929 through 1932 were destroyed. In the whole USSR, collectivization meant the destruction by peasants of roughly 40 per cent of the cattle and hogs, half the horses, and two thirds of the sheep and goats.[12] The grain losses had a cumulative effect, since seed grains were also involved. All this contributed mightily to the ghastly famine of 1933, which killed perhaps a million people in the Ukraine alone.

The losses of horses and oxen were made up by tractor production only at the end of the 1930's. The loss of meat and dairy animals was never made up in Stalin's lifetime. Not all animals are merely economic assets to peasants. Many are prized and beloved pets, fellow workers, and friends. The pathos of the peasant who lost his dear horse to the *kolkhoz*, or who killed it to save it from the Communists, was repeated many thousand times, and often hurt as badly as starvation or arrest.

The course of collectivization was wildly unsteady. An often-published allegation in 1929 was that the regime planned to collectivize 20 per cent of the villages during the First Five Year Plan. In October, 1929, after the harvest, when the big drive began, only some 4 per cent of Russian agriculture seems to have been in any form of socialist farm. By the end of January, 1930, almost 15 per cent of the peasants of the USSR were already herded into *kolkhozes*. In the next five mad weeks, more than another 40 per cent of the peasants were gunned into forming collective farms—a rate far more intense than anyone had planned, and one that provoked the major peasant resistance and reprisals that Stalin and other high Communists had feared.

On March 2, 1930, Stalin published his famous editorial in

Pravda, "Dizzy with Success . . . ," in which he blasted the Communist organizers of collective farms for using hasty, coercive, and violent methods when they should have persuaded the peasants to join voluntarily on a much slower schedule. Stalin has often been accused by his enemies of blaming his agents for atrocities which he himself had secretly ordered. Certainly Stalin had set forth no detailed schedules, and had made no effective administrative provisions against letting the collectivization drive get out of hand. Yet he certainly felt himself sincerely aggrieved at the incompetence of his agents—he did not yet suggest treason as the explanation. Stalin's dim view of the peasants had led him into authorizing the most forceful measures against them when necessary. But his Bolshevik optimism had led him to expect that these measures would not be so invariably necessary. It was not Stalin's way to sense his own error, however colossal. He sincerely blamed others.

Stalin's blast sent the entire collectivization drive into chaotic reverse. By May Day, 1930, the percentage of Soviet peasants in collective farms had gone from 58 per cent down to 24 per cent. Then this wild stampede out of the collectives was reversed by force. Those who had left were made to return, and the formation of new *kolkhozes* was resumed. The decollectivization of the spring of 1930 was more than made up for by the end of 1932, when roughly 60 per cent of the peasants were supposed to be in collectives. By 1936 the figure for socialized agriculture was supposed to be over 90 per cent. All *tozes* and communes, and many state farms, were transformed into collective farms of the *artel* type, either at the beginning of the great collectivization drive or after 1936.

By the end of the 1930's both the socialization of the countryside and the form of the rural socialist institution were set in the pattern they were to retain for the rest of Stalin's life in all the countries he was to rule. The form, the rate, and the manner of collectivization had not been foreseen in Stalin's ideology, but once he had bulled his program through and saw the results, he incorporated a version of them into his ideology, and applied them on ideological grounds to the East European countries he conquered later. After permitting and sharing in the vilification of the "left opposition," Stalin ironically came to pursue a far more violent, bloody, and extreme left strategy than any Trotskyite, even Preobrazhensky, had ever dreamed of.

The collectivization of agriculture between 1929 and 1933 —its earlier catastrophic stage—was one of the most colossal horrors of Stalin's Russia and of all history. The humanitarian and democratic objections of non-Communists to the whole procedure are obvious enough: millions of humans and animals dead, more millions of the former in labor camps. What is more relevant to the Communist world is the tremendous failure of the process by Stalin's own Marxist-Leninist standards. Bolsheviks prided themselves on being scientific, provident planners who map everything in advance and proceed smoothly and efficiently according to precisely predetermined schedules. But Stalin decided on the institutions of collectivization and the distribution among them only after several trials and errors. He indicated the rates of collectivization only vaguely, and blundered into altogether unexpected rates which he had to reverse at least twice. He never guessed that so great an effort would be necessary to force the peasants into collectives. He had no idea that collectivization would be so destructive of Soviet agrarian wealth. He had no plans for the millions of prisoners his agents took in the process.

The collectivization of Soviet agriculture fulfilled its aim of placing Communist personnel in key positions in every village to prevent counterrevolution, but the process stirred up far more counterrevolution than Stalin had ever faced in the 1920's. The regime succeeded in its aim of getting to a position from which it could appropriate a larger share of the crops, but the process resulted in a temporary reduction of plant foods and in a permanent loss of animals. The third aim —to raise total production rapidly through scientific agriculture—was never to be achieved under Stalin. Stalin's Communist planning turned into a bloody adventure using unplanned methods to bring about many destructive results.

Stalin did learn from the fiasco that peasant resistance would be far more adamant than he had thought in 1928. When he collectivized the agriculture of the East European countries after 1945, he took greater care to prevent the wild destruction of crops and animals. So did Mao in China after 1949. But neither Stalin nor independent Communist leaders have been able to eliminate the resistance and destructive response of peasants to collectivization.

Stalin's usual public response to the catastrophe was to deny that it had ever happened. He retrospectively described collectivization as having gone smoothly according to plan. Peasant resistance, destruction of crops and animals, famines, all were fabrications of capitalist slanderers. But on rare occasions he spoke his mind even to foreigners, most notably when he admitted to Churchill at Teheran that collectivization had cost ten million dead, and that it had been a struggle more bitter and more dangerous than his current war against Hitler. That was a gross exaggeration, but it expressed the way Stalin felt.[13]

Once the catastrophe of collectivization had been endured, and once Soviet agriculture had been organized into collective farms (and some state farms), the long third and final period of village life in Stalin's Russia began. Half the animals were dead, and millions of peasants were dead or at forced labor. Such support and trust as the regime had won among the peasants by its "right" strategy after 1921 had been dissipated. The surviving peasants were for the most part an alienated, sullen, frightened mass without the incentives to work hard or well. So far, so bad for Stalin.

But there were certain compensations. The Party did at last control each village from within. The Party was at last in a position to try what the full range of *agit-prop* could do in the villages. The Party could at last plant what its scientists and ideologists thought best to grow, instead of having to rely on peasant habit and peasant cupidity to produce the goods. The Party could now clear away the centuries-old clutter of strip fields, individual holdings and privileges, obsolete equipment, and superstitious backwardness that had made Russian agriculture so world-famously inefficient. The Party could now apply whatever science and machinery to agriculture that its schools, factories, and laboratories could produce, regardless of peasant opposition.

In short, the disasters of collectivization might be overcome by the inherent virtues of science, technology, and planning: A Communist would say the virtues of socialism. Stalin did very little for the peasants materially or psychologically for the rest of his life. Yet sheer socialism, unsupplemented and at its worst, was sufficient to raise Soviet agricultural production from the famine level of 1932-33 to a high point in 1939 and 1940 at which plant crops (but not animal products) exceeded on the average the previous highs of 1913 and 1928. World War II set agriculture back drastically, and earlier peaks were equaled only in 1950 and surpassed only thereafter.

The Stalinist *kolkhoz* has been one of the basic institutions of life under Communism to this day. The form developed during the great collectivization drive prevailed with few real changes to the end of Stalin's life, and still persists in spite of the many modifying reforms of his successors. Every other Communist government has collectivized the agriculture of the country it controls on the Soviet *kolkhoz* pattern—either on Stalin's orders or under his inspiration. Only after his death did China vary from the *kolkhoz* pattern in the direction of the full commune, while Yugoslavia, Poland, and Hungary decollectivized most of their farms in the 1950's. Three-quarters of the Soviet population once lived on collective farms, and this proportion has shrunk to less than one-half because of the growth of Soviet cities, not because of any contraction of the collectives.

When one flies over a Soviet *kolkhoz*, one usually sees large rectangular fields extending for several miles around each village—a very different pattern from the patchwork of strip fields that prevailed in old Russia up to 1929, and which prevails today in much of Western Europe. The village itself in Stalin's day was apt to be a collection of the peasant huts traditional to the ethnic group that lived in it, for Stalin would rarely spend the money to put up modern housing on his collectives. Until 1950 the collective farm usually coincided with a pre-existing peasant village and its lands. After that date three or four *kolkhozes* were merged into a big new one that included several villages, reducing the original 240,000 *kolkhozes* to about 90,000.[14] In the 1930's and 1940's the population of a collective farm ranged from several hundred to several thousand peasants.

A collective farm was officially a voluntary peasants' co-operative in which the peasants owned all major productive assets (including the land) in common, and made all decisions in a democratic assembly—as had been the case in many of the *artels* in the 1920's. In fact, as in the Party's inner ideology, the collective was rigidly controlled by the regime through its usually Communist officials who enforced the regime's economic and political laws and directives, and who were backed up by the regime's police power. The regime's stranglehold on the Stalinist collective farm differentiated it drastically from the earlier *artels,* and reduced its difference from the state farm very considerably.

The large fields and work buildings were the collective's, that is to say the regime's. The collective's officials, aided by agronomists and whatever wise peasants they trusted, decided what and when and how to plough and plant and cultivate and harvest, in the light of the regime's unvarying orders to produce more, and often fluctuating orders about new and different crops. By and large the collectives produced the grains that Russian peasants had always lived on, along with potatoes, turnips, and other root crops. But most collectives came to devote at least part of their lands to some of the "technical crops" that the regime was pushing, whether they were long established like sugar beets and cotton, or newly introduced like soybeans and sorghums. The peasants—men, women, and older children—were compelled by law to work long and hard in the collective's fields. Records of work hours and days were kept against each peasant to ensure that he met the high prescribed minimum load for his job or category.

Nevertheless, the peasants did not usually work very hard or well. No great care was taken to clear the weeds from Stalin's fields, and no great effort was made to harvest the difficult-to-reach portions of Stalin's crops. If a truck carrying peasants to work in a distant field broke down, everybody went to sleep in its shade while the driver walked disconsolately back to the collective headquarters to wait many hours for the Machine Tractor Station to send a repairman.

Why work harder or better, the peasants reasoned. At the end of the agricultural year, the crops from the collective's fields were stored safely in the collective's barns, often under armed police guard. Almost three-quarters of the crop was usually taken off by the regime in the regime's trucks for the regime's purposes, not the peasants'. Fifteen per cent usually went directly to the regime, constituting what Soviet law described as "compulsory deliveries in the nature of a tax," a dead loss as far as the peasants were concerned. More than 15 per cent might go to the Machine Tractor Station, a highly Stalinist institution. When collectivization began, there were relatively few tractors, trucks, or other large pieces of mechanical equipment in the villages of Russia. To distribute them efficiently, Stalin clustered them in a limited number of garage centers called Machine Tractor Stations, from which the use of the scarce equipment was allocated to nearby collectives. Even when mechanical equipment became more plentiful, Stalin retained the institution because it provided so tight a control over the collectives, which had to toe the line or lose the services of the precious labor-saving machinery. Peasants were willing to pay for the services of this machinery, but they knew perfectly well that no set of tractors or tractor drivers could eat anything like 15 per cent of the crops of ten or more *kolkhozes:* The bulk of the payment went on to the regime. Khrushchëv finally abolished the Machine Tractor Stations in 1958, and sold their machines to the collectives at high prices.

Nearly half of most collectives' crops went to various fodder funds, seed funds, welfare funds, and state marketing agencies. All rendered genuine services to the peasants, but all were grossly overpaid, in the peasants' estimation. That left little more than a quarter of the crop—less, if the crops were bad—to distribute to the peasants of the *kolkhoz* in proportion to their work records, minus whatever fines and penalties they might have accumulated during the year. A peasant on a rich collective near a big city might take some of his share to a collective farm market in town, and gain good prices on a relatively free market. But most peasants lived deep in the country, beyond the reach of urban markets save through the regime's intermediaries. The peasants were lucky if their quarter of the crop could be made into enough bread to live on during the year. In fact, they were lucky if their quarter of the crop turned out to be as much as that, after the different agents of the regime had finished taking their shares of the best part of the crop by their own methods of accounting.

Most of the peasants of the USSR would have starved to death under Stalin if they had had to depend on the payments for their labor on the collective's fields. What kept most of them alive in the bad years were their own garden plots and animals. A family's garden plot was small, usually some small fraction of an acre, but it was cultivated intensively with great pains and loving care, and produced a fine crop of heavy-yielding vegetables. No peasant family was allowed many animals—rarely so much as one cow, often no more than a few chickens—but they were lovingly tended, and yielded most of the protein and other rich nutrients that the peasants ever got. The other major sources of additional food for survival were the proceeds of the sale of whatever craft goods the peasants could manage to produce in their huts, and sheer theft from the collective's grain barns, milk cows, and hen roosts.

The obvious difference on almost every *kolkhoz* between the dismal, bedraggled, inefficient agriculture of the collective's fields and herds, and the spruce and sleek private gardens and animals of the peasants has delighted capitalists all over the world, and has presented a major problem to socialist theorists. It is too simple to say that peasants are inherently individualistic and that socialism cannot work in agriculture. Ex-collective farmers now in the West have often said that they would like to be part of a genuine co-operative that could keep its crops or sell them to the state for high prices as it pleased. But it can well be said that the Stalinist variety of socialist agriculture did not work very well, and that it drove the peasants to lavish their real efforts on their remnants of private property.

It is difficult to discuss the peasants' standard of living in Stalin's Russia because so much depends on intangibles. It is probable that most peasants in the USSR were as well off materially in 1928 as peasants ever had been in that part of the world. It is certain that their material standard of living fell drastically everywhere in the country until the crops of 1933 were harvested. From then on there was a recovery on most collective farms until World War II. In spite of the recovery, most Russian peasants in 1940 were living in older huts, burning less fuel, and wearing poorer clothes than in 1928. Against this one must set the reduction of inequality among peasants (which mattered to many of them), the increased education, and the slightly increased health and welfare services. And how is one to quantify the vastly increased totalitarian tyranny? The whole of the 1940's was consumed by war losses and recovery from them. Only after 1950 did the peasants of the USSR begin to enjoy a mild increase in living standards over anything they had experienced before. Only after Stalin's death were they allowed to advance to a significantly higher standard of living.

Clearly the peasant majority of the USSR was not the beneficiary of Stalin's rule. They would have suffered less and gained more under almost any historical alternative save permanent war. Both Stalin and his successors agreed that agriculture was their most important unsolved problem. Yet neither Stalin nor his successors (as yet) have openly repented their basic agrarian policies. Stalin's collectivization drive was a frightful example of what a Communist should not do, yet even Khrushchëv confined himself to criticizing Stalin's acts from 1934 on, after most of the decisions had been taken and after most of the horrors had been inflicted. Although Communist ideology had failed to prove itself a helpful guide to Stalin before and during collectivization, the colossal hole in his ideology was covered over after the fact by a carefully constructed addition to the ideology.

As Stalin looked back in his later years at collectivization and the record of the collective farms, he might well have groaned as he groaned to Churchill. But he might also have had much cause for satisfaction. The agricultural settlement had been difficult, but it did work. The countryside *was* socialist, the threat of counterrevolution *was* gone, the regime *was* getting the lion's share of the crops. Production *was* now more scientific, and it *was* rising, even if it did not outstrip the rise in population. The agrarian surplus appropriated by the regime *had* proved sufficient to support the new industrial plant that had made the defeat of Hitler possible. Stalin *had* in the long run secured the essentials of what he wanted from the peasants. The only sufferers were the peasants themselves. Yet theirs was the glory of having toiled and suffered for the benefit of posterity, which would be appropriately grateful to them. In the last analysis, Stalin thought the sufferings of his peasants were unfortunate, but that they were more than justified by the record of his industry, which the sufferings of his peasants had made possible.

8. THE CITIES

STALIN'S most important achievement was the industrialization of the USSR. He portrayed himself as the man who had guided a backward agrarian country through the course of industrialization to its post-World War II position: the most powerful modern industrial nation in the world except possibly for the United States, whose lead would in any event soon be overcome. Many Western scholars are skeptical of every portion of this claim.

Stalin described the USSR as the world's best-endowed area in natural resources. It is not, so far as scientists can now determine. Its agricultural lands are mostly too far north or too dry to be very productive by the standards of France or Iowa. Its industrial fuel resources are gigantic, but less than the coal of Europe and America, and less than the oil of America and the Middle East. The iron resources of the USSR are huge, but less again than those of Europe and North America. In many other minerals the USSR is even less well-off. Stalin usually maintained self-sufficiency in copper and sulphur, but he could not remotely equal foreign resources. The USSR possesses supplies of many minor minerals, but its riches in some, such as gold and chromium, are balanced by poverty in others, such as tin, tungsten, and molybdenum. Ironically, the onset of the atomic age found Stalin in possession of less than 5 per cent of the world's known uranium and cobalt.[1]

Stalin liked to memorize tables of production and known reserves. He knew the situation. But his Bolshevik optimism led him to believe that resources are a function of technology, that the natural resources of the USSR were just beginning to be explored, and that Communist science and industry would greatly multiply the known raw materials and discover many new ones. His geologists discovered enough during his thirty-year reign, notably some of the coal fields of western Siberia and the oil fields north of the Caspian Sea, to confirm him in his faith. Stalin really believed that the USSR could become the leading industrial nation of the world, and no man knows if he was wrong.

To Stalin the result was inevitable. The problem was to industrialize fast enough to produce a proletarian majority in the USSR before the capitalist-minded peasants could begin a counterrevolution, and fast enough to support a mechanized army sufficient to repel the inevitable attack from the capitalist West. As a socialist of the Marxist-Leninist variety, he had no doubt that the regime should undertake, finance, and guide the process. But how? Methods of economic development of backward countries are now one of the most studied subjects in modern economics, but this branch of the science had not yet been much elaborated in the 1920's.[2] In a sense, Stalin started to industrialize twenty years too soon, before the development of the mathematical and other analytic tools of contemporary economics that might have helped him enormously. On the other hand, his own program of industrialization was perhaps the greatest single stimulus to modern developmental economics.

Communists believed that in Marxism they possessed an entirely adequate economic theory, but Marx had said nothing very helpful about the economic development of a socialist country, and the capitalist economic development that Marx had described with such venom was precisely what the Communists of the 1920's wanted to avoid.

Certain socialist guidelines could be agreed upon. As the socialist sector of Soviet industry was built up, the government would increasingly come to plan investments and production for the entire nation for years in advance, so as to avoid competitive capitalist duplication of productive facilities, misjudgments out of ignorance, and waste. Production would be for the use of the people, not for the profit of the capitalist, and competitive considerations would be disregarded. The economy would be planned, not market-oriented. Production quotas and prices of goods would be set by the government, not by popular demand. There would be an emphasis on heavy industry, because the later production of both military and consumer goods depended on it.

These Marxist-Leninist generalities, some meaningless, some contradictory, and all vague, left all specific questions up in the air. How would the State Planning Commission (the body of economists and technicians charged with drawing up economic programs, shortened in Russian to *Gosplan*) decide whether to send a given imported steam shovel to a coal mine, a copper mine, or a construction site? In a capitalist country, it would be sent to whoever offered to pay most for it, a procedure ruled out on ideological grounds in the USSR. How would *Gosplan* decide whether a new bridge in an expanding urban area should be built with two levels now, or whether a second bridge should be built next to it later, when traffic required it? In capitalist countries, one can aid the solution of this problem by calculating the interest to be paid over the years on the money secured to build the alternative kinds of bridge. But interest was un-Marxist and barred from the USSR, so the concept could not be used to solve *Gosplan's* problems. Where should *Gosplan* locate a new steel plant, and how large should it be? Lenin had bequeathed such un-helpful suggestions as his dictum that a factory should be as large as possible, and as near to the sources of raw materials and to the consumers as possible—which might lead to three contradictory solutions to this problem. Above all, with a highly centralized system and no market for production goods, how could the regime recognize and correct its mistakes in time?

Stalin was a terrible economist, and did not realize the magnitude of these problems for years after 1928, if ever. When launching the First Five Year Plan for industrial growth in 1928, he was chiefly concerned with the size of overall production targets. His impatience drove him to allocate the bulk of government investment to heavy industry, and to increase the proportion of investment devoted to heavy industry almost every year. His Marxist-Leninist principles and grandiose bent led him to the building of very large factories, and of spectacular projects such as the huge Dnieprostroi Dam in the Ukraine and the new city of Magnitogorsk in the wilderness of the Urals. When unforeseen emergencies arose, he shifted resources on an *ad hoc* basis. He mortgaged the future wherever possible by using existing plant to the utmost—for instance the basic railroad network that had been built under the last Tsars—without allocating the resources to supplement it or even to maintain it properly. During the first two Five Year Plans he moved steadily toward his final position that most mistakes were due to bungling and/or treason on the part of subordinates, not to defects of planning, and were matters not for the economists but for the police.

Therefore an unnecessary tragedy occurred. Several Russian economists in the 1920's were working out the mathematical economic analyses applicable to large scale economic development run by the state. The most notable was Nikolai Kondratiev, who is regarded in the West as one of the pioneers of contemporary mathematical economics. Kondratiev attempted to apply his emerging mathematical techniques to the various drafts of the First Five Year Plan, and urged the government to make use of such techniques and to encourage their further elaboration. His methods and his services to *Gosplan* were rejected by Stalin himself, on the ostensible ground that mathematical economics was idealistic rather than Marxist.³ Kondratiev had worked in the tradition of the early mathematical economist, Leon Walras, whom Marxists had long quarreled with. He was associated with Trotskyites. The results of Kondratiev's analyses of the First Five Year Plan were his reasoned conclusions that its goals were unrealistically high. All of these facts offended Stalin.⁴

Stalin continued to discourage the development of mathematical economics throughout the 1930's. He had some of the economists in the field purged, including Kondratiev himself. The Russian who was to make the greatest contribution to the formulation of contemporary economics was Vasili Leontiev, who did his work not in Stalin's Russia but in exile at capitalist Harvard. Even when the United States and other Western countries made such striking progress in mathematical economics during and after World War II, Stalin barred it from the Communist bloc.

His rejection of the whole range of mathematical and technical aids to economic planning and operations went amazingly far. He refused to invest any substantial amounts in the electronic computers of the post-war world, which would have made possible the large scale application to Soviet industrial planning of such highly relevant new economic techniques as linear programming and input-output analysis, to say nothing of the rapid calculation of statistics, which he did desire. Stalin would not even allow any considerable production of such elementary computing devices as desk calculators and cash registers. When Stalin died, most Soviet factories and other technological enterprises (to say nothing of retail stores) still kept their accounts with pencil and paper, and with the abacus. The latter is a very much better calculating machine than most Westerners realize, but it is not an adequate accounting device for modern industry.[5]

The result of Stalin's blindness was an intensification of the already predictable chaos of the First Five Year Plan. One Soviet enterprise purchased its nail supply from a nail factory fifteen hundred miles away, while a nail factory across the street from it was shipping goods a similar distance. In order to requisition a supply of nails another Soviet enterprise found it necessary to secure the signature of Molotov himself, at that time Premier of the USSR. A truckful of bathtubs was dumped on an empty lot in Moscow; three years later the apartments they were intended for began to be constructed on the lot. Valuable and delicate imported turret lathes were plunked down on the wet, uneven ground that served as the floor of a Siberian factory, where they could not be used because they were not level, and where they rusted irretrievably in three weeks. A factory on a tributary of the Volga was completed just in time to be flooded by the lake that piled up behind a dam that had been built a mile downstream.[6] And so on, and so on.

Since Stalin had rejected the most promising method of setting industrial goals and planning the industrial process, *Gosplan* and the *Politburo* were reduced to setting figures based on relatively crude estimates of resources and rates of progress. *Gosplan* had first been ordered to draw up an over-all plan for industrial development in 1926. The Fifteenth Party Congress in December, 1927, at Stalin's instance, approved a version of what was now called the "Five Year Plan," but urged speed in building up heavy and defense industries. After more promptings from Stalin, *Gosplan* in August, 1928, produced the rather brief document that was actually to become the First Five Year Plan. The goals had been raised far beyond what the Party had approved of eight months before. Heavy industry was to expand by 330 per cent over the five years, industry as a whole by about 250 per cent. Economists of both left and right were skeptical. Both Kondratiev and Bukharin presented statistical arguments to persuade Stalin that the more ambitious plan could not be fulfilled. Stalin ordered the plan into operation anyway as of October, 1928. He had the Party adopt the plan formally in April, 1929, and had it raise the goals even higher a few months later. Thus when the goals were finally determined the plan was supposedly nearly through its first year of operation, which gives some idea of the loose relation between formal and actual policy, and between the plan and industrial reality.

Everything went forward in a hectic crash program, in which exhilaration and apprehension combined to produce a sensation of the giddy moving-forward of history. New projects were added to the plan from time to time, notably the development of iron from Magnitogorsk and coal from the Kuznets Basin to form a dual steel combine. By July, 1930, the Party shortened the Five Year Plan to four years. By the end of 1932 the plan was officially proclaimed to have been fulfilled. The fulfillment was more psychological than statistical. The Dnieprostroi Dam had been completed, and the Magnitogorsk mines were in operation. But the regime did not even claim to have expanded heavy industry by 330 per cent. It claimed production rises in the various branches of heavy industry that ranged from 67 per cent to 160 per cent, with higher figures only in the most readily-expandable divisions such as the oil industry.

The Second Five Year Plan followed, and most of the Third, before Hitler invaded the USSR. The Second Five Year Plan was accompanied by claims that the hardest part of industrialization had been achieved, and that greater emphasis on consumer goods could be indulged. This greater emphasis turned out to be very slight and very temporary. The Third Five Year Plan frankly emphasized military preparations for the coming inevitable war, which was psychologically acceptable enough in 1937.

By the end of 1940 the regime claimed that the production of steel—the all-important economic indicator in Stalin's eyes —had risen from 4 million tons in 1928 to 18.3 million. The key power indices were as follows: coal from 35 to 166 million tons in the thirteen year period; oil from 12 to 31 million tons; electricity from 5 to 48 billion kilowatt hours.[7] Automobiles, tractors, trucks, airplanes, and tanks were new mass industries. Tiny villages had become great cities, and new centers of industry had sprung up in the forests and the steppes.

These figures and claims, taken at face value, and apparently confirmed by Stalin's victory in World War II, are the basis of the strong attraction that Stalin's methods of forced, rapid, socialist industrialization have for so many politicians and intellectuals in so many backward countries. If Stalin could do it, cannot others do likewise? The Western response has often been systematic skepticism about the entire process of Stalin's industrialization.

First of all, Westerners say that Stalin did not conjure modern industry out of an entirely agrarian country. He built up the industrial plant of a nation in which the first and hardest steps of industrial advance had been taken under the last two

Tsars. It was Alexander III and Nicholas II who had presided over Russia's first industrial revolution. In their reigns the basic railroad network had been constructed—all the way across Siberia to the Pacific. Under them, both light and heavy industry had been developed sufficiently to make Russia the world's fifth-ranking industrial country. In the last decades of Tsarism, Russia's major cities took on a modern aspect as their main streets were paved and electrically lit, while tens of thousands of their inhabitants received the technical education that enabled them to participate fully in the rising industrial civilization of Europe.⁸

Stalin was well aware of this. Much of Lenin's argument about the possibility of proletarian revolution in Russia had been based on the existence of such considerable industry in the country before 1917. But to Stalin, the crucial phases of the industrial revolution were his. He had started in 1928 with roughly the equivalent of the industrial plant that had failed to withstand Imperial Germany. By 1941 he had built an industrial plant that proved capable of repelling the far more formidable military and economic might of Hitler's united continental Europe.

Secondly, Westerners doubt many or all of Stalin's claims of production triumphs, and with good reason. The figures quoted above were by no means the highest of Soviet production claims for the early Five Year Plans, but rather the soberest, designed for the most elite audiences. Even the soberest claims can be shown to be exaggerated, especially for agricultural and consumer goods, the fields in which Stalin did least and worst. Furthermore, sheer quantitative indices of goods produced say nothing about quality. A one-ton H-block of Soviet steel mixed sloppily from its alloys, and likely to break under stress, was not the equal of a ton of American or German steel that had to meet the higher standards of Western technology and open markets.

Even if the lower range of Soviet production figures is accepted, and considerations of quality are ignored, it can be shown that a number of capitalist countries have experienced sustained periods of economic growth that have surpassed the USSR during the early Five Year Plans—notably the United States, Germany, and Japan at certain times before 1918, and several smaller countries such as Canada since 1945. Communists have always claimed that an essential difference between the Soviet advance during the Five Year Plans and various rapid expansions by capitalist countries lies in the fact that the latter, notably the United States and Canada, were the beneficiaries of heavy foreign investment.[9] *Gosplan* had originally hoped for far more foreign investment than ever came to the USSR, but the capitalists' own great depression ended that possibility, and the USSR had to grow almost entirely by its own efforts.

A Communist economist can give a Westerner a good battle over comparative statistics of growth. He always returns, however, to his central point: Whatever Stalin's failures and whatever Stalin's exaggerated claims, he won World War II with war matériel that was plentiful enough and of high enough quality to defeat the German Army, not with inflated statistics. The early Five Year Plans were not proved failures because Stalin produced only 18.3 million tons of steel a year instead of what he had predicted, or because he may not even have produced that much; they were proved successes because Stalin won the war.

Thirdly, Westerners say that Soviet economic growth during the early Five Year Plans was horrendously lopsided. An utterly disproportionate 75 per cent or so of total investment in most years went into heavy industry and armaments, entailing an uneconomic wear on such existing plant as housing and railroads, and a starvation of the populace for consumer goods. This in turn cut heavily into the labor force's incentives to work, to the detriment of the desired economic buildup.

Stalin always claimed that he was producing far more consumer goods than in fact he was, and that his people were far richer than in fact they were. His successors were willing to admit that the process had been lopsided, and that consumer goods had not received adequate attention. Although his successors have tried to increase the incentives to work hard and well in the USSR, they have joined Stalin in insisting that the Soviet population was wholeheartedly devoted to the construction of socialism during the early Five Year Plans. Again, the essential case for Stalin centers on the war. Had Stalin allocated more investment to the consumer goods industries total production might have been greater, but the number of tanks, heavy guns, airplanes, and the machines to produce them, would have been significantly less, and Hitler's armies might have prevailed. The margin of survival was not very large. If Stalin had opted for more consumer goods, the Soviet people might have been better fed and better clothed as they watched the Nazi troops march through the ruins of better houses.

Finally, Westerners advance humanitarian objections. The rapid pace of industrialization and state control of the process, Western critics often think, ensured mass brutalities that leisure and decentralization might have avoided. The monomaniacal emphasis on heavy industry brought about horrible living conditions for the workers and most other inhabitants of Russian cities. The extreme and violent nature of Stalin's favorite methods magnified the atrocities.

As usual, the Communist reply centers on the war. A Soviet Party member can now admit that much of Stalin's police terror during the 1930's was unnecessary for the economic buildup, and even impeded it. But he must still stand by the core of Stalin's coercive measures during the First Five Year Plan. Communists know from long experience that mere propaganda and other methods of inspiring a people and enlisting its will to sacrifice for a cause cannot keep enough people at work long enough and hard enough to construct the huge industrial plant necessary to win a war such as World War II. Khrushchëv ordered some decentralization of industry in the USSR on the grounds that its developed condition in his day rendered the previous super-centralization no longer necessary. But none of Stalin's successors applied that judgment retroactively to the early Five Year Plans.

One can distinguish three possible courses of action that Stalin might have pursued before World War II. There was the extreme and bloody course he did pursue—which *did* lead to victory over Hitler. There was the opposite course of mild rule coupled with more consumer-oriented economic growth, which was discouragingly likely to have led to defeat at the hands of Hitler. And there was the middle course: a strong coercive buildup of heavy industry and armaments sufficient to stop Hitler, without the foolish methods and self-defeating excesses of brutality that we can retrospectively separate from the core of Stalin's construction.

Before we succumb to the temptation to approve the middle course, we should remember that there is no sure way of distinguishing between necessary and unnecessary brutality in building an economy until years and often decades later. And if we approve the middle course, we are in effect supporting the undemocratic side of arguments over how to industrialize the backward countries of the world. No proponent of coercive industrialization with great emphasis on heavy industry—not even Mao Tse-tung—has ever proposed to repeat all of Stalin's mistakes *in toto*. They all insist that they will use only the necessary amount of harshness to build up their countries in time to avoid capitalist attack (or Communist revolution, or the population explosion). This allegedly middle course is in fact a modified Stalinist course. To support it is to say, as many leaders and intellectuals in backward countries *are* saying, that Stalin's coercive, socialist methods of dealing with the problem of backwardness, if properly modified, are *the* methods to follow, while mild, libertarian, democratic methods, no matter how much they are improved (unless supplemented by massive foreign investment, which is not so easy to come by) will still produce too little and too late.

It is possible to admit that Stalin's Russia provides a poor model for backward countries to follow without denying that some version of the Five Year Plans was necessary for Russia. The underdeveloped countries are all in different geographical and industrial situations from Russia in 1928. None of them face a capitalist attack that requires a rapid military buildup for self-defense.[10] Many face violent revolution, and all face the population explosion.[11] To deal with these threats a backward country requires, among other things, a rapidly increasing supply of the very consumer goods that Stalin's methods produce so meagerly. One can admit that today's backward countries would do better to try the Japanese method of state-guided capitalist growth, or Lenin's New Economic Policy, while insisting that Stalin faced Hitler and a genuine need for huge *military* buildup, for which some version of the early Five Year Plans was the only alternative.

A defender of Stalin who retreats to this last line of defense faces a very different line of Western attack. If Stalin had not ordered the German Communist Party to do the things it did to bring Hitler to power, Westerners often argue, and if Stalin had not aligned himself with Hitler in 1939, he might never have faced the invasion in 1941 that is so often offered as the justification for his economic measures. This supposition will be considered in Chapter 11.

The much disputed but undeniable growth of Soviet industry under Stalin was of necessity accompanied by the growth of the Soviet proletariat. Industrial workers constituted less than 10 per cent of the Soviet population in 1928. At Stalin's death they were more than a third of the people, and their proportion was still increasing. This sheer numerical growth of the proletariat was a great reassurance and comfort to Stalin, for it was one of the major purposes of the industrialization program.

Stalin was certainly sincere in thinking that the workers supported his government, and that they were the ultimate beneficiaries of his policies. Westerners are more apt to believe that the life of the workers under Stalin was an unrelieved industrial hell, making a bitter irony of the earlier Revolutionary phrase, "the workers' paradise."

Admittedly the workers in Stalin's factories had to be compelled to work long and hard for years, for very little material reward, if the Five Year Plans were to be successful. Stalin was faced with an intransigent form of the dilemma that faces so many pro-labor intellectuals: The long-run interest of the workers and everybody else is best served if everyone works hard and forgoes consumption to build up the economy and make future prosperity possible. But the short-run interest of the worker, which is all he usually sees, is obviously served by working less long and less hard, and by getting more and more proceeds from the enterprise and spending them on immediate consumption.

Proposals to change work habits and work rules in the interest of increased production usually encounter bitter and universal worker hostility to management in any form—even if the management is the workers' own socialist government. Workers often want to retain their current low level of petty benefits, instead of risking them by assenting to changes that suspect higher-ups claim will bring greater benefits later. In short, workers will not of themselves consent to the measures necessary for rapid industrial growth, and they are technologically and politically incompetent to run a program of rapid industrial advance even if they can be propagandized into accepting the idea. Apparently industrialization cannot be brought about by industrial democracy.

Lenin had never been sentimentally optimistic about the capabilities of workers. After a brief but dismal experience with workers' control of factories in 1917-18,[12] and the consequent plummeting of production, he came out solidly, in his April Theses of 1918, for one-man management of industrial plants. He now supported efficiency engineering, as well as many of the other practical capitalist methods of industrial management and control that had long been anathema to workers and to the more proletarian-minded Bolsheviks.

The crucial issue was the matter of trade unions. Should they be genuinely independent trade unions, representing the workers' interests as the workers saw them at any given moment, even against the workers' state? Or should they be organizations of the regime to control the workers? The latter was Lenin's choice, with some qualifications, and he never pushed his policy to extremes. It was Stalin's choice with no qualifications whatsoever. Yet the Workers' Opposition—as the proponents of truly independent trade unions were called whenever they clashed with the government—remained in the government throughout the 1920's, until Mikhail Tomsky, the longtime leader of the trade unions of the USSR, was purged from office along with other rightist leaders in 1929.

Tomsky's successors as bosses of the trade unions were Nikolai Shvernik and Lazar Kaganovich, under whom the trade unions became a full-fledged Party "transmission belt to the masses." Their functions from then on were to regulate and propagandize the workers on behalf of the regime—to increase their political loyalty, to stimulate harder, more intelligent, more engaged work. It was up to the unions to persuade the workers to accept new industrial methods, to accept new higher forms of work, to volunteer for extra work and political duty, and to inform on slackers and dissidents. The unions were to select likely workers for Party membership, and to advance their political education and careers.

These are all the functions of a super company union. One might expect that the workers of the USSR would have lost all faith in their union leaders, and regarded them as traitors to their class. Yet the Soviet workers were never so totally alienated from the unions as that. Although the unions in no sense represented the workers against the regime, many sympathetic petty union officials remained, even after the great purges. The unions carried on some functions that the workers could support. Much of the nation's welfare and insurance program was administered through the unions. Housing, especially new housing, was often allocated through the unions, and this was a very tangible asset for the worker to enjoy or sell. Summer camps for children were often run by the unions, and some lucky unions received the use of former resort hotels on the Black Sea, in which to reward ailing or hard-working members with spectacular vacations.

Perhaps most winning of all, many trade unions ran sports programs, both for their members at large and for virtually professional teams that gained the members much prestige, excitement, and betting profits—notably the railroad workers' champion soccer team, *Lokomotiv*. Russian workers had never had a strong tradition of independent trade unions that had ever brought them many tangible gains, and therefore could not miss them. They attributed what advances they had made to political action. They could often get used to doing without the strictly union activities of their unions, and be glad to cheer the union soccer team instead. If athletics serves the function in America of keeping many workers and students from thinking about politics, it was used far more consciously by Stalin for the same purpose.[13] After 1929 the trade unions were in every sense a help rather than a barrier to Stalin's manipulation of the workers. He had reason to make virtually every worker join.

When Stalin decided in the 1920's against producing enough consumer goods to give workers the incentive to work hard, he was caught in a dilemma over wage policy. He never thought that the USSR had advanced far enough along the road to the ultimate communist goal to justify the abolition of wages as the method of payment. Russian workers always received wages—even forced laborers often had cash balances piling up in their names in the state bank. If Stalin decided to pay his workers low wages, he would have to expect the workers to be discontented at not having enough money to buy the scarce consumer goods. If he decided to pay them higher wages, he would be adding billions of rubles to the sum already chasing the scarce consumer goods, thereby stimulating a wild inflation. If he tried to solve the dilemma by setting prices at low levels and imposing rationing and quotas, a vast system of black marketeering, favoritism, and corruption would come into existence.

By and large, Stalin paid his workers more than they could spend on the available goods at the legal prices, although the whole disproportion took place at a low level. There was indeed a great deal of inflation under Stalin, especially during the First Five Year Plan and during the war. Stalin's system of price-setting and rationing did in fact lead to a vast black-grey market system, which exists to this day as an important element of the Soviet economy.

Some surplus worker purchasing power was drained off by hard-sell programs to persuade workers to buy government bonds. The bonds did not bear any such capitalist benefit as interest. But if the worker bought bonds or placed his money in some other form of savings account with the government, he could avoid having his savings confiscated in one of the periodic "currency reforms." These always involved the exchange of existing paper money for a new issue of rubles at an unfavorable rate, while citizens who trusted the government enough to deposit their money with it received a more favorable rate. Such confiscations wiped out a great deal of purchasing power, and systematically penalized the workers and peasants for their lack of co-operation with the regime— it was the workers and especially the peasants, rather than the new Soviet middle class, that were apt to hoard cash. The grandest confiscation of all came in 1947, when Stalin imposed the harshest of his "currency reforms," designed to suck up most of the accumulated cash hoards from the whole of the World War II period—a climax to his anti-inflationary measures.

Since the regime offered few consumer goods to the workers, and saw to it that money was dangerous to keep, it had great difficulty inducing the workers to labor for no great tangible reward. The effect of Communist *agit-prop* should not be underestimated. The "construction of socialism" during the First Five Year Plan and the defeat of Hitler during the "Great Patriotic War" were goals that could be used to inspire millions of workers to sacrifice themselves to some extent for a certain period. If the real driving force was coercion, at least the ideals made many workers feel that the unpleasant process was ultimately justified, even if they loathed all the details. This was not unlike the psychology of an American drafted into the army.

But the real driving force *was* coercion. In Stalin's Russia the worker had to work to live, and in most cases so did his wife, for the wage of one person could rarely support two. A worker who did not work at all would soon be starving, unless he went back to his ancestral village—now a collective farm where everything was even worse—or unless he engaged in a career of crime. There were millions of criminals in

Stalin's Russia, but a whole labor force cannot support itself that way. Needless to say, Stalin suppressed all statistics on crime in the USSR, except to announce periodically (and falsely) that it had been reduced to a new, minuscule low. According to Stalin's laws, anyone who stole anything was a criminal; according to this not-unusual definition practically the entire population of the USSR was criminal once it had outgrown infancy. But full time footpads or black marketeers could never have numbered more than several hundred thousand. The only lucrative crime was theft from the government, and this usually required some position with the government to make it possible. The vast majority of Soviet citizens merely supplemented their incomes by some petty form of theft or conniving at theft, and did not really make a living at it.[14]

So the worker had to work. Both the man and the woman of the family would have to get up early—before dawn in the Russian winter, which lasted many months of the year. The woman might leave her children with elderly female relatives or with older children. She might deposit them for the day in the state nursery in her housing block, if there was one, or take them with her to the factory nursery, if there was one. Millions of Soviet children grew up in the streets, or in their scarcely less freezing rooms. Both man and woman would probably have to walk a long way to the factory, or to the place where the factory's trucks came to pick up crowded loads of workers. Only the largest cities had public transportation networks, and only Moscow boasted a subway during Stalin's reign.

It was a very good idea to come to work on time, for tardiness was penalized by severe tongue-lashings and fines, and repeated tardiness was a criminal offense. When the labor practices of the early Five Year Plans were finally codified from 1939 to 1941, many workers were subject to deportation to Siberia for being twenty minutes late three times. Outright absenteeism tempted fate.

Inside the factory, labor discipline was rigid. Strikes vanished in the First Five Year Plan. One had to be respectful to foremen and other factory officials, and this did not come easily to many Slavic members of the work force. Rest time was very limited. It was hard to convice the factory doctor that one was ill, for he was employed by the regime to increase production rather than to treat the workers. The factory doctor was judged and promoted on his success in keeping sick leave down, that is in denying sick claims. No mere worker could afford a private doctor.

Those who fell behind on their part of a joint task, and those who damaged precious machinery were sure to be fined, and during tense periods they might be charged with sabotage. Officially, hours were rather moderate by world standards: In many industries the regime claimed a forty-eight hour work week. In fact fifty-four and sixty hour weeks were common, and irregularly longer hours were frequent during the last parts of months, when the factory was rushing to complete its monthly quota. Factory officials might call upon workers to keep at a given task until it was completed, and who would refuse at his peril a call to work overtime in Stalin's Russia?

Stalin had some difficulty deciding how to distribute wages. In his inherited ideology, wages were to be distributed during the period of "socialism" (which Stalin was entering with the Five Year Plans) on the principle, "From each according to his ability; to each according to his work." The burden of this dictum was that every man *should* work, including the former leisure class. The strongest Bolshevik tradition was toward equality of wages, regardless of the quality or category or difficulty of the work. It was usually assumed that this dictum applied to management as well. This was all very well for the weaker and lazier workers, but not very helpful to anyone interested in production. In the course of the First Five Year Plan, Stalin abolished such wage equality as had existed in the USSR in the 1920's, and substituted the permanent Soviet system of piece rates. Stalin squared this with his ideology by interpreting "to each according to his work" to mean payments per unit of work well done.

Thenceforth in Stalin's Russia the worker in each job was faced with a production norm for his job: He must cut so many jigs or turn so many thousand screws a day. Failure to meet the norm was penalized by fines; repeated failures aroused suspicions of sabotage. If an able and energetic worker overfulfilled his norm, he was usually paid more money for each unit of work he had performed beyond the required norm. Any striking overfulfillment was singled out for honors. During the middle years of the First Five Year Plan (1930-31) the regime encouraged "shock workers," who volunteered to work longer and harder, to go without rest, meals, and sometimes sleep, for the sake of greater production. At first any given shock worker might set records; sooner or later he collapsed or had an accident. The drive was stopped in favor of the permanent push for more intelligent and efficient work.

In 1935 a certain Alexei Stakhanov, a coal miner in the Donets Basin in the eastern Ukraine, persuaded his crew of fellow workers to collaborate as a team instead of duplicating each other's efforts. They thereby managed to dig out fourteen times as much coal in one day as the norm required. Stakhanov became the regime's hero, and the "Stakhanovite" drive was pressed. Workers and managers were urged to find similar ways of rationalizing production, and were honored and paid when they did so. Then all workers at similar tasks had to reorganize their work on the relevant Stakhanovite model, so that production would rise throughout the industry. But instead of giving all workers in the field more money for their increased output, the norm itself would be raised, and the workers would be back at their original wages for speeded-up work. Workers managed to beat up and murder a number of Stakhanovites in revenge, but they had no way of avoiding the speedup. In fact, the workers themselves were made to beg the regime—through their trade unions—to raise the norms.

It is not surprising to find that the standard of living of the Soviet workers declined sharply during the First Five Year Plan, and that it had scarcely recovered its 1928 level when the war came. The urban population of the USSR almost quadrupled during the early Five Year Plans to a figure of roughly sixty million. Over half the rise in the urban population was accounted for by the flight of peasants and their families from the collectivized farms to the new factories in the cities. The children born to these families after they reached the cities accounted for much of rest of the urban population explosion. During the First Five Year Plan there was a tremendous turnover of labor in the new factories as unskilled and ignorant peasant migrants wandered dazedly from one job to another, and were sloughed off as unsuitable, while the more experienced workers shopped about from factory to factory searching out slightly improved conditions. The regime complained that the average peasant migrant to the cities in 1930 held five jobs in the course of the year, and that one factory with 1700 positions had employed 26,000 people in the course of the same year.[15] Managers of new plants, desperately short of acceptable workers, lured them from other factories with better conditions or promises of better conditions. Hundreds of determined managers kidnapped workers by main force to their plants, and kept them there with combined blandishments and threats.

To prevent this chaos of excessive labor mobility, Stalin decreed various arrangements that amounted to a new serfdom. He forbade workers to leave their jobs until the regime had approved of the final arrangements for the next job. A system of internal passports was used to make sure that a worker could not leave a city unless he could persuade the regime to stamp its approval. Consequently job stability increased during the Second and Third Five Year Plans, and again after the war. But the influx from the countryside continued. At Stalin's death, approximately one hundred million people lived in Soviet cities, roughly three-quarters of them workers and their families. About three-quarters of these workers had been born in the villages, or born to peasant fathers. The urban Soviet worker was not yet divorced from his village forebears.

The new workers were at something of a disadvantage in purchasing food and clothing until they had acclimatized themselves to the local urban system of favoritism and black marketeering. But their most striking disability lay in housing. Throughout the early Five Year Plans, and even as late as Stalin's death, the shrinking majority of the more or less solidly built housing in Soviet cities dated from before 1914, and it was usually in steadily deteriorating condition. It became more and more crowded. A slum room designed in 1910 to hold one wretched family was almost certain to contain three, four, and five families as the 1930's and 1940's ground on. Millions of new workers from the countryside failed to get into existing housing at all, and had to build huts without any facilities in vacant lots or at the edges of towns, on their own time (meaning chiefly at night), with whatever materials they could scrounge. This was least horrible for some of the Muslim peoples of the South, who could build traditional domed adobe huts of river mud. It was most horrible for the northerly Russians who could reproduce neither the materials nor the heating of their traditional farm houses out of scraps picked up in the cities. During and after World War II, millions had to live in cellar holes and caves. Sheer freezing to death was far more common in the cities than in the villages, just on account of the fuel shortage.

In spite of these hardships peasants kept flocking to the new factories, and only some of the psychologically broken went back. Although the housing and fuel supplies were worse in the cities, one is forced to the conclusion that almost everything else seemed better to the incoming peasants, even during the First Five Year Plan, and ever after except during the war years. Those who had lived in the cities before 1928 usually suffered a drop in living standards during the First Five Year Plan, but even this reduced standard of living seemed an improvement to the peasant fresh from the country, who had traditionally lived at a still lower level. The factories did provide money that could be used to buy more and better food than was available to most Russian villagers, in spite of the shortages (except during the war years). Cities of any size, if they had been in existence before 1928, provided more companionship, more public facilities, more excitement, more things to do, and more liquor than the villages. Even a new city such as Magnitogorsk, composed exclusively of factories and slum huts, with virtually no public facilities of any sort, at least offered more variety of companionship than a village.

The consolation of liquor was enormously important. Stalin released no meaningful figures about drink or drunkenness in the USSR, but anyone who walked along the streets of a city in Stalin's Russia at night could find hundreds of drunks. The Soviet drunk in the streets was not usually a neurotic bum, but a worker as healthy and normal as any man could be in Stalin's Russia. It is hard to see why most workers would ever have wanted to be sober under such conditions.

Much of the incredible severity of the Soviet labor codes—against absenteeism, lateness, and damaging machinery—was directed essentially against drunkenness. The peasant could go through the whole of the agricultural year more or less drunk, and do almost as well as his sober neighbors—if any. But if a worker did not get to the factory because he was out cold, or if he smashed a valuable machine by getting his drunken arm chewed up in it, the industrial process suffered. Labor offenses were strikingly lower in Muslim areas where drunkenness was somewhat inhibited by religion and custom.[16]

Some peasants turned out to be among the lucky ones. On a low level, a peasant who went to the city might actually get into one of the new apartments, or he might be picked for a trip to a Black Sea resort. Beyond that, he might rise into the Party hierarchy, if he was able and loyal, and into the cadres of industrial management. And if not he then perhaps his children might succeed, for they would be used to the city and would probably get a better primary education there than on a collective farm. And if one believed in Communism at all, one might well respond to the many propaganda appeals to go to town and help in the construction of socialism.

But at bottom, during Stalin's rule the USSR was not being run for the benefit of the workers. A real skeptic might say that the country was being run for Stalin alone, or for no one. A much more common analysis, with a covert appeal to many Communists as well as outsiders, held that Stalin ruled by and for the new Soviet middle class, Djilas's "new class." The groups referred to—the bureaucrats and managers of the various industrial, state, and Party hierarchies—were regarded by Stalin as "workers with their minds," who were genuine proletarians just like the more numerous "workers at the bench." They were to be employed and driven to build and maintain socialism just like other workers. They were to be paid more and to receive more benefits and privileges solely as an incentive for them to undertake the more responsible tasks that only people with their uncommon intelligence and scarce skills could perform—Stalin asserted. Trotsky looked on the process as a thwarting of the Revolution by a bureaucratic group that had crept into the Party, a group of which Stalin was merely the instrument.[17] Djilas went further, and asserted that this was a *new* class in Marxist terms, with a special relationship to the means of production, distribution, and exchange—they did not own them like the preceding bourgeoisie, but rather constructed, controlled, and enjoyed the fruits of them in the name of the state and the people.[18] Karl Wittfogel saw them as the agents of a return to Marx's Asiatic mode of production, the coercive control of a totalitarian bureaucracy which had spread from old China through the Mongols to Tsarist Russia.[19]

All had a point. Stalin was surely right in insisting that he made decisions, not his managers and bureaucrats, that they served his purposes and not the other way round, that their greater rewards were not the purpose of the system but his means to get it to work. Trotsky was right to emphasize the bureaucratic organization of Stalin's rule, as opposed to any preceding independence or spontaneity on the part of workers or bourgeoisie. Djilas was right to emphasize the newness of the class and its function: It rose by and large from obscure origin, and not from any preceding elite. It created the new means of production that it enjoyed the fruits of, and it controlled them in new ways. Wittfogel was right to emphasize the long Russian tradition under which the autocrat ruled and created new wealth through his all-pervasive centralized bureaucracy. Most Western analysts feel no necessity to describe the phenomenon in Marxist class terms, and speak of "privileged elites," and "ruling" or "managing groups," and then plunge into the details, and into the controversy on whether Stalin ruled his new groups or expressed their will.

They were certainly *new* groups. When Stalin rose to power there were many pre-Revolutionary managers and technologists in Soviet industry, just as there were many Tsarist officers in the Red Army, and Old Bolsheviks in the Party hierarchy. A number of show trials in the later 1920's and during the First Five Year Plan signalized the drive against the older technologists who were not to be trusted, and who were to be replaced by new reliable management cadres from among the workers. The passage of time and the great purges finished off most holdovers from the old bourgeoisie, just as they were ending the importance of other kinds of Tsarist and Leninist elites.

The new managers and bureaucrats who were promoted during the crises of the First Five Year Plan, the great purges, and the war came mostly from below. Some rose from the petty bourgeoisie of provincial cities, like Malenkov, some from the peasantry turned proletariat, like Khrushchëv, some from equivalent groups among the minor nationalities, but relatively few from the peasantry itself. At the end of the First Five Year Plan less than half the factory managers had had more than a primary school education, a sure sign of their low origin. Large numbers of these men had genuine ability, in spite of their lack of education and culture. At least one reason why the Five Year Plans worked at all was that these reserves of talent were summoned up from groups that had never before had a chance to exercise them. On the other hand, the essential talent that was required was the ability to survive in a Stalinist atmosphere, which often meant a safe, colorless, obedient mediocrity, rather than real talent. The First Five Year Plan and the war saw the emergence of the most real talent. The great purges and the post-war period seem to have produced more faceless Party hacks.

Stalin did not trust his industrial managers any more than he trusted his other servants. In each factory there were elaborate controls, from the chief auditor commissioned to watch the manager to the secret policeman disguised as a janitor. But the factory manager's job was usually more difficult than the Party apparatus man's or the peacetime army officer's. He had to produce. He had to meet the ever-rising quotas set for his factory or face demotion or criminal charges. Yet to meet his quota he often had to violate Communist law and custom. He had to assemble the factors of production. If labor was short he had to lure capable workers in his line from other enterprises and other places—even to the point of sending trucks to carry them in, and sometimes he had to resort to outright kidnapping. In emergencies he might even persuade his police friends to lend him prisoners and to arrest some for the purpose. If materials were short, and they almost always were, the manager had to use his influence to buy, wangle, or even steal them from other places. In emergencies he had to cajole or bride repair services or what not. In real emergencies he might borrow finished goods and list them as his own factory's production, or he might falsify statistics outright.

Any amount of black or grey marketeering necessary to meet one's quota was justified in the eyes of most managers, for that was far less an offense in the eyes of the regime than failure to meet the quota. The consequent operations of the black and grey markets were staggering, and have been estimated to account for 10 to 25 per cent of Soviet industrial product of various times by various calculations.[20] This was by all odds the biggest single hole in the fabric of totalitarian state control. Yet it was absolutely necessary to the regime, for the plans were impossible in detail if strictly adhered to. Only black marketeering, corruption, and theft gave the economic system the flexibility to work at all well. Stalin presumably did not buy on the black market, but many of his fellow *Politburo* members are known to have resorted to it to secure needed goods, including Beria, the head of the police that were supposed to suppress the black market.[21]

One result was a large underworld of business men who usually had some legitimate post, but who spent much of their time and received most of their money exerting influence (*blat,* in Russian slang) and procuring goods under the table. A fair proportion of these influence men were Jews, which did nothing to stop the revival of anti-Semitism.

The life of the industrial manager was more fluctuating and more tense than that of any other branch of the Soviet elite (save for Red Army officers during the war). A civil servant or an apparatus man might sit tight in his office and proceed strictly and cautiously by the rule book, but that was precisely the procedure that got the industrialist nowhere. He had to flirt with illegality or commit it outright. He had to cover up his tracks by involving all his associates from the chief auditor on down in his conniving—the custom Stalin denounced as "cronyship." The very rhythm of his life was more unsettled than that of any other officials. Each month began slowly with a necessary period of recovery and repair and replenishing of stock after the rush at the end of the previous month. By the middle of the month things had picked up, and in the last week came the mad rush of "storming" the quota, the frantic, overtime, theft-supported drives of management and workers alike to complete the legal requirements.

It was a more trying but a more imaginative and diverse life than that of most other officials. Not surprisingly, a higher proportion of factory managers turned out to be capable and in some sense forward-looking men, able to serve with distinction in the higher ranks of government service should Stalin or his successors give them a chance.

At home, the managers and other members of the new middle class could enjoy whatever material rewards and signs of status Stalin had to give. The upper ranks were well enough paid: A factory manager might receive seventeen times as much in pay and bonuses for overfulfilling his quota as his average worker (a far greater gap than normally occurs in America).[22] The lower ranks struggled with petty bourgeois poverty, but they might have hope. Even a rich man had little to buy in Stalin's Russia, and the richest were not business men but popular authors and performers, who could collect enormous sums in royalties and fees without having to pay much income tax. (The richest of all was Stalin, the author of books that everyone had to read.)

A member of the new elite would probably have a whole room to live in with his family. He would try to secure an apartment of his own, perhaps by buying the rights to one from a worker who had secured this windfall through his union. Rent itself in Stalin's Russia was set low by the landlord-state. Furnishings would be showily Victorian in style, and would not include many mechanical conveniences. A very important luxury of the well-to-do was the ability to keep one's wife out of the labor force—unless she too commanded an honorable elite position. Even then, many Soviet elites thought that a homebody wife enhanced their reputation for manliness, and certainly their domestic confort, since domestic servants were vanishing, as in many capitalist countries, for all save the very top group.

A bungalow *(dacha)* on a lake in the country for summer weekends was highly prized, and was possible with money. Luxuries such as automobiles were rare in private hands until the 1950's, although official cars could often be diverted for private purposes. Work was hard, and sport or other exercise was infrequent among the elites (although not among their children). But heavy eating was the custom, as it is among the elites of many food-poor societies. Malenkov gained one hundred pounds in the last ten years of Stalin's life. A fair share of income could be spent on cultural activities, which were more available than material goods, and ideologically more desirable. The uncultured rough diamonds among the elites certainly needed polishing. If they had married after success, their wives often saw to it. Much money could be spent on children: on keeping them out of the labor force for higher education, on seeing them through it, and often on arranging a favorable entry into their careers and subsequent advancement.

The first generation of the new Soviet middle class that had so largely risen from below was increasingly replaced after the war by its own children, who were born into the middle class and educated in the technological and engineering faculties of the state institutions. Stalin usually proceeded on the assumption that he needed all the technological elites he could get, but many things interested him more than going through with his plans for mass higher education. There were periodic drives to ensure that some workers' sons received higher education and hence future elite positions. But these did not seriously disturb the establishment of a new class-line between those who could normally provide their children with educational opportunity, and hence professional success, and the worker-peasant majority that normally could not. In these respects, of course, the peasants fared even worse than the workers, and most of the minor nationalities fared worse than Great Russians.

The members of the new Soviet middle class enjoyed much of what there was to enjoy in Stalin's Russia. Some could even derive a certain amount of comfort from the great purges and World War II, which opened up so many higher positions. Yet they could scarcely begin to try to pressure Stalin into giving them the other things they wanted: individual security through the end of police terror for failure to keep up with the frantic pace of industry, relaxation of that pace to make the working month less hectic, an increase in the share of production devoted to consumer goods which they would be in a position to buy, and, for many, a relaxation of personal and cultural restrictions. If the factory manager did not understand the idea of intellectual freedom, he might at least want the chance to go to Sweden and buy goods to show off in his home and on his wife. These desires were catered to only after Stalin's death.

Stalin could ignore their wishes, for it was he who ruled, not the new "ruling" class. Nothing in the vastly changed economic base of the USSR in the decades after 1928 affected the political superstructure in any inevitable way. When Stalin looked back on the rise of industry in his cities he was distressed at the many shortcomings, which he made constant attempts to rectify. But he was immensely proud of the total result. An agrarian country was fast becoming half urban. A largely agrarian economy was now overwhelmingly weighted toward industry. The postulated inevitable industrialization of all countries was coming true in his own country under his own guidance. Because of the size and riches of the country, the industrialization process had produced the second largest and mightiest industrial plant in the world.

The workers at the bench did not yet have much, true, although Stalin thought they had more than they did have, and he certainly thought that most of them had as much as they deserved. The new managers, he knew, were looking after themselves effectively enough. They had to be watched all the time—theft, embezzlement, black marketeering, and treason were everywhere. But no matter, the great enterprise of industrialization had vindicated socialism, the Communist Party, and Stalin, by meeting the supreme test of history: the mightiest war to destroy it launched by the worst capitalists. If Stalin ever had any inner doubts, victory in World War II removed them all. And he was well aware that most of his subjects and much of the outside world assented, enthusiastically or grudgingly. No wonder Stalin looked on his creation and saw it was good.

9. THE MINORITIES

*S*TALIN'S treatment of the national minorities of the USSR forms one of the most paradoxical chapters in his career. He valued unity above all other organizational principles, and often subsumed other values under that ideal. One might have expected him to stress Soviet unity above the diversity of the national minorities, centralized administration above minority rights, and the Great Russian core of the USSR above the smaller, peripheral peoples. And so he did, increasingly, throughout his reign.

Yet the situation was more complicated than that. The resolute pursuit of total unity that characterized Stalin's construction of his power machine and economy was less striking in his nationalities policy. Stalin ruled the minority peoples as he ruled the Great Russians, and often more harshly. He made them all work, fight, and suffer for his own larger goals. Yet in this field alone he not only tolerated but encouraged a certain amount of diversity of behavior. Here alone he favored the idea (if not the reality) of an un-hierarchial agglomeration of independent equals. He devoted a great deal of time throughout his life to flattering and manipulating minority susceptibilities. He designed much of the constitutional structure of the entire USSR to embody the privileges of the minorities. Behind this façade of national diversity and freedom lay the reality of centralized Stalinist control, but in no other field did Stalin build such a façade—and he decorated it very richly.

Why did Stalin go to such lengths to formulate and carry through this elaborate minorities policy? He could easily have reasserted Great Russian domination with theoretical simplicity and crushing effectiveness. First of all, he was himself a member of a noted national minority; he could not unthinkingly adopt the attitudes and prejudices of a Great Russian chauvinist. If he had pretended to do so, his Georgian origin and accent would have made him ridiculous. Secondly, Stalin had first risen to intellectual eminence in the Bolshevik Party through his theoretical work on nationalities. It would have been possible for him to suppress his early writings on behalf of the minorities, but it would have been both difficult and painful. He had invested much of his own emotion and self-esteem in his position on the subject. Thirdly, Stalin's career in the early Revolutionary period and during his rise to power had been much involved in the nationalities question. He had been the first People's Commissar for Nationalities, he had set up the first national autonomous areas, and he had written the very Constitution of the USSR along nationality lines. All these things would have been even harder and just as painful to erase.

Ultimately, Stalin did not reverse his youthful stands on behalf of the nationalities because he still believed in their correctness. He was profoundly convinced of the moral legitimacy of nationalities. He never ceased to assert the Marxist-

Leninist tenet that economic classes are a more fundamental division of mankind than nationalities, but within the Marxist-Leninist spectrum, he emphasized the importance of nationalities as much or more than anyone else, and became widely known for it. The eccentric Marxist-Leninist linguistics expert, Nikolai Marr, had asserted during the 1920's that language is a class matter, that rulers and oppressed masses of a nation really speak different languages. After allowing Marr's supporters to conduct a reign of terror against dissenting linguistics experts for two decades, Stalin finally, in 1950, came out against these absurd theories, and reasserted the obvious truth that language is not a class but a national matter.[1] The ideological point was significant: In one all-pervasive aspect of human activity, at least, the nation was more important than the class.

And Stalin was glad that the world was filled with diverse nationalities. Part of his sentiment was doubtless a matter of maintaining his own Georgian identity against the Russians he often looked down on, but there were moral and aesthetic considerations of a more general nature. Stalin loved the rich variety of folk costumes, folk music, and folk dances of the different nationalities, and gave them enormous support and propaganda. He was much less interested in the high arts of the aristocracies of the different nations, especially if they were religious arts—but he granted money for others to excavate the monuments of those arts, to preserve them, and to display them in museums. He was delighted with the more dramatic incidents of a nation's past, especially if these included popular uprisings against the local "feudal" nobility (e.g., Stenka Razin's rebellion), or better yet, heroic popular resistance to outside invasion (e.g., the victory of the Novgorodians under Alexander Nevsky against the Teutonic Knights). He was uneasy about heroic popular resistance to *Russian* invasion: As the years went by, he played down and finally suppressed all favorable mention of the eminently heroic revolt of Shamil, the Imam of Daghestan, who checked the Russian advance into the Caucasus for three decades under Nicholas I and Alexander II. Stalin's attraction to selected features of many national cultures—part Marxist, part popular, part aesthetic—was fairly accurately reflected in the left wing American folk song enthusiast who collected and sang Appalachian mountain songs, Negro spirituals, and strikers' ballads.

A nationality, Stalin wrote in 1913, is a group of people with certain common characteristics. The group must possess a territory of its own. It need not be the majority group anywhere (the Armenians were not in 1913), and it might have lost its national territory through historic oppression (this proviso was written mainly to account for the Jews). The essential test for a nationality is the possession of a separate language. Stalin knew that the distinction between language and dialect is tricky. He tended to grant the claims for recognition as separate nationalities of sub-groups speaking local dialects (e.g., the Belorussians and the Ukrainians). This proved useful in his decades of power for breaking up large and dangerous minorities, such as the Turks, into many small, impotent fragments.

Race and religion help to define nationality, Stalin admitted, but he wished to play both factors down. He recognized the Jews and the Kalmyks of the USSR as separate nationalities ostensibly because they possessed separate languages, not because of their Judaism and Buddhism, which in fact set them off from their fellows. Only in the case of the American Negro did Stalin grant special nationality status based solely on race—and that was never a very effective decision. A nation ought to have a sense of nationality based on common customs and historical experience, he said, although some nationalities (such as the Belorussians) had lost theirs through centuries of oppression. A nation could be brought to self-consciousness as a social class could—and Stalin set about the task vigorously throughout his reign.

The vaguest and most Hegelian criterion was "common historical experience." Separate nations might branch off from one common stock, as the Slavic peoples did a thousand years ago. Or different groups might merge into one common nationality, as had happened in both France and England. Late in life, Stalin was willing to grant the Indonesian claim to West New Guinea, ostensibly because the Papuans, in spite of all apparent national differences from the Indonesians, were really Indonesians through the sharing of a common historical experience in the Dutch colonial empire.[2] The matter of customs was a clouded one, for Stalin wanted to eliminate the religions that were the bonds of many national groups, and the nomadic, backward-peasant, or aristocratic ways of life that characterized many more. In fact, few customs remained for a developed Stalinist nationality, atheist in its factories and collective farms, save language and folk arts.[3]

In Stalin's view, then, nationalities exist and ought to continue to exist during the foreseeable future—although he sometimes hinted that in the distant future humanity would speak one language. But the sentiment of nationalism was another matter. All the nationalities of the USSR except the Great Russians had experienced some degree of specifically national oppression at the hands of the Tsars. This had stirred up dozens of national movements in varying stages of development. Lenin had proclaimed that "the national question must be subordinate to the class question," by which he meant that Bolsheviks must use the discontents of the national minorities in the Russian Empire to help break down the structure of that Empire, and to help the Bolsheviks seize and keep power during the ensuing Civil War.

But the phase of history during which the nationalist aspirations of the minorities were useful to the Bolsheviks came to an end with the Civil War in 1921. By the time Stalin came to power any further nationalist impulse toward independence from Russia was disruptive to the socialist state, and therefore reactionary. The genie of nationalism had somehow to be charmed back into its bottle. The peoples of the USSR had somehow to be persuaded to live in peace with each other and with the Great Russians. They had to be urged to develop "Soviet patriotism," and to believe that their national aspirations had already been satisfied, while they were bound tightly together for the sake of state security and the forthcoming industrial drive.

Since Stalin was ideologically in favor of diverse nationalities, he would not solve this problem by liquidating the Ukrainians and the rest as nations (save for six small nationalities during World War II), as he had liquidated the *kulaks* and bourgeoisie as classes. He expressed his compromise between his insistent demand for unity and the continued separate existence of the nationalities by the formula, "national in form, socialist in content," which was to describe the arrangements in the various Soviet Socialist Republics and lesser minority areas.

From the early days of Communist rule, Stalin experimented with the setting-up of ostensibly autonomous areas for the national minorities, first and most notably the giant Tatar-Bashkir Republic from the Volga to the Urals. When, by 1921, the Red Army had reconquered most of the minority areas of the former Tsarist Empire, Stalin set to work to reform the constitution of the Communist state. The result was the much-touted Constitution of 1924, which first proclaimed officially that the country was henceforth to be known as the "Union of Soviet Socialist Republics"—without the word "Russian" in the title. The Russian word for "union," *soiuz*, had the political advantage of meaning any kind of bond from a loose federal ararngement to a tight centralized government, according to interpretation.

In this Union, the Russian Soviet Socialist Republic was officially only one of four federated republics, along with the Belorussian, Ukrainian, and Transcaucasian Republics. These republics had voluntarily joined the Union, it was proclaimed, and could voluntarily leave it to become completely independent. Furthermore the smaller national minorities were allowed to form various categories of allegedly autonomous areas within the Union Republics. Presently a number of these autonomous areas themselves became Union Republics through the split-up of the Transcaucasian Republic into the Georgian, Armenian, and Azerbaidzhani Republics, and the breaking-off of five Central Asian Republics from the Russian Republic. In 1939 and 1940, five new Union Republics were set up in the newly conquered Baltic states and parts of Finland and Rumania.

The supposedly governing parliament of the USSR was the Supreme Soviet, divided into two chambers, one of which was the Soviet of Nationalities. In this chamber each Union Republic was equally represented (with twenty-five seats apiece after the reorganization of 1936), and each of the other minority areas was similarly over-represented. Thus the minor nationalities allegedly had a veto power and a considerable initiative in legislation. The rights of minorities were lengthily proclaimed in all Soviet constitutions. While military and foreign affairs were almost entirely reserved to the All-Union government, many administrative, economic, and cultural affairs were specifically placed under the control of the Union Republics. This Constitution of 1924 and its successor in 1936 seemed to embody the brotherly democracy of the nationalities that Stalin so often proclaimed.

This constitutional structure was a farce. The various

nationalities had really joined the USSR only after they had been conquered by the Red Army. Anyone who suggested secession from the USSR would have been shot. The Soviet of Nationalities, along with its brother chamber, the Soviet of Union, constituted not a parliament but a rubber-stamping body in which propaganda speeches were made before unanimous approvals were voted. The difference between the All-Union people's Commissariats in Moscow, and the Union Republic people's commissariats, was a matter of frequently reshuffled administrative procedure, especially in economic matters. The great bulk of constitutional forms and all the constitutional guarantees to the nationalities were the merest window dressing.

Nor did the national minorities get much of the substance of their desires. All the developed peoples of the USSR had possessed national movements by the Revolutionary and Civil War periods. These movements demanded either complete national independence from Russia, or the loosest federal ties to a larger union in which Russia would pay money and provide defense, but otherwise leave the minority peoples alone. The purpose of such independence was to be free of Russian oppression and exploitation. The minority peoples wanted their own religions, their own languages, their own customs, their own finances for local development, their own social systems (which were in no case socialist), and above all their own sense of identity and freedom. Under Stalin's compromise they had no independence, no protection from Russian exploitation, endless coercion from Moscow, severe restrictions on their religious and other social customs, and forcible replacement of their own way of life by Stalin's brand of socialism. Stalin secured everything he wanted from his compromise, and almost everything there was to dispute. Yet he did give the minorities some things that they desired.

First of all, Stalin conveyed to the minority peoples a

genuine impression that they were in some sense being taken seriously. No people felt unanimously from the start that Stalin's whole nationalities program was a complete fraud. The Union Republics and other legal minorities areas were in fact set up. More than 175 nationalities were listed in rollcalls and schoolbooks.[4] Their languages were legalized and encouraged, and made compulsory in the local schools, even for resident Russians.[5] The smaller and less developed the nationality, the greater these concessions seemed. The key issue was language. To a foreign skeptic, secure in his own national state, it might seem that Stalin had granted the minorities only the right to hear Communist propaganda in their native tongues. But for many peoples who had endured linguistic Russification under the Tsars, the very right to use their own language in their own homes, much less in the streets, at work, in schools, and in public offices, was the precious palladium of national identity, and the all-important liberty.

Secondly, Stalin's search for local cadres to carry out his orders at the local level really did give a sense of importance and participation to many peoples who had been systematically excluded from public life under the Tsars. The proportion of positions held by most national minorities lessened as one went up the various state and Party hierarchies, but the presence near the top of any member of one's group was a source of immense psychic satisfaction and prestige to many. Most Georgians could take pride in Stalin's supremacy, even if they hated everything he did with it. During much of the 1920's Jews could reflect that Zinoviev, the head of the Communist International, was officially the top Communist in the world.

Thirdly, the very industrialization and modernization of the USSR gave many members of national minorities a sense of participation and satisfaction. Modern industry in Tsarist times had been confined to certain areas of Great Russia,

Poland, Finland, some eastern provinces of the Ukraine chiefly inhabited by Great Russians, and the city of Baku. During the Five Year Plans the drive to exploit minerals and power sources in remote areas, and the drive to industrialize the "East" brought factories, mines, dams, and certain associated amenities such as some paving and street lighting, to many of the most backward places in the USSR. It was possible to be grateful for Stalin's helping hand that pulled a people into the twentieth century, even while hating the often unnecessary accompanying brutalities. Even the Ukrainians could take pride in the great Dnieprostroi Dam, built not in the Russianized east of the Republic but on the classic Ukrainian river, the Dnieper. So much more could the primitive Siberian peoples be persuaded to glory in much larger dams going up in their wildernesses.

And finally there was a widespread feeling of participation in the victory in World War II. Stalin, in a toast to a largely Great Russian audience at a victory banquet just after the war, drank to the Great Russian people as "the foremost of the peoples of the USSR." But the other peoples had their losses, and their home front efforts, and their bemedaled heroes, and their sense of contributing to the common triumph.

These things may seem like trifles for which to bargain away one's freedom. But no people bargained; no people submitted voluntarily to Stalin's compromise. The minorities assented to the bargain only insofar as they did not continue desperate active resistance. But this slight degree of assent was important. It distinguished Stalin's rule over his minorities very sharply from Hitler's rule over occupied Europe, which never gained even such minimal assent in most countries. It was not only Stalin's armed force, police vigilance, and propaganda that tied the USSR together; it was in small part these minor attractive features of his system. The compromise between Stalin and the minorities was very lopsided, but it was the only compromise with diversity that Stalin ever willingly made.

The extent of the compromise can best be seen by examining the occasions during World War II when Stalin revoked it. His apprehensions led him to deport the entire Volga German people to Soviet Asia during the initial German invasion in 1941. As the Red Army recovered Soviet territory during 1943 and 1944, Stalin deported five more peoples eastward: the Buddhist Kalmyks of the lower Volga steppe, the Crimean Tatars, and three small North Caucasian peoples —the Chechen-Ingush, the Karachai, and the Balkarians. The charge against them was collaboration with the enemy. The Crimean Tatars, the largest of these groups, may have numbered half a million at the time of deportation. They are certainly not so numerous now, since the death toll during deportation and before adjustment to their new harsher homes was something between 25 and 50 per cent.[6] In these cases Stalin for the only time in his career treated minor nationalities as he treated all other forms of diversity: by liquidating them, as he had liquidated Party oppositionists, objectionable social classes, and all other groups that resisted his homogenizing machine.

Three minority peoples must be considered separately because of the peculiar problems they presented to Stalin: the Ukrainians, the Jews, and the Turks.

The Ukrainians have long been the largest non-independent people of Europe. When Stalin came to power he ruled over more than thirty million of them. After he conquered the western Ukraine from Poland in 1939, he had over 95 per cent of the world's thirty-eight million Ukrainians in his power. More than five million were killed in the War, however, and their numbers have not yet been made up.

The Ukrainian nationalist movement under the Tsars had

always been peculiar and somewhat artificial. The Tsars, the liberals, and even most of the revolutionaries of Russia would not admit that the Ukrainians formed a separate nationality, much as Americans have never admitted that the Southerners are a different nation. Much that was special in the Ukrainian way of life involved relations with a much-persecuted sub-minority, the Jews—another often-noted parallel to the American South and its Negroes. Although some Ukrainian leaders professed brotherhood with the Jews of the region, anti-Semitism has always been a large and essential component of Ukrainian nationalism—still another parallel to the American South, and this too alienated liberals and revolutionaries from the movement.

It was never certain how much of the Ukrainian peasantry had been attracted to the nationalist movement before World War I. When the Ukrainian nationalists had their chance at independence between 1917 and 1920, their governments often depended on foreign support while the peasants showed more enthusiasm for the guerrilla armies of anarchist and brigand chiefs. (The most notable was the movement led by the remarkable anarchist commander, Nestor Makhno, the closet parallel to Emiliano Zapata to emerge from the Russian Revolution.)

Alone among the Russian revolutionary groups, the Bolsheviks came out strongly for the separate nationality of the Ukrainians. This won them little support in the Ukraine, since their natural proletarian allies in the region were chiefly members of the Great Russian (e.g., Khrushchëv) or Jewish sub-minorities. Such Ukrainian forces as there were in the field during the Civil War usually fought the Reds. The Bolsheviks had to conquer the Ukraine three times, in 1917, in 1918, and in 1919-20—the last two times with considerable bloodshed. This did not bode well for the acquiescence of the Ukrainians to Stalin's rule, and the situation was all the more dangerous because of the Ukraine's huge economic resources. Nevertheless, Stalin was willing to try to make the Ukraine the largest single example of the workings of his nationalities policy—a Union Republic, national in form but socialist in content.

What complicated the situation immeasurably was the fact that when Stalin rose to power, the Ukraine possessed the only meaningfully independent Communist Party in the USSR, and one of the few in the world. This was the fruit of Lenin's apprehension and impatience late in the Civil War. In 1920, when the Reds were winning the Ukraine for the third time, and when the situation was still chaotic, Lenin violated his cardinal principle of Party unity by permitting the merger of the Ukrainian section of his Bolshevik Party (headed by a Ukrainian, Mykola Skrypnik, and a Bulgarian, Khristian Rakovsky, who were no sticklers for rigid centralism) with a larger and looser group of revolutionaries called *Borotba*. The Borotba group contained more Left Socialist Revolutionaries than Marxists, and many in it were genuine Ukrainian nationalists. Lenin's purpose was to gain support immediately for the Bolsheviks in a crucial struggle. The result was a paradox: The Ukraine was conquered by the Red Army, giving Moscow a potential stranglehold on the area, but the conquest was followed by the partial political surrender of the Ukraine to a nominally subordinate but actually autonomous Party organization.

This was the world's first example of what was to be called "national Communism" after World War II. It lasted for six years, since Lenin did not wish to press conclusions with his co-operative Ukrainian allies immediately, and since Stalin did not feel strong enough to crack down seriously until 1926. Since this was the period of the New Economic Policy, the Ukrainian Communist Party's rightist tendencies were then in line with Moscow's orders. Rakovsky, Skrypnik, and their allies spent much of their time "Ukrainianizing" the Republic: promoting the language and its speakers in schools and in public offices. They recalled some non-Marxist Ukrainian nationalists from exile abroad, notably the historian Mikhail Hrushevsky, to play a leading role in educational and cultural affairs. In Kiev it was possible to keep up even closer relations with the "modern" Western culture of the 1920's than were allowed in Moscow in those relatively free days. These right strategies and Ukrainian nationalist policies gained the Ukrainian Communist Party a certain degree of popularity among the Ukrainian people.

Stalin did not approve. He regarded the whole state of affairs as a major breach of sacred Party unity, and feared that the Ukraine would become a dangerous power center for oppositionists in the Party (Rakovsky eventually joined forces with Trotsky).[7] The Ukrainian Communist Party, Stalin thought, was degenerating into an organ of petty bourgeois nationalism. Stalin's fear and disgust at the national Communism of the Ukraine hardened into a permanent ideological rejection of any national Communist movement. This was to have important consequences in Eastern Europe after World War II.

Stalin had the military power in the Ukraine to crush the Ukrainian Communist Party—which he did not have twenty-five years later in Tito's Yugoslavia. He rammed his new Constitution through the All-Russian Party Congress in 1923 (and proclaimed it the next year) against the protests of the Ukrainian representatives and those of some of the other minorities, who saw quite clearly that the façade of national equality covered the centralized power of Moscow to do as it pleased. He removed Rakovsky as head of the Ukrainian Party in 1926 and appointed Kaganovich, a Jew, which was something like appointing a Negro as boss of the American South. Conspicuous nationalists were removed from office and silenced, notably the Bolshevik novelist, Mykola Khvylovy, who had proclaimed "Away from Moscow!" as the slogan for Ukrainian intellectuals.⁸ By 1929 the process of persuading Ukrainian Communist leaders to capitulate was well under way.

G.P.U. terror moved into higher gear with the great collectivization drives, which hit the Ukrainians harder than any other people in the USSR save the Kazakhs, and which was most bitterly resisted by them. The crops of the Ukraine failed in 1932 due to a combination of collectivization and drought. As mass starvation increased in the first half of 1933, Stalin denied the existence of any famine and refused to send grain in any adequate quantity from other parts of the USSR—apparently a straightforward measure of retaliation and discipline. At least a million Ukrainians died in this arranged famine: the greatest single atrocity of collectivization.⁹ Stalin later admitted that the early 1930's was a period of virtual war in the Ukraine.

Show trials of dozens of alleged conspirators at a time began in the Ukraine as early as 1930. Both Skrypnik and Khvylovy killed themselves in 1933 to avoid worse. Stalin appointed a Pole, Stanislaw Kossior, as boss of the Ukraine— another hard blow to nationalist sensibilities—and had him conduct most of the great purges in the Ukraine, which hit non-Party Ukrainians, ex-national Communists, and Stalin's own supporters with impartiality and great severity. In the grand climax to the purges in 1938 Kossior himself and all his associates disappeared without a word of notice or explanation. The new boss appointed to complete the killings and bring them to an end was a Great Russian born in the Ukraine, Khrushchëv. Thereafter the Ukrainians had fewer members in the Party in proportion to their numbers than any major national group.

After such a decade, it is not surprising that the Ukrainians resisted the Germans with little vigor during the first months of the war. Hundreds of thousands of Ukrainian soldiers surrendered to the Germans long before the bitter end. The elders of hundreds of villages met the incoming German troops with traditional peace-offerings of bread and salt. In the summer of 1941 the Germans found plenty of collaborators in the Ukraine, but their harsh occupation and atrocities soon soured the bulk of the Ukrainian population.

In addition to the two great armies warring back and forth over the Ukraine, there were Red Partisans (many of whom were not Ukrainians) and three major groups of nationalist partisans. These last were strongest in the former Polish Ukraine, and they fought the Russians more often than the Germans. The most important group, led by Stepan Bandera, harassed the Russians early in the war, and turned against the Germans too by 1943. Confined in Berlin by the Germans, Bandera was released in 1944 and continued to resist the Russians even after the Germans were driven from the Ukraine. He gave up the fight and escaped to the West only in 1947.[10] Of the nearly three million Soviet citizens whom the Germans drafted for forced labor in Central Europe, more than half came from the Ukraine. In all, more than five million Ukrainians died in the war. Of all the peoples of the USSR, the Ukrainians suffered more horribly than any save the Jews. The one consolation for many Ukrainians was that they had helped the Germans see to it that the Jews suffered even more.[11]

With such a war record, the Ukrainians drew Stalin's vengeance after what he called "liberation." Most of the nearly two million surviving Ukrainian war prisoners and forced laborers in Central Europe were voluntarily or forcibly repatriated to the USSR (some only with the armed help of Western troops) to face investigations for collaboration and, in many cases, deportation to Siberia. Khrushchëv and

Zhdanov were sent to the Ukraine to conduct purges. Stalin arranged his allocations of investment for recovery to guarantee that the Ukraine would never again reach its pre-war dominance in Soviet heavy industry. Khrushchëv reported that Stalin had expressed the wish to deport all Ukrainians to Siberia (probably no more than a savage wisecrack on Stalin's part).

Whatever Stalin hoped to achieve through his nationalities policy, he was less successful in the Ukraine than anywhere else. And yet if Stalin had not completely secured his aims in the Ukraine—he had neither won their hearts nor deported them all—he had done his third best. He had smashed their independence drives and crushed national Communism permanently (to date) in the USSR. He had socialized the Ukraine along with the rest of the USSR, and put all recalcitrants to work. The immense agricultural resources of the Ukraine were being exploited, albeit at a low level of efficiency, and the even more important mineral and industrial resources were the heart of his early Five Year Plans. Stalin wanted the love of the Ukrainians, but he was really interested in their economic wealth—and that he secured.

For Stalin, the Jews were a perplexing but less serious problem than the Ukrainians. Although Tsarist Russia had contained at least 5,250,000 Jews, the world's largest concentration up to that time, only about 2,500,000 were left in post-Civil War Russia after Poland and the other western provinces broke away. During the reigns of the last two Tsars, the Jews had succeeded the Poles as the most persecuted minority in the Empire. Jews had become very prominent in all three of the revolutionary parties, but neither so prominent nor so numerous as reactionaries maintained. Lenin had been a genuine egalitarian in ethnic matters. He had repeatedly chided his former mentor in Marxism, Georgi Plekhanov, for his anti-Semitism, and had welcomed Jews into his Bolshevik Party and into his personal circle. Trotsky, Sverdlov, Zinoviev, Kamenev, Radek, and dozens of other leading Bolsheviks who helped make Lenin's victory possible were Jews. Insofar as the Jewish masses took part in the City War, they fought for the Bolsheviks who stopped *pogroms*, not for the Whites who committed them. In the 1920's the Jews of Russia were a largely urban community, with the highest incidence of literacy and education in the country, and with a flourishing Marxist minority among them. One might have predicted that the Jews would go further under Stalin than any other nationality save the Great Russians. Instead, their descent to renewed persecution and massacre was precipitous.

Stalin was not personally anti-Semitic when compared to the average anti-Semite of his day in Central and Eastern Europe. In private conversation he spoke of Jews as little, physically unfit, cowardly, over-clever, excessively intellectual, selfish, money-grubbing people. He told derisive Jewish stories, and used such Russian and Georgian phrases as "stingy as a Jew," and "to Jew a price down."[12] This sounds anti-Semitic by today's high Western standards, but in Eastern Europe in Stalin's lifetime, anti-Semitism meant far worse things.[13] When serious and when speaking in public, Stalin insisted on the absolute equality between Jews and other human beings. He liked to cite a group of medieval Turkish Jews of the Volga steppes as brave cavalry warriors. He always kept some Jewish colleagues, and he was rumored, probably without foundation but not without credibility, to have taken a Jewish woman (Kaganovich's sister) as his third wife. Neither Stalin's petty anti-Semitic attitudes nor his heritage of Leninist egalitarianism accounted for his policies toward the Jews of the USSR and the world.

Stalin had an ideological explanation for the Jews as for everything else. They had been an ordinary people until they had lost their national territory in Roman times. They had suffered from distorted development ever since that catastrophe. They were caught in a vise between the petty capitalism they had been forced to resort to and the consequent anti-Semitic reaction. Only the Revolution could free them from this vise. To normalize the Jewish community, it must be given a national territory, where Jews could once again become normal peasants and workers, and free themselves from the unnatural, exploitative, persecuted life of the petty bourgeoisie suffering from alienation.

Until this was accomplished, Stalin expected many Jews to have less loyalty to the USSR than to their fellow petty bourgeois Jews abroad. The comradeship of workers across national boundaries was progressive and desirable; Communists called this "internationalism." But the ties of Jews and other bourgeois groups across national boundaries were reactionary and dangerous; Communists called this "cosmopolitanism." The Jews had stronger ties with their fellows outside the USSR than any other people, Stalin said, because "the jealous God of Israel is Mammon," (a quotation from Marx). The most reactionary form of Jewish cosmopolitanism, to Stalin, was Zionism, which was a throwback to the epoch of ancient religion and slavery. The language of the Jews of the USSR was Yiddish, but Zionists wished to revive reactionary Hebrew. The Jews of the USSR were participating in a modern economy, but the Zionists wished to re-establish an antique theocracy. Furthermore the Zionists were collaborating with the British imperialists to steal land in Palestine from the Arabs. The harshest measures would have to be taken to keep the Jews of the USSR from being corrupted by Zionists and other Jewish cosmopolites.[14]

These things Stalin was willing to say throught his reign, phrasing them in increasingly harsh ways as the years went by. As he rose to power, another consideration darkened his view of the Jews, which he did not usually include in his public ideological discussions. Trotsky was a Jew, and most of the important Jews in the Communist Party came to support Trotsky against Stalin, along with much of the rank and file Jewish membership. Stalin was able to use a certain amount of covert anti-Semitism in his struggle to get rid of Trotsky. When he succeeded, the *Orgburo* and the *G.P.U.* found themselves purging a high proportion of the Jewish Party office-holders and members. In foreign Communist parties too, Jews were often prominent in the Trotskyite factions. Stalin's previously postulated petty bourgeois cosmopolitanism of the Jews now took on the more sinister form of an alleged Jewish-Trotskyite conspiracy to overthrow Stalin and recapitalize the USSR.

Consequently, from the first days of his power, Stalin believed it would be wise to sap the position of Jews in his Party. In 1922 Jews had made up 4.2 per cent of the Party; the percentage fell steadily thereafter. Toward non-Party Jews Stalin was lenient enough in the 1920's. A disproportionate number of NEP-men were Jews, which aroused Stalin's hostility toward them for their very success. Atheistic propaganda was encouraged among Jews in order to end religion, religious customs, and the authority of the rabbis among them. Yiddish was encouraged as the Jewish national language. Its classics were printed in large editions. Yiddish writing, theatre, and other secular arts were encouraged by the state—and they experienced one of their finest flowerings. But the use and teaching of Hebrew, along with the other activities of religious schools, was discouraged. This mild persecution did not harm the core of Russian Judaism, although many young Jews were attracted away from their parent's religion.

Stalin was in no hurry to fulfill his prescription for the Jews as a nation by forming a national homeland for them. It was a Great Russian peasant, Milhail Kalinin (one of the few who reached the top ranks of the Party), who pushed the matter. In 1928 he moved Stalin to "reserve" an area along the Amur River as a Jewish Autonomous Area. This region, Birobidzhan, contained about fourteen thousand square miles, half again as large as Palestine. It was largely uninhabited, unlike Palestine, so Stalin could point out that the Jews were not stealing it from anyone. It was an undeveloped wilderness most unappealing to the urban, middle class Jews of European Russia. But it was not north of the Arctic Circle, as Stalin's enemies often alleged. It is magnificent country, with rolling mountains covered with noble forests, through which prowl the world's largest tigers.

Only a trickle of Jews ever went out to this Jewish Autonomous Area in eastern Siberia, not more than 50,000. Most of them did not farm, but mined or manned frontier stations against the Japanese across the Amur in Manchuria. Life was hard in the wilderness, and was made doubly hard by Soviet inefficiency in sending supplies thousands of miles out along the Trans-Siberian Railway during the hectic Five Year Plans. As it turned out, it was unfortunate that millions did not volunteer to go. In retrospect, one even wishes that Stalin had arrested and deported every Jew in Russia to Birobidzhan, for it was far beyond Hitler's reach. As a solution to the Jewish question and a device to soothe Stalin's apprehensions, the Jewish Autonomous Area was a failure.

Jewish NEP-men suffered heavily during the First Five Year Plan, but the largely urban Jews suffered relatively little damage from collectivization. Throughout the 1930's Stalin formed more and more suspicions about Trotskyite plotters and became more and more wlling to play on Slavic national sentiments, some of which were anti-Semitic, to drive his machine along. What Stalin's enemies called his "return to Great Russian chauvinism" boded worse for the

Jews than for any other nationality. The great purges resulted in a disproportionate number of Jewish deaths—almost a hundred thousand—and in the arrest of nearly half a million. Stalin's alliance with Hitler in 1939 was followed by the annexation of about two million more Jews in eastern Poland and the other conquered territories. In the next two years Jews were often singled out in classrooms and meetings to praise Hitler, the new Soviet ally.[15]

At the time of Hitler's invasion, the Jews of Russia once again numbered five million. Stalin had told them little of what was happening to Jews in Hitler's Europe, although they heard many rumors. He did not of course warn them of the impending invasion, for he was not expecting it himself. When the war came in June, 1941, the first German and Rumanian pincers surrounded most of the newly annexed Jews in the border areas. The majority were rounded up and either shot or deported to death camps. The Jews who lived within the pre-1939 boundaries of Belorussia and the Ukraine, and in the western provinces of the Russian Republic, had a little more time. Most of them escaped east—with no thanks to Stalin, who did not warn them of their special peril even after the invasion began, and who supplied them with no scarce transport. Something like 750,000 Jews from the pre-1939 USSR were caught and killed, most shot in mass executions at the edges of Belorussian and Ukrainian cities by the "special groups" of the SS. The worst and most notorious massacre took place on September 28 and 29, 1941, in the ravine of Babi Yar outside Kiev, where some 34,000 Jews were murdered (not 80,000 to 150,000 as is often reported). Stalin never commemorated the spot with any marker.[16]

Something like 2,250,000 Jews survived the war in the USSR. The figure is uncertain because Stalin never released any census figures after the war, and Khrushchëv's census of 1959 failed to list the hundreds of thousands of Jews who were by then claiming to be Great Russians in order to save their careers and lives. Nevertheless, it is certain that Hitler killed over two million of Stalin's Jewish subjects. Another half million seem to have been killed in battle, by starvation and disease while hiding behind German lines, or by similar deprivation as refugees behind Soviet lines.

The survivors were lucky if they got themselves officially registered as Great Russians on their passports and other documents, for Stalin's worst persecutions of Jews came during his last years. After the creation of the state of Israel, Stalin was hardened in his conclusion that the Jews of the USSR were shot through with incorrigible cosmopolitanism. He suppressed the public expression of Yiddish culture by closing down all Yiddish presses, newspapers, and theatres, and by deporting most of the Jewish intellectuals connected with them to Siberia during 1948 and 1949. Jews were continuously purged from positions of status and influence. A special effort was made to reduce the prominence of Jews in scientific, technological, and cultural professions by limiting their admission to higher education and by restricting their careers even if they had secured the training. Popular anti-Semitism was encouraged in the western parts of the country. Thousands of Jews were arrested in the middle of the night in phase with the show trials of Jewish "Titoists" then going on in Stalin's East European satellites. At the end of Stalin's life came the "doctors' plot," in which eight prominent physicians, six of them Jews, were accused of killing Zhdanov and other high Communists under the guise of medical treatment. The crescendo of persecution stopped only with Stalin's death, to give way paradoxically to the less extreme anti-Jewish policies of his personally more anti-Semitic successors.

As Stalin saw it, his hopes of reviving the Jews as a nation and purifying them of their capitalist vices had largely failed, for too many of them were hopelessly capitalist-minded and cosmopolitan. But he believed he had taken giant strides toward the second best solution to the Jewish question. He had unmasked the worst offenders and sent to corrective labor, and he had cut down the unhealthy concentration of Jews in elite positions where their treachery could do so much damage. He had provided the chance for future generations of Jews to become proletarians in mind as well as in fact, and to take their place in the glorious future among the brotherly peoples of the USSR.

The Turkish peoples of the USSR are the second most numerous minority after the Ukrainians, and the most complex and widely scattered. Before World War II there were roughly twenty-five million Turks in the USSR and roughly twenty-five million Muslims—the world's largest Turkish population and third largest Muslim population (after British India and the Dutch East Indies). There are non-Muslims among the Turks—chiefly the Chuvash of the Middle Volga and the Yakuts of east central Siberia. And there are non-Turkish Muslims in the USSR—chiefly the Iranian Tadzhiks north of Afghanistan and the incredibly mixed population of Daghestan in the east Caucasus. But about 90 per cent of Soviet Turks are Muslims and about 90 per cent of Soviet Muslims are Turks, so that Stalin, for practical purposes, was faced with the problem of a huge Turkish Muslim minority.

Furthermore, as Turks this minority had ties with their fellow Turks who constituted almost half the population of Afghanistan, almost one-third of Iran, and 85 per cent of Turkey. As Muslims they had strong ties with hundreds of millions of brother Muslims to the south. And these were not Ukrainians and Jews, peaceful peoples who had been walked all over for centuries. These were Turks, known for their skill and tenacity as warriors even in the warrior House of Islam. Many of them could still remember the days of independence and armed vigilance in defense of their way of life, and armed forays against their neighbors. The central institutions and customs of their civilization were intended to produce tough, tenacious, and intransigent men. This was an awesome block of peoples for Stalin to try to control. He knew it from his childhood in the Caucasus, and he respected them enough to proceed warily.

The Ukrainians and certainly the Jews were more Europeanized, more "advanced" than the bulk of the Great Russians. But the Turks were the leading non-European, non-Christian, largely undeveloped people in the USSR. The relationship of the Great Russians and the Turks in the USSR had much in common with the relations between other European peoples and their Asian and African colonies, which we often call "imperialism." Communists define "imperialism" as the invariably harmful exploitation of weaker peoples by capitalists, which excludes their own activities. Anti-Communists often retaliate by defining "imperialism" as the wicked exploitation of weaker peoples by anyone they don't like, especially Communists. If the older and more useful definition of "imperialism" is revived—the relations between an advanced (usually European) people and the backward, often non-white, distant peoples it controls or influences heavily—then the Turks can be seen as the most important subjects of Russian imperialism, and Stalin's imperialism among the Turks can be compared to contemporary developments in the other European empires.

Like most of his imperialist contemporaries, Stalin denied that his policies were exploitative and for the most part believed it. Unlike his contemporaries he explained everything in terms of a socialist class analysis, and his operations in his "colonies" were directed entirely by his regime while those of his contemporaries were partly in private hands. Unlike the other imperial powers, Stalin's regime governed its Russian "metropolis" and its "colonies" in much the same way. Neither Stalin nor most of his imperialist contemporaries intended their colonies to evolve into independent countries. Yet most of the European powers were forced to grant most or all of their colonies independence in the years after World War II, while Stalin was not. This distinction occurred chiefly because Stalin's harsher methods crushed all open nationalist movements in his colonies, while the milder methods of the other imperialists failed in that purpose.

Stalin's ideal was an intermingled comity of peoples in the USSR. The British Commonwealth and the French Union always implied continuing geographic separation of their components. This distinction came about chiefly because the mountains, forests, grass, and sand of the USSR were not such great barriers between metropolis and colonies as were the oceans between Great Britain and India. Stalin wanted his colonies to lose most of their cultural distinctiveness and merge into the new culture of the Russian metropolis. Some West European imperialists had this ideal, especially in France; others rejected that path, especially in Great Britain. Stalin, like his imperialist contemporaries, made great efforts to rule his colonies through agents recruited from the local population. He granted them higher positions but less initiative (by and large) and was probably more successful. Like his imperialist contemporaries, Stalin developed many of his colonies more rapidly than his metropolis.

Many colonials and ex-colonials today judge Stalin's policies in comparison with Western imperialism by reference to two basic points. Stalin by and large industrialized his colonies more rapidly than his Western contemporaries were able to—although some favored colonies of the West were built up even more rapidly than the Soviet East. And Stalin systematically attacked all open manifestations of discrimination built on color as such, while Western imperialists were very slow to attack the problem, even after World War II. Westerners are more apt to inquire whether they or Stalin treated their colonies with more brutality and terror, a question that loads the scales against Stalin in most cases—but definitely not in all.

The Turks had been the subject of Stalin's first major experiment with the nationalities problem. In May, 1918, he had set up the Tatar-Bashkir Autonomous Republic covering a large area from the Middle Volga to the Urals, in which Turks were only a minority. This Republic vanished behind White lines later in the year, but was re-established within smaller boundaries after the final Bolshevik conquest in 1919. As its leader, Stalin appointed Mirza Sultan-Galiev, who became thereby the leading Turkish Bolshevik. At that date, no colony of a West European power had yet seen a native governor-general of non-European ancestry. Sultan-Galiev was built up by the Bolsheviks not only as the leader of the Volga Tatars, the most advanced Turkish people in Russia, but as a magnet for all the millions of Turks in Turkestan, where fighting was to continue for three more years. He was needed to counter the attractions of Enver Bey Pasha, the former leader of the Ottoman Turks who had fled the collapse of his empire in 1918 to begin a new career as a Turkish nationalist in Central Asia.

When Enver Bey was killed in battle in 1922, the serious fighting in Turkestan was over. Stalin felt that he could now come to grips with the obvious problem of nationalist deviation among the Turkish Communists, led by Sultan-Galiev, who favored a genuinely autonomous Communist Party for the Muslims (such as the Ukrainians then possessed), and much real freedom for the Turks under a loose federal constitution for the USSR, which was then being debated. Stalin saw to it that Sultan-Galiev gained the distinction of becoming the first high Bolshevik to be arrested by the *G.P.U.* and purged from office—although he took no further measures against Sultan-Galiev so early. Stalin's hold on the Party in Turkish areas was solidified in the 1920's while the Turkish populace was enjoying the relaxations of the New Economic Policy. But guerrilla bands known as the *Basmachi* continued to fight Communist rule in the mountains of Central Asia until 1926, and sporadic *Basmachi* outbreaks continued to plague Stalin until after World War II.

In 1925-26, Stalin instituted the "alphabetical revolution" among the Muslims of the USSR: the substitution of Latin letters for their previous Arabic script. This was designed to secularize Turkish culture, and to cut the Turks off from their brothers south of the Soviet border. Unfortunately for Stalin, Atatürk imitated him in 1928 by Latinizing the alphabet in the Turkish Republic, which neatly trumped Stalin's ace. It was Stalin's custom when dealing with minority peoples to subdivide them as much as possible in order to weaken them and cut them off from each other. This process was carried to great lengths among the Turkish peoples, whose tribal and dialectical diversity lent itself to such maneuvers. The Turkish minorities living in Slavic territories were given different kinds of "autonomous areas," notably the Tatars of the Volga and the Crimea. The Azeri Turks of Transcaucasia, who were mostly Shi'ite Muslims (unlike their normally Sunnite Turkish brethren), were made into a Union Republic. The solid, contiguous areas of Turkestan were renamed "Soviet Central Asia," and divided into four Turkish Union Republics and one Iranian, with many sub-minority areas within them, such as that of the famous Black Hats of the oasis of Khwarizm on the lower Oxus. The technique of dividing and conquering was plain enough, but it met no special resistance from the readily fractionable Turkish groups.

So far, Stalin had perfected his rule, reduced race prejudice, and appointed many Turks to office, but had not basically changed the life of most Soviet Turks. By 1929 it was time to bring Sultan-Galiev to trial for nationalist deviation, and to purge many other Turkish Communists in Asia and Europe. Collectivization hit the Turks a particularly hard blow. The agricultural peoples such as the Uzbeks were forced to grow larger quantities of cotton and other inedible technical crops on their new *kolkhozes*. Since the regime could not and would not send them enough food in return, many of them starved.

The effects on the nomadic Turks, especially the Kazakhs of the dry steppes of North Turkestan, were the most disastrous in the entire USSR. The entire Kazakh economic and social system depended on their animals. After Allah, the Kazakhs' values, sense of virility and status, and very identity depended upon their horses, which Stalin tried to seize. More than four-fifths of the Kazakhs' horses and herd animals were killed in the course of settling these nomads on unsuitable permanent farms. Judging by later census records, Western analysts conclude that about a million Kazakhs died in the holocaust. The heart of the Eurasian steppe became an area chiefly inhabited by incoming Slavs. So passed the heroic life of a gloriously barbaric people.[17]

The Five Year Plans did provide for the introduction of many new mines and factories among the Turks. Tashkent, the capital of the Uzbek Republic, became a city of over 800,000, dotted with cotton mills and other light industrial plants. Public improvements, schools, and other paraphernalia of the modern industrial world appeared with sufficient frequency among the Turks to contrast impressively with the continued absence of major economic development across the USSR's southern borders. Stalin strung up miles of electric lights along the Soviet side of the Oxus to propagandize the Turks across the river in the darkness of Afghanistan.

The great purges hit the Turks less heavily than most

peoples of the USSR. In the middle of them Stalin tried a second alphabetical revolution, changing all the new Latin alphabets to Cyrillic, in order to cut the Turks off from Turkey again. The war reached only the Crimean Tatars and some of the North Caucasian Turks—whom Stalin deported east as soon as he "liberated" them. The bulk of the Turks were as well off in the war as any Soviet people. They were out of the battle zone, by now relatively favorably supplied with food, and the beneficiaries of a great deal of emergency relocation and construction of war industries. The influx of millions of refugees from Soviet Europe, a large minority of whom stayed on after the war, helped build up the Turks' country, after initial dislocations, at the expense of diluting its Turkish character. In his last years Stalin trusted his Turks enough to use their area as the scene of showcase tours for Muslim visitors from south of the border. He even displayed the few remaining active mosques and the severely limited Muslim religious exercises for their benefit, but he did not allow the resumption of pilgrimages to Mecca.

All told, Stalin was more successful in taming his Turks and in modernizing their areas than most outsiders would have predicted in the 1920's, perhaps more so than he himself predicted. Considering the Turks' previous reputation as warriors and fanatics, it is surprising how easily their military resistance and their Islamic institutions collapsed before Stalin's assault—while Islam was also retreating with relatively little resistance before Atatürk in the Turkish Republic. There may yet be a Turkish revival in the USSR, as there is now an Islamic revival in Turkey. But Stalin could look back at his handling of the Turks with some satisfaction. Some had resisted like true Turks, and had had to be destroyed. However most of these magnificent peoples had rather easily been brought to modern civilization and to socialism. This showed, Stalin concluded, that under the Soviet system the East can be built up to the level of Europe and beyond in one generation: a tremendous triumph for socialism, the USSR, equality, and Stalin.

Perhaps Stalin and the rest of us exaggerate the degree to which he succeeded in taming the national minorities with his compromise, but he seems to have gotten what he wanted, and so have his successors. So far, there has been no Yugoslavia, Poland, or Hungary within the USSR. Stalin certainly believed that the creation of the new Soviet brotherhood and supra-national patriotism in a giant industrial state was better than the murderous communal strife of Tsarist days, or the establishment of dozens of squabbling, economically impotent, little new countries. And the strength of the national minorities, nearly half the population of the USSR, had been harnessed, without crippling concessions to any nationalism, to his real purpose—the industrial and military drive for power.

10. THE CULTURE

STALIN believed himself to be a profoundly cultivated man, and the greatest patron and promoter of culture in all history. His opponents often pictured him as an utterly vulgar boor, who put an end to one of the great ages of Russian culture with an atrocious police terror, and who plunged a whole generation into the dark night of the mind.

Stalin's education had chiefly been secured on his own. It was spotty by European standards, and by those of more fortunate Russian revolutionaries. But he had acquired one of the two things needful: an enormous respect for and interest in intellect, science, and culture. This respect for what he believed to be true culture was not negated by his frequent philistine attacks on "bourgeois," "formalist," "negative," "degenerate" culture. A commitment to culture does not mean a commitment to everything that alleges to be culture. Stalin believed that he was maintaining standards.

Most Western observers denied that Stalin ever possessed the other thing needful: an intelligent understanding of cultural matters.

The place of culture in Stalin's ideology was very high, certainly one of his ultimate values. The Revolution could not be brought about, Lenin had taught, without correct ideology, highly devolped science, and supporting arts and letters. And the ultimate purpose of having a Revolution, of building up socialist and then communist societies, of assuring material plenty for all mankind, was not to transform men into well fed hogs, but to make it possible for them to lead a rich life: which meant as much as anything else a rich cultural life. Stalin insisted on the intimate linkage of science and every other branch of culture in a way that was very common in the nineteenth century, and very rare in the mid-twentieth century.

Stalin's cultural views were the ones he inherited and developed from his European and Russian Marxist forebears: overall philosophical questions, he thought, had to be answered first. Until one masters the essential nature of the universe, one cannot proceed to examine or manipulate any part of it correctly. Dialectical materialism was the true philosophy which alone made possible true progress in any modern science. Science should not be the activity of a few aristocrats contemplating the universe; that would be neither moral nor practical. What aristocrats allege to be "pure" science divorced from technology and practical problems can no longer get us anywhere. The purposes of science are to solve material problems, provide material abundance and material means of defense, and so to bring on the Revolution and to preserve and build socialism. The sciences and other branches of culture must be endowed and encouraged by the socialist state. To all these Marxist-Leninist sentiments Stalin added his own contribution to the ideology of culture: Culture must be regulated with the full coercive powers of the state, lest dangerous errors creep in.[1]

The arts and letters, Stalin was convinced, must serve a similarly practical function. Any doctrine of "art for art's sake," any indulgence by rich people in a life of art aside from art's contribution to the social struggle, any use of art to criticize or impede the Revolution or the Revolutionary government—all these, Stalin thought, were evil, and should be chastised. Each and every artist and writer should use his full talent and energies to help the Revolution. Any slackening of effort, any devotion of the artist's time to purely aesthetic concerns or to purely private and emotional matters, was loafing on the job and tantamount to treason against the Revolution.[2]

Cultivated Westerners find all of this hopelessly wrongheaded. In the last two hundred years we have built a complicated aesthetic according to which we judge that most of the best writing and art of the modern world has been created precisely by emotionally intense, privately oriented neurotics, whose essential subjects have been private feelings and/or pure aesthetics devoid of social or even natural content. Our artists, if they pay any attention to public events and the state, usually express alienation and rebellion.

Stalin believed that such alienation and rebellion had had their place during the bourgeois phase of history. Rebellious writers and artists, such as Zola and Tolstoy, Courbet and Repin, even if they were not socialists, stirred revolutionary sentiments by their art. But now in the socialist phase of history alienation from the state was reactionary. Only ideologically correct, healthy-minded, positive artists could now properly serve the cause.

Westerners, in moments of great crisis such as the two World Wars, are apt to take a similar view. Then our writers and artists too volunteer for military service, devote their energies to performing for the soldiers and encouraging the home front, and gladly write stories and draw posters that exalt our ideals, denigrate the enemy, and exhort our forces. Stalin highly approved of all this. However, *he* believed that the forces of progress and reaction were *always* at war, that the world of exploited and starving humanity was always a battlefield on which every man was morally obliged to fight without respite. Our artists usually recognize the battle only in case of wholesale international hostilities or catastrophic depression, and in the long intervals of apparent peace they do not usually feel the obligation that Stalin felt to answer the cries of agonized mankind.

One of Stalin's major assumptions about the arts and letters was that they are enormously important influences on public opinion and hence on public events. Bertrand Russell once quipped that the English allowed freedom of thought because they never took ideas seriously enough to imagine that they could matter. Stalin took ideas with deadly seriousness. He drew twin logical conclusions from his position: The arts had to be enlisted on the side of progress, and artistic dissent had to be suppressed. He so respected culture that he greatly exaggerated its political impact. The cheapest and most vulgar propaganda blast over the state radio moved the masses far more than the finest novel, but Stalin continued to invest enormous sums in art, claiming that it was politically worthwhile.[3]

The most horrifying aspect of Stalin's cultural program was of course his total censorship of dissenting art and his total terror against dissenting artists. It was dismal enough for Stalin to finance tons of pompous garbage posing as art, but his cultural *pogroms* require a further explanation. It is difficult to see what harm would have come to Stalin's political and economic drives if he had allowed a few people to scribble incomprehensibly about their own neuroses or drip blotches of paint on canvas somewhere in a back room (and that was how Stalin described modern culture as early as 1928).[4]

But to Stalin, a man's cultural superstructure was determined by his politics, which was in turn determined by his economic position. A good socialist writer's work reflected his good socialist satisfaction with his position in a good socalist society. Artists in bourgeois countries, unless they had gone over to the proletariat and its party, concentrated on the private and the formal precisely because they and their capitalist paymasters desired to distract their audiences from the real and public worlds, the scene of the forthcoming revolution. Soviet artists who created the same sort of art, Stalin was sure, did so in order to express their political sympathy with the bourgeois order. They were attempting to convert the people back to capitalism, or at least to distract them from their proper task of helping the Party. Dissident art *was* dissident politics in Stalin's ideology. And the USSR could not afford to take a chance with treason, encircled as it was by capitalist powers.[5]

Stalin's particular theory of what was good in many of the arts was what he came to call "socialist realism." He thought the meaning of "realism" was obvious enough: detailed, accurate representations of everyday human life, as opposed to primitive clumsiness or deliberate distortions, and to supernatural, remote, or consistently upper class subject matter. A realist always expresses a social if not a political point of view. "Naturalism" was the word Stalin reserved for what he thought was the necessarily false or deluded attempt to portray reality without expressing any values.

Realism, he thought, had always been the most desirable form of art. It was scientific. It was directed toward this material life instead of some idealistic theological otherworld. It tended to be critical, satirical, indicative of the horror of social reality, and hence subversive. Realism was originally the bourgeois mode of art, he believed: Classical realism accompanied the triumph of the Greek bourgeoisie over the tribal aristocrats and their hieratic art. It declined into Christian distortion and formalism when the bourgeoisie gave way to rising feudal aristocrats. Likewise realism was reborn among the Italian and Flemish bourgeoisie in opposition to the feudal lords and the feudal Church. The triumph of realism in various waves from the early Renaissance through the nineteenth century followed on the triumph of various bourgeois class movements.

Bourgeois realism, Communists asserted, reached its height in the nineteenth century. But since the bourgeoisie had now triumphed, the best bourgeois artists ceased to attack the old upper classes on behalf of the bourgeoisie and, as a result of the artists' alienation, instead excoriated the bourgeoisie itself. In bourgeois revolutionary France, novelists such as Balzac and Zola and painters such as Daumier and Courbet portrayed the declining aristocracy, the rising bourgeoisie, and the sufferings of the early proletariat with devastating effect, visibly fomenting the coming socialist revolution even when they did not personally sympathize with it. The Russian realist writers from Pushkin on down, the Russian *narodnik* painters such as Repin, and even the Russian Slavophile composers such as Musorgsky, performed the same revolutionary task in their country.[6]

But by the end of the nineteenth century the bourgeoisie had fulfilled its historically progressive role, Stalin thought, and had turned reactionary in the face of the rising threat of proletarian socialism. As the life went out of the bourgeoisie as a class, so its artists lost their touch. They turned to their private worlds and to experimentation with form, to blind themselves to their coming doom and to distract others. At this point, however, knowing, self-consciously socialist writers and artists took up the torch, notably (Stalin thought) the one major Bolshevik novelist of pre-Revolutionary days, Maxim Gorky. His realistic method of "superfluous detail" patterned on Tolstoy, combined with his Bolshevism, deserved the new title, "socialist realism."

Before the Revolution, a socialist-realist novel was one that was as detailed and critical as its bourgeois predecessors, with the additional feature of socialist, especially Bolshevik, exhortation—for instance, Gorky's *Mother*. The hero of bourgeois realist novels might be a "negative hero," a vicious expression of the social *status quo* such as Gogol's Khlestakov and Chichikov, or a crushed victim of degenerative social forces, such as Zola's Gervaise and Nana. But in socialist realism the hero had to be a "positive hero," who exemplified or at least foreshadowed the virtues that could be fully developed only after the Revolution. Such a hero may fail or be killed, but he will pass the torch on; he will inspire others in the novel, and hence among the readers. For Stalin as for Lenin, the model of the positive hero was to be found in their favorite novel, Chernyshevsky's *What Is To Be Done?*, with its rational and emancipated young men and women who had inspired three generations of revolutionaries, as Stalin wanted a novel to do. A socialist-realist writer would not engage in formal experimentation, because Stalin was satisfied with existing realist methods, and assumed that all experiments would end in failure, and would prove incomprehensible to the masses.

After the Revolution, the field for socialist realism in the various arts was enormously expanded. A novelist might do retrospectively what Chernyshevsky and Gorky had done for their contemporaries. He might go further back in the past and write historical novels, praising and blaming the historical figures whom the Party had previously judged. He might celebrate Bolshevik heroism and Party correctness during the Revolution and Civil War. But his central task would be to write in support of whatever happened to be the Party's most pressing current task—the Five Year Plans, the war, or what not. In all these socialist-realist novels ostensibly laid in the present, there was the obligation to foreshadow the socialist future—to make the hero nearly perfect as future men will be under communism, to make the Party perfect as it soon will be, to make many of the conditions of life superior as they soon will be.[7]

All of this had to be done in a realistic style, with simple, comprehensible language, plot, and characters, so the masses would readily understand and not run the least risk of being puzzled or confused. For the esoteric writer catering to a small group must be inherently reactionary and anti-popular.

Although the novel was the genre for which the doctrine of socialist realism had been formulated, all other forms of literature and art had to be socialist-realist as well. The drama was regulated by the same strictures as the novel, and was thought to be a particularly effective medium for swaying the populace. Controversy raged during the 1920's and 1930's between the partisans of Konstantin Stanislavsky's school of acting which emphasized the creation of each role by the individual actor himself, and Vsevolod Meyerhold's school which emphasized close guidance of each actor by the director. Since Meyerhold's close control of all individuals on stage in the interest of a larger plan was analogous to Stalin's guidance of the Party and country, one might have expected Stalin to come out emphatically for Meyerhold, but this never happened. Meyerhold was instead condemned for excessive "leftism" in his theatrical productions, and was purged in 1939.

Socialist-realist poetry was supposed to follow in the footsteps of Nikolai Nekrasov, a mid-nineteenth century *narodnik* poet who reworked the forms of folk poetry to celebrate the peasant and lament his lot. What Stalin really wanted was rather far from Nekrasov's production: heroic and inspiring odes and marching songs about the Revolution and its leaders. History and other non-fiction was to record the triumphs of the Party and its predecessors, under correct guidance.

Architecture was supposed to display the triumph and grandeur of the Soviet state. Painting was to represent photographically (as was photography) heroic moments in the life of the Party leaders, or the people at work, or in other positive attitudes. Painting was to be colorful enough to interest the masses, but not so so colorful as to distract them from the subject or to distort reality—the faults Stalin found in the early French and German expressionists. Stalin's favorite painting portrayed himself and Marshal Voroshilov pacing along the wall of the Kremlin, confidently facing the storm clouds of the future.[8] Sculpture was to celebrate leaders and people in massive, muscular, heroic poses.[9]

Socialist-realist music was to stress edifying vocal texts if possible, as did Prokofiev's last cantata, *On Guard for Peace*. Stalin liked music best in conjunction with other arts, as in the opera and ballet. Both these genres permitted the simultaneous display of folk music, folk dance, folk costumes, and individual and group virtuosity while an edifying plot was unfolded. Even if non-verbal, a piece of music was to be programmatic and didactic, as was Shostakovich's *Leningrad Symphony*, which included a famous movement with a "fascist theme" that expressed the German invasion, and orchestral development that expressed successful Soviet defense.[10] The musical texture of a piece was to be simple, comprehensible, and at least as melodic and harmonious as the Romantic composers whom Stalin loved. If possible, the composer was to use themes from folk songs that reflected and attracted the people. (Prokofiev wisecracked that socialist realism in music meant tunes that Stalin could whistle.)

Stalin rejected the harshly discordant and apparently formless strain in modern music as he rejected similar movements in literature and the fine arts. It was a sick, bourgeois flight from reality that would offend the common people and distract some from their true tasks. One might have expected Stalin to welcome the "neoclassic" strain in modern music, the return to some of the formal principles of Bach worked out by Stravinsky and others during the 1920's. But Stalin liked Beethoven, and Bach left him cold (although he was respectful). He dismissed the new polyphonic music as the fruit of self-conscious desire by the aristocratic exile, Stravinsky, and his despairing bourgeois supporters, to set society back to the late feudal days of Bach.[11]

Stalin believed that this ideology of socialist realism went back to the aesthetic writings of Chernyshevsky, and its roots can certainly be seen there. The full elaboration of the doctrine came only in the early 1930's. Its institutional underpinning, the various unions of Soviet writers and artists that were to regulate and discipline their members, was developed after a number of false starts during the same early Five Year Plan period. Full-fledged Stalinism in culture is often thought to have begun with the formal proclamation by a congress of the Union of Soviet Writers in 1934 that socialist realism was the only permissible mode of Soviet writing.

That date marked the end of the big change that Stalin inflicted on Russian culture. In the early and middle 1920's Russia was still enjoying what we now call its silver age of arts and letters. Since 1890 Russian poetry, fiction, dramatic art in all its branches, ballet, music, painting, and finally the film had all flowered with a vigor that belied the catastrophes in public affairs. This cultural renaissance had survived World War I, Lenin, and the departure into exile of many of its leading figures. It had by no means run its natural course when Stalin began to tighten censorship and impose positive controls in the late 1920's. Stalin murdered it. It was the richness of the culture that Stalin transformed along with the terror that accompanied the transformation that makes socialist realism so odious to cultivated people in the West. The great variety of self-consciously Bolshevik arts was swept away along with non-Party culture to make way for unified ideological prescriptions. The suicide of the liveliest Bolshevik poet, Vladimir Maiakovsky, in 1930 is often taken as the death of independent Communist creativity in the arts.

And there was a peculiar vileness in the extension into the arts and letters of Stalin's methods of coercing victims into becoming accessories to their own punishment. The sight of Prokofiev, Shostakovich, and Khachaturian repenting in unison their "anti-popular" music in 1946, Eisenstein's nearly simultaneous description of the second part of his *Ivan the Terrible* as "my worthless and vicious film"—all on the prompting of Stalin's hatchet man for culture, Andrei Zhdanov—was somehow worse than seeing Zinoviev or Kamenev capitulating again. The disappearance of Meyerhold in 1939 after a speech in which he finally refused to mouth all of Stalin's sentiments, accompanied by the murder of his wife by the police, was somehow worse than the disappearance of Yezhov.

We are convinced that socialist realism ought never to have come into existence, and that it was an integral part of a system we detest. Consequently we are unable to evaluate a piece of socialist-realist writing or even to look at a socialist-realist painting without thinking of the great purges. It is time to try to examine the products of Stalin's culture without political prejudice. Reconsideration, the author believes, will usually confirm one's prejudice, but not in every case.

A clear case of Stalin's butchery of art can be found in the film. In the 1920's the film was sometimes touted as a new technological art specifically suited to Bolshevism. Sergei Eisenstein was at once a true Communist and a great founder of the new art. In 1927 he released his full-length picture about the Revolution, *October*. Stalin was already cutting out parts of films—in this case all the scenes with Trotsky in them —but he was not yet directing the camera. The climax of the film was the climax of the October Revolution: the Bolshevik assault on the provisional government holding out in the Winter Palace in Petrograd. Eisenstein used the gigantic Winter Palace itself as the most spectaular set in the history of film. He showed the giant crystal chandeliers of the palace trembling ponderously under the impact of nearby exploding shells from the cruiser *Aurora*. A ragged and disorderly mob of Bolsheviks, led by a wild-eyed, flowing-haired, rat-faced actor playing the Bolshevik leader of the assault, Antonov-Ovseenko, charged the palace. One man in dramatic silhouette climbed the great grilled iron gate. The crowd poured into the palace, some of it finding the imperial wine cellars and plunging into an orgy of stealing until some soldiers came down and furiously smashed rows of bottles with their rifle butts.

Ten years later Stalin had the whole film redone and called *Victory in October*. It was taken on some stage set in the Stalin style of columned architecture. Stalin appeared everywhere, correctly guiding the *Putsch*. No chandeliers. A disciplined troop of tunic-clad soldiers marched up to the palace. No mention of Antonov-Ovseenko: He was being purged. A number of men crossed the gate in acrobatic unison. No wine cellars.

Socialist realism could do better than that, even in the novel, the genre that Stalin wished to transform above all others. Considering Stalin's own purposes, it was a pity that his admiration for Tolstoy and Zola led him to insist on their detailed, realistic description as the only proper mode of writing. The precise description of endless details usually induces revulsion in the reader—as Zola intended, or a feeling of the vanity of human endeavor—as Tolstoy often intended. It is usually quite inappropriate to the portrayal of a positive Bolshevik hero. Stalin might have had more success if he had promoted socialist fantasy—Bolshevik Paul Bunyans and whatnot—for which Russian folk tradition could have supplied many examples. Such fantasy was in fact employed in animated propaganda cartoons for children. These short epics of super-heroes wrestling with tigers, Trotskyites, and Germans remain as the most charming products of Stalin's propaganda.[12]

Stalin further limited himself in dealing with novels by his theory that a reader will take any figure or event in a work of art as typical of that class of figures or events in real life. If a stupid or dishonest Communist appeared in a novel, Stalin believed that the author was expressing his opinion of all Communists. Stalin's agents in the arts denied all pleas by writers that they were portraying atypical individuals—such writers would mislead the people, and were probably not even honest.

This doctrine sealed the exclusion of tragedy in any modern Western sense from the Soviet novel and other literary genres. Stalin's idea of a tragedy was the death of a hero after he takes several dozen Germans with him. The tragedy of a man with great virtues but one flaw was excluded because it was atypical and unedifying. The tragedy of a man in conflict with himself was excluded for the same reasons. The tragedy of a man in conflict with his environment was excluded because the socialist environment was good and anyone in conflict with it could not be a hero. The tragedy of any genuine conflict of values was excluded because socialism is a consistent, rational system, and contradictions exist only in capitalism.

In spite of all this, Stalin found it possible to accept as socialist-realist Mikhail Sholokhov's memorable novel, *The Quiet Don*, which was a Revolutionary tragedy of the first water. This long novel about the lives of hundreds of characters through peace, World War I, Revolution, and Civil War was a deliberate imitation of *War and Peace* in scope, subject, and realistic style—and Stalin approved. The first chapters appeared in 1928, when Stalin had just begun to close in on the writers. The novel's hero, Gregor Melekhov, is a Cossack peasant of the Don. He perfects his masculine skills and the integrity of his soul in his primitive village on the Don, and amid the horrors of World War I. During the Revolution, Bolsheviks appear and are treated favorably, but not incredibly. As the book came out in sections until 1940, it is surprising how little Sholokhov was compelled to modify his story and style to suit Stalin's drastically increased demands.

Melekhov endures the confusion and bloodshed of Revolution on the Don and is revolted by the excesses of some Bolsheviks, which lead to the rising of the Don Cossacks on behalf of the Whites in 1919. As Stalin read and commented on each installment of Melekhov's alternating course between Reds and Whites, his stated expectation (a very strong hint) was that Melekhov would end a good Bolshevik. But no, even after the great purges Sholokhov had the courage to try and the prestige to succeed in publishing his own conclusion.

Melekhov, so far from emerging as a decisive, positive hero and a true Bolshevik, is swept into a band of White bandits, a useless, hopeless, vicious crew. Escaping with his much battered romantic love, Aksinia, he sees her shot dead by

Bolsheviks, which drives him to despair. He wanders for days, throws away his arms, and finally rides home to see his sons, the positive element left in all the bloodshed and despair, probably to fall victim to the implacable vengeance of the Bolsheviks he has betrayed.

Here was true tragedy in a Bolshevik framework. The Bolsheviks, although faulty, were the Revolutionary future. But chance and human weakness led them to destroy a genuinely great and tragic man. The Revolution crushes many people while wrenching history forward. The politics of the novel was slightly askew, but the art was true. No such work was to be produced again in Stalin's Russia.

Stalin sensed that *The Quiet Don* was the greatest work of art to emerge from the Russian Revolution, and granted Sholokhov the unique privilege of finishing it as he thought best. Even in his last years he confined himself to censoring from the 1953 edition certain Bolshevik brutalities, certain Bolshevik bed scenes, and certain crudities such as the references to a Bolshevik's "horse-like" body hair or to Aksinia's "unashamedly parted" legs.[13] *The Quiet Don* was thus violently atypical of novels in the Stalin era, but in this case the exception was more important than the rule.

The first major line of closely controlled Stalinist novels came out during the First Five Year Plan, and dealt with the stirring industrial scene. These novels usually sound like unbearable propaganda when described, yet some of them were good second-rate tales. Valentin Kataev's *Time Forward* combined the best elements of many. It told a lot about machine production, as Balzac told a lot about barrel-making in *Eugénie Grandet*. It conveyed the sense of frantic rush in the new factory, and the dizzying passage of time. It provided a fine suspense yarn about a good Communist factory manager and his troubles organizing the factors of production, and overcoming Trotskyite wreckers who set fire to his plant.

There was comic relief—the secretary who thinks the manager wants to seduce her, and who is helpful at the wrong time. There was a striking portrait of an American engineer who comes to the USSR to pile up a balance in his bank in Chicago: The bank crashes in the depression, of course, destroying his capitalist *raison d'être*.

Time Forward was certainly not *The Quiet Don*, but it was probably better than any socialist-realist novel that came after it. In the later 1930's and after the war, the industrial novel was made to degenerate into a propaganda piece in which boy meets tractor and girl meets quota. World War II in the USSR was an event so Stalinist in its nature and so distracting to Stalin's censors that a fair quantity of readable war literature emerged. But only the sufferings inflicted by Germans could be described, not the inner psychic horror of war.[14] It is fair to say that no one need read a post-war Stalinist novel for its literary value.

If Stalin finally succeeded in throttling the Soviet novel, the situation was quite different in architecture. Westerners usually think it was the same. A great burst of free and modern experimentation in architecture in the 1920's was limited by lack of money for major building, not by socialist realism, a doctrine which applied to architecture only by extending the term. The chief survival from this period is a number of interesting "cubist" monuments and pedestals of statues to Lenin, notably his tomb in Red Square, for which Stalin himself had approved the plans.[15] The Stalinization of architecture involved the usual prohibition of free and diverse experiment, the policing of architects through their union, much self criticism, and rigid state-imposed uniformity, as in every other field of culture.

But what was Stalinist architecture to be? There was no ideological basis or Leninist precedent to follow, as there was in literature. Stalin had to choose for himself. As in many other cases, Stalin reached his decision after some false starts by seeking the most nearly analogous leads in his ideology, and by following his own taste. And when he had formulated his views, he worked up a theoretical underpinning and incorporated them into his ideological system, to serve as precedents for all later efforts in the field.

Stalin might have followed the lead of certain German revolutionaries, who believed that socialist architecture should exploit the latest achievements in science and should express the freedom given man by new scientific techniques—in short the boldest experimentation in modernistic architecture with new materials and light, sheer, free forms. He did not. He might have followed the many Russian and other revolutionaries who have thought that the people's architecture should be a magnification of traditional peasant styles. He did construct some such buildings—notably the pavilions of the various Union Republics and regions of the USSR at the permanent world's fair at the edge of Moscow called the Moscow Agricultural Exposition. These were very elaborate variations of peasant buildings, or in the case of the Central Asian Republics, of Iranian Muslim buildings.

But what turned out to be the Stalin style of architecture was neither of these. The public architecture of the USSR, Stalin said, must express the might of the people and the dignity of their state. Many forms of building, though not all, could do that. He liked huge buildings—to show the people's might and his own. He liked regularly symmetrical piles standing wholly or partly in the open, the better to be seen. These were usually topped by tall central towers. Evident symmetry and hierarchical ordering of parts was dignity. He liked to break up his big complexes, notably Moscow State University, into strongly articulated blocks. A huge central tower with some setback stages was set off by outer square towers connected by lower masses to the center. Major architectural lines were rectangular, sometimes radiating straight from the center, but rarely curved.

Entrances were colossal in scale, involving either monumental colonnades with flat pediments, or huge Florentine rusticated arches. The colonnades or the rustication might extend along the whole façade (or the ground floor of it) and even all around the building. The rising walls with regularly placed windows were usually graced with elaborate window frames and often balconies. On top of the great tower blocks were several setbacks, often in the form of flat-roofed peripteral temples, or some Romanized version of sixteenth and seventeenth century Muscovite round segmented towers. The upper parts of these tower blocks were usually decorated with huge clocks, heroic statues, plaques or coats-of-arms or hammer-and-sickles enclosed in wreaths, and were often topped by colossal spikes tipped with illuminated red stars, with or without wreaths.

Stalin's interiors were usually far more sumptuous, colorful, and decorated with overall patterns than his exteriors. The large interiors were often characterized by symmetry, colonnades and other grandiose motifs to emphasize colossality, surfacing with expensive materials, huge chandeliers, decorations of plaster scroll work derived from the Baroque, and large spaces for socialist-realist paintings or mosaics. The best known Stalinist interiors are the various staggering stations of the Moscow subway, each of which blasts the eye and mind in a different way.

The sources of all this are clear enough: first Imperial Rome, then a surprising amount of Mannerist and Baroque Rome in its monumental aspects rather than its fugal complexity, Louis XIV's France, a very important element of Imperial Russia of the eighteenth and early nineteenth centuries, some French Revolutionary-Napoleonic motifs such as the heavy metal wreaths, some of Lenin's revolutionary iconography, and finally a touch of Mussolini. The monumental, opulent, statist magnificence of most of these sources is striking. Stalin expressed his regime well through these borrowed architectural forms.

Yet the result was not an eclectic hodgepodge. No one would confuse a Stalinist building with any other. The tall central tower blocks with setbacks topped by spikes (a creative variation of the Tsarist Admiralty and several other buildings in old St. Petersburg) were only the most obvious distinguishing feature. The decorative scheme was uniform and distinctive in its assemblage of elements. In the course of choosing among the various plans presented to him in the early 1930's, Stalin set himself in the architectural tradition of the Tsars, as he became their successor in other ways. The buildings of the Tsars from Peter the Great through Alexander I are among the wonders of the world. Stalin took off from them to evolve a style of his own that will mean *Stalin* as long as the memory of the buildings survives, for it expressed so much of his personality and that of his system.

Hardly anybody likes these buildings now except the Russian people and humble visitors from abroad. Cultivated Westerners have always ridiculed them as gross, heavy, overdecorated wedding cakes. Sophisticated Russians are now in agreement. There are many charges made against these buildings, some more just than others. First there is the moral charge: Stalin should not have spent so much on these showy buildings when his people lived in crowded squalor. This may be true, but the same charge can be made against all public architecture as long as the people are not well housed—and they never yet have been well housed. The more general moral charge is that Stalin was evil and therefore whatever he did was bad. His buildings do, in a sense, drip with blood, but that is not an architectural fault.

Then there is the structural charge: These were rapidly constructed, slipshod, jerry-built edifices that are already decaying. This was often true of Stalin's buildings before 1950, although Moscow State University was solidly enough built in 1950-53 when Stalin had the money to spare. It is similarly charged that many of Stalin's buildings are literally façades, vast street-front structures with nothing through the monumental gates save unpaved courts and pre-existing slum buildings. This was often true, notably along the Stalinallée in East Berlin. In such cases, architects should judge them as façades. The Alhambra and many other masterpieces are jerry-built.

Finally there are the specifically architectural charges: The buildings, it is said, are too big, too showy, too decorated, and obsolete. They make little use of any twentieth century building materials or techniques, even construction with reinforced concrete. The insides and the outsides were both planned for show instead of for use, and neither the structure nor the interior arrangement is reflected in the exteriors. The style is self-consciously *style*—it could be pulled off and replaced by a different decorative scheme without affecting the structure. The styles are obsolete, a grandiose rehashing of outmoded Classical, Renaissance, and Baroque motifs with a few bizarre, tasteless novelties such as the stars and spikes.

In a word, the Stalin style was unmodernistic. It was indeed, self-consciously and belligerently so. Beyond the sheer fact of its connection with Stalin's tyranny, it is the unmodernism of the style that condemns it in our eyes. If we condemn Stalin's buildings because we don't like his politics, we are guilty of one of his sins. If we condemn his buildings because they don't conform to our current fashion, we are as narrow as he. If the viewer is not impressed with the grand monumentality of Moscow State University as he sees it looming up over the endless Russian plain when he drives in from the airport, he would do well to think whether he is responding to the buildings he sees or to his antecedent prejudices. The same may be said for our judgments of many other specimens of socialist realism. Too many Western critics reject an effective and absorbing propaganda piece, such as *Time Forward,* as if it were no better than the later tractor sagas—which bored Soviet readers through their failure to live up to their own socialist-realist standards—because both are equally remote from Kafka and Joyce.

If Stalin killed the novel and suppressed all architecture save his own, there was one cultural field in which he was truly and beyond dispute the greatest patron of all time: chess. Chess had long been popular in Russia, but Russia was in no sense *the* chess country of the world until Stalin made it so. Stalin had played chess from youth, but he had never devoted the time to become very good at it. He was confirmed in his liking when he found that chess was Lenin's favorite game and only relaxation. (He cherished one more of Lenin's few jokes: "There are three things no woman can do—understand Marx, play chess, and fold a newspaper.")

Chess is a peculiarly appropriate game for a conspiratorial revolutionary, especially a Bolshevik. It is a game, providing needed relaxation, but a mental game for those who will not or cannot take physical exercise or afford equipment. It is a conflict situation which forces the player to a scholarly mastery of theory and history, yet it provides infinite new possibilities. Chess is in fact what the world at large is in Communist ideology: a perfectly ordered, theoretically guided, eternal conflict. Consequently chess is good psychological training for Communism.

The Communist government had always encouraged chess in a minor way. Communists established chess clubs and competitions in factories and trade unions. Chess was cheap, easy to win people to, democratic in the Bolshevik sense of crossing class lines in all activities, masculine—although women were encouraged too, in spite of Lenin's wisecrack. After

Lenin's death, chess took on a sentimental memorial quality. In 1925 Stalin arranged a major international chess tournament in memory of Lenin, which turned out to be the first gathering of any category of people save Communists for which most of the world's leaders went to Communist Russia. Stalin's tournament in honor of Lenin was won by Evfim Bogoliubov, a White Russian living in exile in Germany, to which he promptly returned in spite of tempting offers to stay in the USSR as an honored grandmaster.[16] This somewhat dampened Stalin's enthusiasm for chess as a political weapon.

It was further dampened in 1927 when the world chess championship was captured by Alexander Alekhine, an exiled White Russian nobleman, who kept it, save for a two year interval, until his death in 1946. Alekhine was very anti-Bolshevik, and was willing to be the court chess player for Hitler and later for Franco. The whole world chess scene was disturbing to Stalin. Chess has reflected the major cultural currents of Europe. Philidor's small and elegant game was suitable to the French Rococo; Morphy's loose, daring, highly personal king's side attacks were of the Romantic age; the systematic, theoretical, erudite, flexibly symmetrical openings worked out by Steinitz and Lasker were appropriate to the Victorian age of science.

But in the 1920's the wild burst of free, experimental modern art was reflected in the "hypermodern" school of chess, in which the principles of orderly step-by-step unfolding of the pieces and domination of the center gave way to bizarre, dramatic, asymmetrical openings that usually ignored the center and emphasized the far queen's side—notably Alekhine's Opening, introduced by that master in Budapest in 1921. Stalin disliked these features in modern chess as he disliked their equivalents in other arts. But so long as Hypermoderns continued to win over other schools, there was nothing Stalin could do about it.

But others could. In 1933 a twenty-two-year-old Soviet Jewish engineering student, Mikhail Botvinnik, startled the chess world by winning a tournament in Prague against a very strong field, including some leading hypermoderns. He won through a modified return to late nineteenth-century principles, especially through his renewed use of the French Defense. Botvinnik and his school developed their neo-orthodox strategies, which much appealed to Stalin, who thus saw his cultural principles vindicated in chess in an unarguable way. Once again, chess proved to be in fact what Communists hoped the world would be.

Botvinnik's rise stimulated Stalin to support chess on a fairly large scale. He allocated the sums and cadres for the study of chess all over the USSR, the training of masters, the running of a full hierarchy of tournaments, and extensive participation in international chess. Botvinnik and other Soviet citizens won many international prizes, and gained much prestige for the USSR as Stalin hoped, but they could not persuade Alekhine to a match. Alekhine died in 1946, and two years later the tournament to determine a successor was won brilliantly by Botvinnik, and has been kept by Soviet citizens ever since. Stalin never interfered in chess in any harmful way; he never, for instance, made his players adopt the Russian Defense or the Slav Defense for nationalist reasons.[17] Since Jews were very prominent in Soviet chess, he largely exempted them from his anti-Semitic campaigns. The Yiddish chess journal was the last Yiddish publication to close (1950), and it was merely transformed into a Russian language chess journal under its old editors. Whatever Stalin and Communism have done in other fields, they have proved to be the best patron and the best political system for the game of chess.

One field of culture in the USSR interested Stalin relatively little: religion. He treated non-Orthodox religions (harshly) as part of his nationalities policy. He paid as little personal attention to the Russian Orthodox Church and sects as possible, in contrast to Westerners' intense interest in the subject. Lenin had proclaimed that religion was a minor, not a major, class enemy of the proletariat. He meant that the Russian Orthodox Church was too weak to damage the Bolsheviks much once its military bulwarks in the Tsarist regime had been smashed. Sweeping changes had come to the Russian Orthodox Church in the Revolution and during the next ten years. The Church was disestablished, its wealth was confiscated, its schools, seminaries, charitable activities, and missionary efforts were closed down. Many churches were shut and neglected. Priests were often persecuted and sometimes killed. The Party and its League of Militant Atheists propagandized millions of young people away from their *pro forma* religious allegiance. Those who had been Orthodox because of custom or expediency lapsed into passivity, leaving only the core of seriously believing Christians.

All these changes had taken place before Stalin rose to power, and Stalin had had little to do with them. He did not much fear the Church. He maintained the restrictive controls he inherited, and launched a fairly vigorous anti-religious campaign in 1929. More churches were closed, along with most monasteries, and their bells were seized. Sunday became a work day for a spell. The League of Militant Atheists was pushed until it had enrolled five million members. Some priests and believers were arrested. All of this sounds like a major persecution, but compared to the drives against Party oppositionists and against *kulaks*, whom he did fear and in whom he did take a personal interest, the drive against the Church was minor.

The anti-religious campaign was flagging by the late 1930's —although several renewals were proclaimed. The Party had not destroyed Christianity first of all because it had not seriously tried to. It had not tried to because Stalin did not think it was worth such an effort to crush so minor a threat. When the war came, Stalin uttered his famous remark, "If they won't fight for socialism, perhaps they will fight for Holy Russia."[18] He re-established the Patriarchate of Moscow with pliant clergymen whom he had been grooming for years, and called off the vestiges of the anti-religious campaigns. Much restrictive legislation remained in force after the war. The higher clergy served Stalin at home and abroad, incongruously but faithfully. Christianity continued its decline among the population, especially in the cities, not so much because of Stalin's religious policy as because of the spread of industry and education that he had promoted. At Stalin's death, there were perhaps fifty million Christians left in Stalin's Russia who cared enough to make their beliefs known to their fellows. These were mostly peasants. Christianity seemed to have little appeal to the educated elites of the USSR.

When Stalin died and his successors adopted milder policies of cultural control, most branches of the arts and letters began to revive, at first slowly and diffidently, then with increasing vigor. The religions have experienced no such revival, although recent persecutions have been even milder than Stalin's. One cannot be sure, but the evidence suggests that the older religious cultures of the Soviet peoples, especially Christianity and Judaism, are in irretrievable decline, whereas the new secular culture of the USSR may yet bounce back from the Stalin era to become one of the richest of the late twentieth century.

II. THE WAR

STALIN believed that the Second World War was inevitable. He was ideologically convinced that any attempt to avoid the attack on the socialist fatherland by apprehensive capitalist powers was futile. Yet most of Stalin's foreign policy up to the day of Hitler's attack was directed toward avoiding the war, postponing it, or trying to secure allies to fight it more successfully. Stalin's faith in the inevitability of war did not paralyze his will to take active measures to avoid it, although it seems to have rendered him pessimistic at times when greater faith might have led him to make concessions to the Western powers for the sake of a meaningful alliance.

In foreign policy as in other fields, Communist determinism coexisted comfortably with intense activism. Insofar as Stalin's foreign policy aimed at avoiding war or entering it on favorable terms, it was a colossal failure. But the results of World War II made Stalin's foreign policy seem in his own eyes and in those of many others the most astounding triumph in all history.

Lenin had believed that once the Revolution was established in Russia it would spread throughout the world—that is, the advanced nations of Europe. Then there would be no need of any traditional foreign policy, since all peoples would live together in peaceful, disarmed, co-operative brotherhood. By the time Stalin came to power these hopes had vanished, and Communists had reconciled themselves to a period of "temporary stabilization of capitalism," during which the USSR would have to carry on systematic relations with foreign capitalist countries. The purpose of maintaining the USSR was supposed to be to serve as the base for the future World Revolution—which was an unusual national aim to assert. But the purpose of Soviet foreign policy was to preserve the USSR and to increase its power, which did not distinguish the Communist state from others.

The question that has been asked for forty years—was Stalin's foreign policy directed toward the national aggrandizement of the USSR, or toward the World Revolution—cannot be answered by examining Stalin's foreign policy itself, for that was not a field in which the distinction could be made. According to Stalin's ideology the World Revolution could only be promoted by preserving the USSR and advancing its power. There could be no instance in which Stalin might sacrifice the USSR for the sake of the World Revolution, for that would destroy the very base of the World Revolution. There could be no instance in which Stalin might sacrifice the World Revolution for the sake of the USSR; he could only cut back certain exposed foreign positions to preserve the USSR for the sake of the World Revolution.[1]

Unlike any other foreign country, save perhaps the Papal States in the millennium before 1870, the USSR had two distinct modes of conducting foreign policy. The traditional mode, diplomatic relations with existing powers, was employed essentially for defensive purposes during Stalin's first twenty years of power. The People's Commissariat for Foreign Affairs was supposed to keep the capitalist powers from combining against the USSR by playing them off against each other, providing distractions nearer home, and luring them to temporary friendship with offers of trade, which the USSR needed for its own buildup. Theoretically, Soviet diplomats might always be used to advance the World Revolution directly, but no real chance occurred before World War II unless one interprets Soviet diplomacy in the Spanish Civil War in that way. In Stalin's first years of power, traditional diplomacy was much inhibited by the angry and suspicious refusal of some powers, such as the United States, to recognize his government, and by the touchiness of others, notably Great Britain, which would break off relations when they thought the Comintern was trying to stir up revolution among their own peoples. This problem persists to some extent to this day, but the hump was crossed in 1933, when the USSR was recognized by the United States, and in 1934, when it was admitted to the League of Nations.

The other mode of conducting Soviet foreign policy was the Communist International. Stalin inherited this world-wide organization of Communist parties. To foreign diplomats, Stalin and his People's Commissars for Foreign Affairs could claim that the Comintern had nothing to do with the Soviet government. They said that the Comintern was a genuinely international body in which the Communist Party of the Soviet Union had just one vote, like any other party. But according to Communist ideology, the Comintern was the institution whereby the other truly revolutionary parties of the world could be rightly guided and co-ordinated by the correct leadership of the Soviet Party. Without that correct leadership, the other Communist parties would fall into disastrous errors and failure, as had Bela Kun's Communist government in Hungary in 1919.

In Stalin's early years the Comintern's functions were also essentially defensive. During the temporary stabilization of capitalism, it was to help safeguard the position of the various parties of the world, or at least to minimize their losses. It was to direct the efforts of the foreign Communist parties chiefly against other socialist parties, so that when the World Revolution became possible the Communists would have in their ranks as many active workers as they could. To this defensive end, Communist parties had to organize labor movements, foment strikes, take vigorous stands on current political issues, and sometimes push electoral campaigns. All these activities struck both capitalists and other socialists as highly aggressive and subversive. Since such subversions were known to be directed from Moscow, the issue of Comintern revolutionary efforts proved to be the sorest point and greatest obstacle to normalizing official Soviet foreign relations.

All told, Stalin's foreign policy during the 1920's was feeble. No notable new alliances were secured, and the alliances with Germany, Turkey, Iran, and Afghanistan (all inherited from Lenin) proved more useful to its partners than to the USSR. The various trade agreements had no great effect on the Soviet economy. The one really important venture was the Comintern's effort to bring about a Communist revolution in China. Stalin's heavy-handed machinations managed to wreck the position of the Chinese Communist Party in 1927, but it would probably not have been able to seize power in any event. Stalin's major concern with the Comintern and the foreign Communist parties was to purge them of all supporters of Trotsky and Zinoviev, who were numerous, since Zinoviev had managed the Comintern since its foundation in 1919, and Trotsky's forward policy had more appeal to foreign Communists than Stalin's caution.

With the beginning of the great depression in 1929, Stalin decided that the temporary stabilization of capitalism had given way to a "renewed general crisis of capitalism," a period that would offer greater opportunities to extend the Revolution but would also bring greater threats of attack by desperate capitalists on the USSR. The rapid industrial buildup of the USSR under the early Five Year Plans contrasted strikingly with the mass unemployment in most capitalist countries, and made Communism attractive to many workers and intellectuals. But the early years of the great depression brought major Communist gains only in Germany, where Hitler was gaining more rapidly still.

Stalin misinterpreted Hitler as another Mussolini, and he had misinterpreted Mussolini from the start. Fascism, he thought, was the open and terrorist dictatorship to which big business and its allies resorted when a revolutionary threat tore away their mask of bourgeois democracy. He minimized Mussolini's personal appeal (although he imitated some of Mussolini's trappings), his nationalist appeal, and his mass appeal across class lines.[2] Hitler's Nazi Party, Stalin thought, was German fascism (it was the Communists who turned "fascism" into a generic term for modern rightist movements). Hitler was really the tool of the Krupps and the other big industrialists; his war policy was designed to maximize the profits of arms manufacturers. Furthermore, Stalin reasoned, since fascists overthrew bourgeois democracies, they contributed to the decay of the bourgeois order, of which fascism must be the last stage.

Consequently Stalin was not worried by the possibility that Hitler might come to power—that would bring on the end of German capitalism. He was more worried that the German Social Democrats might take over in the ensuing revolution, so he continued his policy of ordering the German Communists to attack the German socialists above all other enemies.

The German Communists tacitly co-operated with the Nazis in the *Reichstag* by voting with them against most constructive measures, so as to bring down parliamentary government. Stalin had the German Communist leader, Ernst Thaelmann, run for President of the Republic in 1932, in order to split the Social Democratic-led coalition against the candidacy of Hitler.

It is too much to say that Stalin wanted Hitler to come to power and made every effort to help him. But he did nothing effective to stop Hitler, and much to prevent an effective coalition against him. We cannot be sure that Stalin could have stopped Hitler between 1930 and 1933 if he had adopted the united front tactics then that he was to adopt in 1935. But the burden of proof lies on those who deny that Stalin's ideologically motivated mistakes were an essential element in Hitler's rise to power. The issue is clearly of supreme historical importance. The most nearly convincing justification for the hardships that Stalin imposed on the peoples of the USSR during the early Five Year Plans was that they were necessary to build the industry and the army to stop Hitler. If Stalin might have stopped Hitler before the latter took power, merely by giving a few orders to Thaelmann to reverse policy, then all those who suffered in Stalin's Russia from 1928 to 1941 suffered unnecessarily. If Stalin could have stopped Hitler before 1933 and did not, then all those who suffered at the hands of Hitler after 1933 were partly Stalin's responsibility. The only thing that can be said in defense of Stalin is that we cannot be certain.

Within a year of Hitler's taking power it was apparent that he was *not* a weak way-station to the German revolution. He was powerfully entrenched; he had crushed the Communist Party and all other opposition groups alike. He was successfully rearming for openly announced expansionist purposes. At this early period, Hitler was neither speaking nor preparing for a conquest of the USSR. But Stalin read *Mein Kampf*, and was aware of Nazi ideology about living-space, the drive to the East, and Jewish Bolshevik Commissars. He did not take Hitler's racist complex of ideas seriously as the mainspring of Hitler's motivation, but he did take Hitler's long-range foreign policy objectives seriously.

Therefore Stalin made his first major shift in his foreign policy. Resolved at last in 1934 and 1935 to stop Hitler, Stalin told his diplomats to secure military alliances with the major powers against Germany. He reversed the Comintern line, and ordered the various Communist parties to stop their fifteen years' war against other socialist and radical parties, and to combine instead with those very parties to build "united front" governments that would enter into such military alliances with the USSR. He ordered a Far Eastern counterpart to this change of policy, to stop Japan. This new strategy would also trump Trotsky, who was making advances among left wing French socialists at this time—for Trotsky figured centrally in Stalin's fears as the master traitor, villain, and organizer of opposition coalitions.

As explained by the current head of the Comintern, the Bulgarian Georgi Dimitrov, at the Seventh (and last) Congress of the Comintern (held in Moscow in July-August, 1935), the united front strategy was to proceed in certain definite stages. First the Communist Party of a given bourgeois democratic country was to form an electoral alliance with the other "antifascist" parties, whether socialist or merely bourgeois reformist, and if possible a merger of their respective trade unions, youth groups, and so on. Then the alliance was to win the next election and to form a government. Communists should concede to their allies the prestigious posts of the new government: the prime ministry and the foreign ministry. But Communists should seek if possible the real power positions within the cabinet: the ministries of defense, interior, and information. Communists would secure the adherence of each united front government to a hard alliance with the USSR against Hitler. From then on the Communists would use their positions in the government to pack their various departments with their own supporters, building up a position of overwhelming power. Finally the Communists would eliminate their allies from the government and rule alone.[3] These tactics were carried furthest in Spain during the later 1930's, but they were fully pursued only after World War II in Eastern Europe, especially Czechoslovakia. The united front technique was thus to pass smoothly from a defensive measure against Hitler to an offensive means of spreading the Revolution, if and when the opportunity presented itself.

No opportunities presented themselves. The united front had first been tried in France, where the Communists were able to sign a limited agreement with the Socialists in July, 1934. Meanwhile Soviet diplomats were negotiating a pact of mutual aid and assistance between France and the USSR in case of attack by a third party, presumably Germany. This pact was signed in July, 1935, but Stalin drove on for a united front government in France in hope of making certain that France would observe its treaty. Consequently the French united front was expanded to include the Radical Socialist Party, a mildly liberal bourgeois group. This success encouraged Stalin to have the united front strategy proclaimed on a world-wide basis at the Seventh Congress of the Comintern.

There followed an international united front period, during which many Communist parties attempted to form alliances against "fascism." In France, the united front coalition won the election of May, 1936, and the Socialist leader, Léon Blum, became Prime Minister with Communist support. Blum used Communist votes to pass a number of New Dealish reforms into law but kept them from infiltrating into any significant government positions, and he ably prevented their take-over of the newly reunited French trade union movement. Nor did Blum's government do anything for the USSR beyond maintaining the existing treaty. Blum manipulated Stalin, rather than the other way round. In China, the strangest of united fronts was brought about when one of Chiang Kai-shek's dissidents generals kidnapped him and forced him to join the Chinese Communists in a pact against Japan. Chiang never lived up to the spirit of the pact, nor did it prevent Japan from invading China the next year.

Contrary to Stalin's hopes and expectations, which were centered on France, the most important united front was the one in Spain. The tiny Spanish Communist party joined the socialists, the bourgeois radicals, and even the anarchists to win the election of February, 1936. This provoked the rising by most of the Spanish Army in July, and led to the prolonged Spanish Civil War. To Stalin this was an unplanned and embarrassing distraction. He was reluctant to commit the USSR to the struggle for fear of offending France, with whose supposedly powerful land army he was most desirous of maintaining an alliance. On the other hand he realized that leftists of the world expected him to give aid to the Spanish Republic, which was going through a number of workers' and peasants' revolutions.

At first Stalin merely let foreign Communists and fellow travelers go to Spain and form International Brigades, which played a crucial role in the defense of Madrid against Franco's attack in the last months of 1936. To keep the Republic alive Stalin found that he had to send some of his precious arms, but he was too stingy and too apprehensive about French reactions to send enough to win the war. The arms he did send gave Stalin a powerful voice in Republican Spain, which he used to impose Russian military and police "advisers" on many branches of the Republican government and army.

The Communist strategy in Spain was to soft-pedal any

revolutionary aims in order to engage as many Spaniards as possible in the struggle against Franco. Consequently the Communists came to constitute much of the right wing of the Republic, for most of the socialists and all of the anarchists favored and were engaging in immediate workers' and peasants' revolutions. These revolutionary parties retained the support of most of the toiling masses of Spain, while the Communists became the largest bourgeois party in the Republic and the only mass bourgeois party in Communist history. The Communists of Barcelona were the spearhead of the Republican government's drive in May, 1937, to crush the anarchists, who had been ruling Barcelona with revolutionary abandon since the beginning of the Civil War. Stalin ordered his *N.K.V.D.* agents to kill the leaders of an anarchist splinter group that contained some former Trotskyites, warning that these Trotskyites were a worse threat to the Spanish Republic than Franco's troops.

To Stalin, this was the wrong war in the wrong place at the wrong time. While Communists gained influence in the Republican government by suppressing the Spanish revolutions, Franco was gaining victories at the fronts. Stalin slowly cut off supplies to the Republic during 1938 and left it to its fate, which was conquest by Franco—freshly armed again by Hitler—in the first three months of 1939. The united front strategy had proved a failure. In no case had a Communist party come to share power in a major government long enough or strongly enough to make an airtight military alliance with the USSR to stop Hitler. While Hitler built his strength and territory, Stalin still had only his own growing strength to rely on for defense. The enormous attractiveness of the various Communist parties due to their apparent firm resistance to "fascism" did not bring Stalin the tangible aid to his defenses that he wanted above all else.

The popularity of Communism during the 1930's attracted

many new members into the Western Communist parties, and provided greatly increased opportunities for spying on Western governments. By the end of the 1930's spying had replaced subversion as the greatest irritant to the relations between the USSR and many foreign countries. Both the Red Army and the N.K.V.D. ran spy networks abroad without any proper co-ordination. It is difficult to estimate the value of the information secured through spies. *If* Alger Hiss really was a Communist spy, the information he is alleged to have passed on to Moscow included such items as a dispatch from an American representative in Vienna in 1938, assuring Washington that Hitler would never march in. Such stuff is not worth the money spent to secure it, much less the ill will involved in running a spy system.

Some Russian spies did apparently pick up worthwhile military information during World War II. The "Red Orchestra" network in Berlin and Switzerland secured valuable information on German operations, and Richard Sorge's spy ring in Tokyo informed Stalin of such items as Japan's intention to bomb Pearl Harbor—which it was not to Stalin's interest to pass on to the United States. The really vital information, Hitler's plans to invade Russia, reached Stalin from the British and American governments as well as through spies, and Stalin did not act on the information anyway. The greatest spying coup of the war is popularly supposed to have been Stalin's "theft" of the atomic bomb. This might have been important if World War III had broken out in the following ten years, but by this time Soviet scientists would long since have caught up with the United States in atomic weapons even if they had not received help from Stalin's spies. After the war, the most important information the Soviet and American governments received from their spies was the continuing assurance that the other super-power was not preparing a proximate attack—a matter on which neither government would take the other's word. So long as spies perform this function, they serve the cause of international peace well.

As Stalin lost faith in the united front strategy as a means to secure the solid adherence of France and other countries to the USSR in the coming war, he turned increasingly to the idea of direct arrangements with Hitler and Japan. This was of course a task for his diplomats, not for the Comintern, which sank steadily to its dissolution in 1943. Simultaneous negotiations with both the Western allies and Germany in 1939 led Stalin to choose the German connection; the Stalin-Hitler Pact was signed on August 23. Stalin agreed to let Hitler attack Poland, to help him finish Poland off, to split Poland with Hitler, and to supply Hitler with oil, food, and other raw materials of war in return for German industrial goods during the expected—and forthcoming—German war with France and Great Britain. A somewhat similar "non-aggression pact" was concluded with Japan, in April, 1941.

The Stalin-Hitler Pact had a horrifying moral effect on Communists and other opponents of Hitler in the West. Tens of thousands of party members tore up their membership cards, and many thousands of non-Communists lost all faith in Stalin's regime. Yet the pact with Hitler was in full accordance with Stalin's ethical position. In Stalin's ideology, Hitler's open police terror was little or no worse than the covert and economic terror that he thought prevailed in the capitalist democracies. War was apparently inevitable, just as Lenin had predicted it would be—so better an internecine war among the capitalist powers than an attack by Germany, supported economically by the West, on the USSR. Stalin's expectation, like that of most of the world except Hitler, was that the bloody stalemate of trench warfare would prevail on the western front as it had from 1914 to 1918. Then the neutral and growing USSR could intervene decisively on behalf of the World Revolution in the exhausted combatant countries.

If the French Army, supported by British forces, *had* succeeded in fighting Hitler to a prolonged standstill, Stalin's diplomacy would in retrospect have been thought brilliantly successful. As it was, the Stalin-Hitler Pact was the Soviet Munich. A "Munich" may perhaps be defined as a morally revolting agreement one makes with an enemy in order to gain time to improve one's position against him, which in fact leads to the enemy's improvement of his position far more.

During the nearly two years of the pact's operation, Stalin conquered Eastern Poland where his troops were to meet disaster in 1941. He warred on Finland to get Karelian territory which he thought (with no real basis) that he needed to defend Leningrad. His slow victory cost the Red Army immense prestige. Without fighting he annexed the Baltic states and seized Bessarabia from Rumania, again justified on grounds of defense, again to lead to military disaster in 1941. During the two years of grace, Stalin pushed his armaments industries at a rate which he and everyone else at the time believed was furious, but which his successors have denounced as inadequate. Direct military expenditures, which had comprised only 12.7 per cent of the budget during the Second Five Year Plan, were pushed up to nearly 30 per cent. Plans were put into effect, but not successfully achieved, to increase the production of certain key armaments including aircraft by 100 per cent in the two years. The weapons that were to prove crucial during the war, such as the MIG-3 fighter plane, the "Katiusha" mortar, and the T-34 tank, were put into mass production before the end of the two years. During the same two years Hitler knocked France, which might have been Stalin's ally in 1939, out of the war, and added French industry and that of most of Continental Europe to his war machine, which was thus incalculably strengthened vis-à-vis the USSR beyond the ratio that had obtained in 1939.

The year between the fall of France and the invasion of

Russia was a strange one. The USSR supported Hitler with its oil, food, and diplomacy, and the Communist parties of the world were ordered to help him too.[4] After Hitler became convinced that he could not succeed in invading Great Britain or in bombing it into submission, he returned to his long-cherished plans for the invasion of the USSR. He sent preparations into high gear in November, 1940, after which he made almost no diplomatic replies to Molotov's pathetic notes begging for a resumption of friendly intercourse and settlement of mutual problems.

As Hitler's gigantic armament completed its preparations for the grand attack, Stalin received many warnings of what was coming: from his spies, from Washington (as early as January, 1941), and from London (as late as four days before the invasion). Churchill telegraphed personally to Stalin on April 3 to convey some of the latest information.[5] Apparently, Stalin would not believe it. In an address to the new graduates of the Soviet military academies on May 5, Stalin came closest to recognizing the threat. He stated that a German surprise attack could not be ruled out in the immediate future, but that the government would try by diplomatic means to put it off till autumn, too late in the year for the Germans to attack. War with Germany was almost inevitable in 1942.[6] The Soviet government did indeed try diplomatic means, but the Germans never answered its notes. A week before the invasion Stalin had TASS publish a communiqué in which any suggestion of an imminent break with Germany was ridiculed. That might have been mere propaganda, but throughout the last week of peace Stalin kept millions of troops near the frontiers in *offensive* postures—where many were to be readily trapped. He brought up few reserves. He did cancel furloughs, but he kept most of his best planes on the ground near the borders, where they were mostly destroyed the first day of the war. The invasion came as a shocking surprise, catching Stalin and the Red Army off balance, with almost fatal effect. Churchill later concluded that "Stalin and his commissars showed themselves at this moment as the most completely outwitted bunglers of the Second World War."[7]

This was fantastic and incredible. This was the most puzzling point in Stalin's entire career. Why did the super-suspicious, paranoid or paranoiac tyrant, who regularly saw vast plots where none existed, ignore the many warnings of an obviously real invasion that had been predicted by his ideology anyway? No one knows. Stalin's entire relationship with Hitler strained even the Communists' ethic of dramatic opportunism. Stalin must have known that many of his subordinates thought the policy unwise. He may have had an emotional investment in thinking himself right about trusting Hitler for the immediate future, even while preparing the USSR furiously and (he believed) effectively for an inevitable conflict the following year. Although he did not believe the fatuous boasts his propaganda machine was grinding out about the utter invincibility of the Red Army, he does seem to have respected his own armed forces too much to believe that Hitler would wantonly risk an attack without even presenting demands, with which Stalin would apparently have done his best to comply.

At any rate, Hitler never presented any demands. He attacked with his full armed might on June 22, 1941. The USSR was invaded by the most formidable capitalist army in history—twenty years after the end of the previous intervention, and ten years after Stalin had warned that he had only a decade in which to prepare for invasion. Stalin's foreign policy had utterly failed. Stalin's Russia had no assurance of any allies, and only its own untested strength to rely on.

Yet Stalin's Russia met what he, other Communists, and the rest of the world could only regard as the supreme test. Hitler's great army was thrown back from the gates of Moscow, and almost four years later Soviet troops captured Berlin. The reasons for Stalin's victory are essential to any judgment of his career.[8]

Stalin's own later official view was that correct ideology had predicted the war and dictated what measures to take to win it. Stalin had accordingly strengthened the Soviet state, purged it of traitors, built up its heavy industry by necessarily Draconian measures, rushed military production, annexed new territories on the frontiers essential for defense, and so been ready for the war. Then the Red Army under correct leadership fell back in a planned manner so as to blunt and exhaust the treacherous enemy thrust, and so as to give the correctly guided heroic Soviet people opportunity to harass the Germans behind their own lines. At the properly foreseen time, the Red Army skillfully concentrated its forces and made a decisive counterattack before Moscow, smashing the myth of German invincibility and permanently crippling its major offensive capacity. The remaining German offensive strength was destroyed the next year when its far weaker offensive was allowed to extend itself into a trap at Stalingrad, brilliantly closed by the Red Army under Stalin's leadership. After that the end was just a matter of time as Soviet strength inexorably pressed the Germans back to their own borders and to spectacular final defeat at Berlin.

This complex thesis has been attacked from various sources at almost every point. Westerners often claim that Stalin could easily have prevented the war before 1933 by making Hitler's rise to power impossible, and that the war might still have been prevented if Stalin had allied himself to the Western powers instead of to Hitler in 1939. The tangled problem of Soviet production-drives in the 1930's has been examined. The great purges, East and West now agree, weakened the USSR, especially the Red Army, which lost more than 3,400 higher officers. Stalin is now universally described as having blundered catastrophically in not expecting the surprise attack and in not disposing his forces to meet it.

Through 1964 Khrushchëv and some of his generals who

took his hints maintained that the Party did indeed plan and guide victory, but that Stalin had little role in it. Stalin was described as having sat in the Kremlin almost paralyzed during the early months of the war, rousing himself only to impose some new horrific blunder on his protesting subordinates, and was reported to have gone through the motions of planning the later stages of the war idiotically on a globe.[9] (Stalin's globe was almost seven feet in diameter, and would not have been at all bad for planning overall strategy.[10]) Meanwhile his generals and Party men such as, by curious accident, Khrushchëv, planned and executed all basic strategies and victories.[11]

The German generals in defeat have come up with a strikingly different explanation for the loss of the war, which has been adopted fairly widely in the West. The Germans could have won the war, their generals usually say, if certain things had not gone wrong. The most important mistakes, they say, were imposed by Hitler himself on a reluctant and anxious military. First of all, Hitler should never have abandoned his own maxim against fighting a two-front war; he should never have invaded Russia until England had made peace. (This is equivalent to saying that Hitler should never have invaded Russia at all.) This attribution of Russian survival to British strength and tenacity has been very popular in Great Britain and among Anglophiles everywhere. Even so, the German generals argue, they could have won in Russia if Hitler had not made most or all of these four fatal mistakes in the East in 1941:

(1) For the Russian campaign Hitler halved the panzer strength of each infantry army, in order to spread his panzer divisions over the huge front. In fact, this weakened the cutting power of the panzers when they were never needed more. (2) Hitler became furious at the Yugoslavs for throwing his friends in Belgrade out of power on March 27, 1941. He

forthwith invaded and conquered Yugoslavia, Greece, and Crete, at the cost of delaying the whole Russian campaign for a fatal five weeks from May 15 to June 22. (3) After a promising start on the central front in which Field Marshal von Bock's Central Army Group captured 585,000 prisoners (the Russians don't admit so many) and swept to Smolensk, two-thirds of the way to Moscow, by July 16—only the twenty-fifth day of the invasion—Hitler called off the advance until September 30. He ordered the panzer divisions that were driving toward Moscow to turn north and south to help the other German armies, because he was distracted by the prospect of victories at Leningrad and especially in the Ukraine. Hitler conquered the Ukraine, but let slip the precious period in which Moscow was relatively undefended, to resume the attack too late in the year, after the Russians had been given the chance to build up a defense. (4) As panzer General Heinz Guderian remarked, "On Hitler's orders we began to mistreat the Russian population too soon." This caused a stiffening of popular resistance that clogged the supply lines just when they should have been most fluid.

After the chance of victory was lost before Moscow in 1941, Hitler managed to ensure catastrophic German defeat, their generals say, by insisting on holding Stalingrad in 1942 when he should have retreated; by ordering an attack on the central front at Kursk, in July, 1943, that lost much of the remaining German armor, and by ordering a rigid and inflexible defense throughout the long, ghastly retreat, which lost more and more of the army in futile, un-military stands.

Furthermore, the German generals maintain, the Russians had inexhaustible reserves of manpower, so that no matter how many millions were killed or taken prisoner, Stalin could draft more millions from the depths of Eurasia to make up the difference. The Russian soldier, moreover, was a primitive peasant with far less need of food, clothing, and the decencies of life than the German. This enabled him to survive by living off bare country even though Russian roads were few and terrible, and even though the Russian army lacked any coherent system of supply. The primitive Russian was far less sensitive to the famous Russian winter, which came earlier and colder than ever, than the Germans who froze without their issues of winter clothing, while the Russians fought on through the ice. And finally, the Russians had the benefit of infinite supplies of war matériel from America.[12]

At least the Germans agree with Stalin that the campaign of 1941 was decisive, and not the campaign of 1942 for Stalingrad, which is so often spoken of in the West as the turning point of the war. Neither side claims that the Germans never had a chance. If Stalin's version is incredible in its Bolshevik consistency, the German version contains many unbelievable allegations, and many inconsistencies as well.

Stalin disposition of troops was certainly a disaster. He had conquered eastern Poland and the Baltic states in order to have forward positions from which to defend the Soviet heartland in depth. According to announced pre-war strategy, the Germans (whose attack would be expected) were supposed to be bogged down by Soviet resistance in eastern Poland and ground to a halt at the "Stalin Line"—a somewhat loose system of fortifications at the 1939 boundary of the USSR—from which quick, triumphant counter-attacks would be launched. In fact, of course, the Red Army was taken by surprise, and Stalin's forward troops and airplanes in the newly occupied territories were exposed too far forward. Most of the planes were bombed to pieces on the ground; most of the troops were cut through in three weeks. They had to retreat in desperate haste, without much air cover, losing hundreds of thousands of prisoners to the Germans.

Yet the bulk of the Russian frontier armies did manage to

retreat across the Dnieper, which suggests that Hitler's weakening of the panzer divisions that might have surrounded many more Russian divisions was a serious mistake indeed. Hitler's five weeks' delay for the Yugoslav-Greek venture was also serious, for it turned out to mean that the final drive on Moscow was pushed off into the period of autumn rains, which bogged down German transport even before it froze in the snow. Yet these five weeks might have been retrieved if Hitler had not diverted the panzer divisions and other resources of the Central Army Group until the end of September, when Moscow was far better defended, and almost fell nonetheless.

It is far less certain that German atrocities against the Russians mattered much in the 1941 campaign. Russians like to emphasize the role of partisans for patriotic and ideological reasons, and German generals, blaming the cruelties on Hitler, can shift the responsibility for the subsequent military losses from themselves. But it cannot be demonstrated that popular resistance seriously impeded the German advance in 1941, whatever havoc it wreaked later in the war when partisan units were better organized and armed. Russian soldiers stopped surrendering by the hundreds of thousands after October because the panzer divisions were no longer able to surround them, not because their will to fight was stiffened by reports of German atrocities. It is even harder to show that Great Britain's persistence in the war had any effect on the Moscow campaign. Hitler sent all the troops he thought necessary to the Russian front, and calculated correctly that the British would not be able to launch any significant campaign against him while he was preoccupied with the East.

Still, three of Hitler's famous mistakes may well have accounted for the Germans' failure to capture Moscow in the summer and autumn of 1941. Was that the turning point of the war? Would the USSR have surrendered or collapsed if Moscow fell? Moscow was a holy symbol, but symbols are ambiguous. The last two falls of Moscow (which were not especially analogous) had stimulated the Russians to greater resistance. It has been claimed that the topheavy centralized structure of the Communist regime made it unlikely to survive the loss of its bureaucratic heart—and also its largest single industrial center, and the hub of its railway network. In fact, most of the bureaucracy fled to Kuibyshev on the Middle Volga in October; the USSR *did* survive the shift of administration from Moscow. Stalin stayed with the military command in the Kremlin for propaganda reasons, as well as to have his hand on the campaign. During the crucial months many local governments and many industrial enterprises proceeded on the basis of previous orders in a little supervised and decentralized manner, without Moscow.

The theory that the capture of Moscow would have destroyed the super-centralized administration, industry, and transport of the Soviet regime is highly inconsistent with the theory that Russia survived because of its primitive, roadless, supplyless, pre-rational nature. To argue that Hitler lost Moscow by diverting troops and armor to capture the Ukraine is also to admit that if Hitler had *not* diverted the troops and armor, and therefore *had* captured Moscow, he might then not have taken the Ukraine. And the Ukraine was a far greater prize than Moscow for its industrial and agricultural wealth—as Hitler recognized—and just as potent a symbol.

It can be granted that Hitler might have won Moscow if he had decided things differently, but not necessarily the war. The war was presumably decided, as most wars are, by the size and equipment of the armies, and by their morale and leadership. The Red Army never outnumbered the Germans by very much in the early years of the war. The Germans had 160 divisions for the campaign of 1941; the Russians (according to Stalin) had 175 divisions. This means that about five million Russians faced about four million Germans, plus their

Rumanian and Finnish allies. (The Rumanians had planned to invade Russia alongside Germany, but Stalin seems to have brought Finland into the war by bombing Helsinki on the first day of the invasion. Hitler had fooled him into thinking the Finns were attacking also.)

The Germans claim they captured from 2,500,000 to 3,330,000 prisoners in 1941 (the Russians admit far less), and that they must have killed a million and a half men. This would have left Stalin with at most a million men, but he was pouring his reserves, his Far Eastern troops, and new draftees into the front, so that by the end of the battle for Moscow, the Germans claim, he had 2,330,000 men against them. Meanwhile the Germans had lost less than a million men, and had replaced most of them. In short, the Germans and their allies greatly outnumbered the endless hordes of Russia during the crucial battle for Moscow. But the Russians admittedly had slightly more men than the Germans in front of Moscow in December and January, because they moved men from the other fronts to the most active and important one. This implies excellent use of an at least semi-intact transport net, not hordes sloshing through the snow.

The German generals later confessed they had not known how much war matériel the Russians had at the beginning of the war, or how much was being produced. If the Russian soldiers ate little and fought primitively, that would not have mattered. But in fact Russian successes came only in battles in which they were better armed. When the German Central Army Group reached Smolensk on July 16, it was held up east of the city for some weeks by the first relatively successful Russian defense of the war—achieved by a concentration of some scarce airplanes and a superior assemblage of artillery. This constituted a relatively weak defense of Moscow compared to what was to come later. The German Central Army Group could have smashed it, and later did so. But the strength of Russian resistance based on its temporary local advantage in heavy guns was one of the factors that led Hitler to refuse to order an all-out assault on Moscow at a Central Army Group conference on August 4, and definitely to postpone the assault on Moscow by diverting the panzer divisions on August 23.

When the Russians launched their counterattack to save Moscow on December 5, they had not yet concentrated enough men and matériel to equal the Germans in that sector. But by January 1, 1942, they were locally somewhat superior in manpower and decisively superior in tanks and planes, and were therefore able to throw the Germans back from Moscow. This implies considerable production amid the catastrophic dislocations of 1941, and intelligent strategic concentration of resources. Even the Russian peasant soldier needed ammunition for his artillery and gasoline for his tanks and airplanes. The Russian supply system was good enough to meet the supreme test.

Nor was Moscow saved by war matériel from America. Almost none of the eventual eleven billion dollars worth of American Lend-Lease aid to the USSR arrived in time to save Moscow. American assurances of aid may have made Stalin more willing to throw matériel reserves into the struggle for his capital after October. But all told, Lend-Lease came to only 6 per cent of Russian war matériel, most of it coming after Stalingrad. The thesis of Russian primitivity is inconsistent with the theory that Russia was saved by importing huge amounts of American goods along thousands of miles of railway.

The war matériel with which the Red Army saved Moscow and the bulk of the USSR was produced at home. The USSR produced 16,000 airplanes in 1941, 10,000 of them *after* the invasion. The production of munitions almost tripled in the second half of 1941—in spite of all the German victories and the chaotic dislocations involved in removing much Soviet industry eastward out of the Germans' reach. In 1942, when two-thirds of European Russia was occupied, the USSR produce 23,000 tanks (of better quality) to the Germans' 9,300; 25,000 airplanes to the Germans' 14,700; and 34,000 heavy guns to the Germans' 12,000.[13] We now know that German production was to increase steadily till the third quarter of 1944, which indicates a foolish low use of resources before then. The invasion of the USSR seems to have stimulated a diversion of all available economic resources to military production, which made even the Third Five Year Plan with its announced emphasis on military goods seem like a similarly foolish low use of resources.

In short, the Russians outproduced the Germans in the mechanized weapons of war in every year throughout the conflict. The Germans started the invasion with a larger accumulation of heavy weapons, and destroyed much of what the Russians had in the first five months. But the Russians eventually succeeded in maintaining their superior production —often in quality as well as quantity—and in concentrating their armaments (after the first five months) more rapidly and more effectively to achieve local superiorities and win key battles.

Except for the early months of the war, before Stalin abandoned most of his disastrous strategic ideas and removed some of his incompetent friends left over from the Civil War (notably Marshal Semën Budënny, who managed to lose 665,000 prisoners in one big bag in the Ukraine in August, 1941),[14] the Russians were as well led by their generals as the Germans were. After the first few months, the Russian troops displayed as high a morale as the Germans, and steadily greater confidence in victory. Stalin made many costly mistakes even after the first few months, but his over-all strategy thereafter avoided the irreparable disasters that Hitler imposed on his army.

Perhaps the war was a less narrow thing than is normally thought. If Hitler and his generals had made none of the mistakes they did make (which is asking a lot of history), and Stalin had made all of his mistakes, then the Germans *might* have forced Soviet surrender, but that is impossible to feel confident of, much less prove. As it was, the Germans invaded a country that was colossal in size, somewhat superior in military and civilian manpower, potentially much superior in armaments, as good in generalship, greatly superior in top leadership as far as the war was concerned, and possessed of defensive supply lines that had not been war-ravaged. Other things being equal, the stronger power wins the war. The Germans' superior accumulation of armaments at the beginning of the war, their successful surprise (one wonders how far Hitler would have gotten if Stalin had *not* been so unbelievably stupid as to be taken by surprise), and other elements of strategy went a long way toward offsetting the Russians' overall superior strength. These early German advantages made the war seem close in 1941, and even in 1942: but Russia's superior strength was never altogether overcome, and eventually won the war. The outcome was by no means certain, but it was, we can now see, probable.

It is difficult to assess Stalin's personal contribution to victory. We cannot tell if another Soviet leader might have prevented the war. Stalin was not responsible for the size of the USSR, and its manpower in 1941 would have been larger without him. Although his successors hold him responsible for the Red Army's shortages of top quality armaments in June, 1941, it seems probable that no other leader would have built up the war machine of the USSR even that quickly in the preceding thirteen years. The early Five Year Plans may not have been necessary to avoid capitalist attack, but they were very probably necessary to stop Hitler once he did attack. Stalin's purges and controls certainly reduced the effectiveness of the Red Army until the autumn of 1941, and his extraordinary blindness to the impending invasion could hardly have been duplicated by an alternative leader. Stalin's later conduct of the war was quite sufficient, if unnecessarily costly; presumably a number of alternative leaders could have done as well in playing his winning hand. Essentially, one must balance the Five Year Plans against the surprise attack. The latter made defeat a possibility, but the former actually led to victory.

The cost of Stalin's victory was greater than that of any other victory or defeat in history. Stalin was very cagey about his losses; he hinted at something like seven and a half million military and civilian dead. Since the newer Soviet histories of the war and the census of 1959, it has been clear that seven million soldiers died, and that total losses, while incalculable within several millions, were somewhere in the twenty millions. The economic losses were so huge as to be meaningless when estimated in numbers. Two-thirds of European Russia, inhabited formerly by seventy million people, was ruined, and the rest was ground down by the only slightly less ghastly war effort. The psychological damage to the wounded, the bereaved, and the deprived can hardly be told, nor can the end of it.

Yet Westerners generally agree that the result was somehow worth it. It was certainly worth it to the West to have millions of Russians killed to bring victory to Great Britain and America. The Russians destroyed the bulk of the German forces, as no other power, even America, could have done, and they suffered *one hundred times* the number of the American war dead, enabling Americans to enjoy the best fruits of victory. One wonders if it was really worth while for the peoples of the USSR to suffer so frightfully in order to keep Stalin instead of exchanging him for Hitler. Whatever the doubts in moments of loss and despair, it is all but impossible to find a Soviet citizen who will not judge the war losses worthwhile.

Clearly Stalin found them worthwhile. Those who suffered and died, he was sure, did so in the greatest of causes. If the USSR had given up to avoid the losses, the whole Revolution would have had to start all over again, entailing greater losses in its course. The earth was rich, men resilient, women fertile, and Communist leadership all-foreseeing. The losses could be made up soon—in some branches of the economy only five years were needed.

And when Stalin thought in comparative terms, he knew that the USSR had emerged from the war infinitely stronger than before, without a rival in Eurasia, or anywhere save perhaps in distant America. The second of the world wars brought about by capitalist imperialism had finally wrecked capitalism in Europe and Asia. Half of Europe could be won for the World Revolution right away, China and parts of its neighbors in a few more years—and the irresistible march of socialism could never again be stopped. The Soviet peoples were hero peoples, and the Soviet leader was a hero leader, generally acknowledged by the entire world, even by the capitalists. Marx and Lenin and Stalin had proved absolutely and unshakably right and great. Other trials lay before the workers of the world and their leaders, but this Great Patriotic War was surely the decisive turn in world history, perhaps more so than 1917. Out of the greatest evil came the greatest good. Glory to the great name of Stalin!

12. THE END

FOR the sake of his reputation with posterity Stalin, like Roosevelt, should have died at the end of his war. Had he died in 1945 he would probably have lived in history as one of its most stormy, controversial figures. He might have had at least as many admirers and defenders as Peter the Great, whom he recognized as a predecessor. Official patriotic histories would have presented him as a harsh but effective modernizer, defender, and builder of his country. Dissenting historians would have doubted whether so much harshness was necessary even in backward Russia.

But Stalin lived on for more than seven years, and ruled in a manner that reminded many literate Russians of the last "seven mad years" of Tsar Nicholas I, after the revolutions of 1848 scared him into paranoid outbursts of police terror. The enormous respect which Stalin had won from Soviet citizens by winning World War II was dissipated by his renewal, on an apparently permanent basis from 1946 on, of peacetime police terror and totalitarian pressures against the individual, and by his persisting economic austerity in the interests of heavy industry and new armaments even after most physical war damage had been repaired. His high reputation with his former allies was likewise dissipated by his extirpation of the liberties of the East European countries, especially Czechoslovakia, by the Iron Curtain he rang down across the heart of Europe, by the reports of his continued tyranny at home, by his intransigent diplomacy from the Berlin *Autobahn* to the United Nations, by his promotion of subversion in many European and Asian countries, and by his ambiguous movements toward World War III, culminating in his invasion of South Korea in 1950.

What went wrong? Many observers think that advancing age rigidified his ideology, isolated him from the real world, and increased his paranoia. Others suggest that Stalin was only carrying on as he always had, but that after Hitler's death the outside world provided no more mad monsters to coincide with and partly to justify Stalin's mad world-view. Certainly Stalin's ideology ceased to evolve much. No novel situation led him to work out a new policy or outlook that could then be incorporated into his previous ideology, as had happened so many times in the 1920's and 1930's. He cast the United States in the role of chief enemy power, previously played by Great Britain and then Germany. Tito succeeded Trotsky as the master traitor. Stalin repeated in his East European satellites much of what he done in the USSR in the 1930's. He ruled the USSR itself with less fury and more steadiness. This did *not* indicate full-fledged paranoia, which is often characterized by increasingly violent paroxysms with advancing age.

During Stalin's seven last years, and ever since, people have thought that he used the vastly increased strength of the USSR to expand his power over much of Europe and Asia, by direct military force and by Communist subversion directed and supported from the USSR itself. Actually, it can be argued that Stalin lost ground more or less steadily during the post-war period of his rule. He had his greatest and widest influence just at the end of the war, in 1945. At that point the Red Army occupied most of Eastern Europe (including strategic points in Finland) while Communist partisan armies held Yugoslavia, Albania, and most of Greece for him. In the Far East the Red Army was in possession of Manchuria and North Korea. Beyond his immediate military grip, Communist parties under his thumb commanded huge minorities in France and Italy, and smaller but often influential minorities in many other European countries. In most of the victorious Allied countries, the governments and the majority of the non-Communist political parties bore a considerable amount of good will toward Stalin and the USSR for their leading part in the war, and were prepared to co-operate with him on a friendly basis for the reconstruction of the USSR and the rest of Europe, and for the maintenance of peace forever.

In the later 1940's, Stalin consolidated his grip on Poland, East Germany, Czechoslovakia, Hungary, Rumania, Bulgaria, and Albania, all of which he already possessed in 1945. It was this process of Stalinization that people cite as a major gain of Stalin's, forgetting that these areas had been his to dispose of since the Red Army's victory. A major consequence of his superfluous oppressions in these seven countries was the loss of most of his influence in the rest of Europe. Finland, which had been compelled in 1944 to accept Soviet bases and garrisons on its diminished territory, Communists in key government positions such as the Ministry of the Interior, and the jailing of many of its patriotic statesmen as "war criminals," foiled an attempted Communist *Putsch* on the Czechoslovak pattern in June, 1948, dismissed the Communists from the government, and recovered effective internal independence.

Austrian leaders fooled Stalin and Molotov into agreeing to the effective union of all Austria including the Soviet-occupied eastern zone under one non-Communist government. Stalin's foolish pressures on Tito drove Yugoslavia out of the Soviet bloc in June, 1948, and failed to overthrow him in the following years of cold war. The Greek Communist guerrilla army consequently lost the civil war in its country in 1949, and was mopped up before Stalin's death. The great Communist parties of France and Italy lost their posts and their influence in their countries' governments by 1947-48, which led to an enormous decline in the French Party's membership and to some decline in Italy. In other European countries and in the Americas, the Communists lost almost all of their positions and influence. Stalin's apparent aggressiveness in Eastern Europe, France, and Italy, provoked a major re-entry of American military and economic power into the European Continent. This culminated in 1949 in the establishment of the North Atlantic Treaty Organization, by governments of countries from Canada all the way to Turkey that were for the most part genuinely fearful of Stalin's further advance. Stalin's operations had become a self-fulfilling prophecy once again: His measures to secure himself in Eastern Europe against the capitalist West had produced an unprecedented military alliance against him of almost the entire West.

While conceding that Stalin was "stopped" in Europe (a mild word for his great losses), Westerners point to East Asia as the scene of his most enormous post-war gains. Mao Tse-tung's Chinese Communist Party did of course win its civil war against Chiang Kai-shek and establish a regular government in 1949, after which Mao "leaned to one side" in the world struggle, Stalin's side. During Stalin's lifetime, Mao's victory seemed a tremendous triumph for Stalin and the Soviet Party. We can now see that it was the beginning of the end for direct Soviet influence in most of East Asia, and perhaps many more distant countries as well. A direct consequence of the rise of Mao was the Soviet withdrawal from all of Manchuria (save for the naval bases of Port Arthur and Dairen) at the beginning of the renewed civil war in 1946, and the abandonment of northern Sinkiang to Mao in 1949. For Stalin, the chief result of his invasion of South Korea in June, 1950, was the loss of his North Korean satellite to the Chinese that November.

Far more important than geographic and political losses, Stalin witnessed the end of what he regarded as one of his most precious legacies from Lenin: world-wide Communist unity. Tito's open and successful defiance of the USSR after June, 1948, was the first successful open Communist opposition to Stalin, the first successful "national Communist" movement. It drove him to frenzies of impotent hatred and apprehension. On the other hand, every public word of his concerning the new regime in China indicated Bolshevik joy and comradely fellowship. But unlike much of the outside world, Stalin was well aware that he did not give any orders in China. Mao, who did give orders in China, had been a successful quiet rebel against Stalin's orders and Stalin's ideologically based formula for proletarian victory in China, until Stalin himself had swallowed his words and accepted Mao back into the fold in 1935. We can only speculate what forebodings Stalin may have had about the future of Communism under two commands, but we know that in this case any forebodings were fully justified.

In the last year of Stalin's life, his traditional apprehensions and new fears for the future found fitful and ambiguous expression. He rushed work on his atomic armament while reaffirming his ideological view that World War III would result in the decisive world-wide victory of the Revolution, and not in mutual atomic ruin of the combatants. In his last published work, a lengthy pamphlet called *Economic Problems of Socialism in the USSR*, he hinted that the ideological scheme of renewed capitalist attack on the USSR might be modified or postponed for a long while because the capitalists might once again fight among themselves for the spoils of the British and French Empires. In the autumn of 1952 he summoned the first All-Union Congress of the Communist Party of the Soviet Union since 1939, but he treated it contemptuously, never appearing before it, and overshadowing its proceedings with his own statements which were hardly complimentary to much of the Party. Just before his death there were suspicious arrests of doctors and others, accompanied by rumors of a new purge of much or all of the high Party leadership. When last interviewed by a foreigner, the ambassador from India, Stalin was allegedly seen doodling fierce pictures of wolves and heard to mutter, "None of them can be trusted!"

Then the great tyrant died in March, 1953,[1] while the world debated whether there would be any changes in the USSR. It is impossible to quantify such matters, but the continuity between Stalin and his successors is certainly greater than the changes introduced by the latter. But there have been many important changes, and most of them would have been galling to Stalin. Most important, his giant police empire was dismantled, his labor camps largely emptied, and his terrorist methods largely discontinued. His top-heavy emphasis on heavy industry was somewhat reduced, and the Soviet people were granted more consumer goods than ever before in their history. His Iron Curtain was parted a bit, and the cultural life of the USSR was permitted to stir within less narrowly limited bounds. His steely grip on most of Eastern Europe and on most foreign Communist parties was blundered away or deliberately relaxed. His intransigent and in some cases violent cold war with the United States and other Western powers was called off in favor of the less intense form of world conflict called "peaceful coexistence." The two greatest heresies in Stalin's ideology, "polycentrism" (the word coined after his death to denote the genuine independence of foreign Communist parties from the USSR) and "revisionism" (the permanent relaxation of domestic political control and foreign revolutionary conflict) were both encouraged to some extent by Stalin's successors, and both flourished beyond their control all around the world.

This destruction of much of what was specifically Stalinist in the Communist movement and ideology, as well as the abandonment of some of Lenin's legacy, was of course climaxed by Khrushchëv's violent repudiation of Stalin's person and his post-1934 activities—Stalin's second death. It is very doubtful if this last would have taken place had Stalin died at the end of the war. The ultimate victim of the blunders of Stalin's last seven years was Stalin himself.

It has been the major thesis of this work that Stalin really was the effective ruler of his Russia and that most of what happened there happened because he wanted it to happen. When his will was not enforced it was because of his own false outlook and blunders, the dead weight of the human material over which he ruled, and the opposition of foreign powers—not because any colleagues, groups, or classes within the USSR, or any inexorable social processes beyond his control, forced his hand. The author has attempted to approach each problem by examining Stalin's views and hopes, tracing what actually happened, and noting the unusually frequent conformity between the two.

It has also been maintained throughout this work that Stalin operated ideologically, that he saw everything important in ideological terms, that he acted chiefly in accordance with his ideology, and that he frequently did things that were irrational and inexplicable save by reference to his ideology.

By Stalin's ideology, it should be repeated, the author has meant not only the Marxist-Leninist doctrines and sentiments that Stalin inherited, but all the new doctrines that he worked out and new sentiments that he adopted in the course of the crises of the first twenty years of his rule. These he systematically incorporated into the structure of his previous world-view, to serve as precedents for all future judgments and actions of the same category.

Stalin's ideology, the author has attempted to show, had the structure of a paranoiac delusion—systematized megalomania and belief in plots and persecutions, motivating violence. The extremity of the violence that Stalin resorted to on ideological grounds, it has been suggested here, indicates but cannot prove that Stalin was indeed suffering from a form of thoroughgoing paranoia, which drove him on to do the dreadful things he did in his mature years, quite independent of any supplementary pressures from political or international events.

Finally, it has been the purpose of this work to show that Stalin, during the really significant central period of his rule from 1928 to 1945, was remarkably effective in spite of many dysfunctional policies and sheer blunders. He built a huge industrial and military machine rather rapidly in a rich but only semi-developed country, to the point at which he could fight and win the greatest war in history. He transformed the USSR into one of the two super-powers of the world. In the course of raising his country to such a pinnacle of power and influence, Stalin demonstrated that his totalitarian socialist system of government and economic growth could not only survive, but could "work," in terms of the problems that seemed to be pressing, with dramatic success. This success has made some variation of his dictatorial, coercive methods of industrialization an attractive option for many influential people in many countries of the world. The power Stalin built in the USSR and the methods he broadcast within the USSR and beyond it will be extraordinarily important features of the world for the foreseeable future.

This historical reconsideration of Stalin's Russia may at times have seemed to be a partial justification of Stalin's career, in the eyes of some readers. The author has tried to avoid the political and moral tendentiousness of much existing work on Stalin. He has tried to explain how the monstrous things that Stalin did can usually be traced back to Stalin's highly moral and idealistic world-view, many elements of which were shared by millions of good and harmless radicals and protesters against injustice throughout the world. Nor has the author tried to minimize the fact that it was Stalin's Russia, not Great Britain or the United States, that was primarily responsible for the stopping and the overthrow of Hitler, a feat which most of Stalin's critics were once willing to approve, and of which they still enjoy the benefits. Stalin *was* probably the most *important* man who ever lived.

Explanation, however, is far from approval, and importance is not always beneficence. Stalin did well to become a revolutionary and seek effective means to alleviate the injustices of the world in which he grew up. And he could not help becoming a paranoiac. But though his will was good, though he did many good things and destroyed much evil, Stalin *was*, on balance, one of the two or three worst men who ever lived. It now seems far more probable than it did toward the end of his life that the world will survive Stalin and his system. The day may come when his system will even collapse in his homeland. But grave dangers persist. Where there is no vision, the people perish. If men have a care for their future, they would do well to consider and reconsider over and over again the astonishing and fateful history of Stalin's Russia.

NOTES

Chapter 1

1. Harry Schwartz, *The New York Times*, March 19, 1955, p. 6.
2. Merle Fainsod, *How Russia is Ruled* (Cambridge: Harvard University Press, 1953).
3. Leonard Schapiro, *The Communist Party of the Soviet Union* (New York: Random House, 1960).
4. This view of Stalin is particularly strongly expressed in Alexander Magid, "Did Stalin Rule?," *British Columbia Historical Review*, Vol. IX, No. 2 (May, 1963), pp. 168-181.
5. Chernov phrased this view strikingly in his article, "Uchast' Stalina" ("Stalin's Destiny"), *Finskii Vestnik*, May 1, 1938, p. 4.
6. The records of the Smolensk provincial government have been very thoroughly examined in Merle Fainsod, *Smolensk under Soviet Rule* (Cambridge: Harvard University Press, 1958).
7. The culmination of these studies was Abram Bergson, *The Real National Income of Soviet Russia Since 1928* (Cambridge: Harvard University Press, 1961).
8. Trotsky's final and most thorough work on Stalin, on which he was working when he was murdered by one of Stalin's agents (his blood dripped over some of the pages), was published in English as Leon Trotsky, *Stalin, an Appraisal of the Man and his Influence* (New York: Harper & Brothers, 1941).

9. Khrushchëv's "secret speech" at the Twentieth Congress of the Communist Party of the Soviet Union in 1956 is best analyzed in editions by Bertram D. Wolfe, *Khrushchëv and Stalin's Ghost* (New York: Frederick A. Praeger, 1957), and Boris Nicolaevsky, "The Crimes of the Stalin Era," *The New Leader*, July 16, 1956, Section Two.

CHAPTER 2

See J. V. Stalin, *Sochineniia* (Collected Works), Moscow: State Publishing House, 1946-48; Bertram Wolfe, *Three Who Made a Revolution*, New York: Dial Press, 1948; Boris Souvarine, *Stalin: a Critical Survey of Bolshevism*, New York: Alliance Book Corp., 1939; Isaac Deutscher, *Stalin, a Political Biography*, New York: Oxford University Press, 1949.

1. Geoffrey Gorer and John Rickman, *The People of Great Russia, a Psychological Study*, (New York: Chanticleer Press, 1950), especially Appendices I and II.
2. Margaret Mead, *Soviet Attitudes toward Authority* (New York: McGraw Hill Book Co., 1951).
3. An example of heavy Communist jocularity on the subject can be found in *Pravda*, June 11, 1952, p. 2.
4. Karl Wittfogel, *Oriental Despotism, a Comparative Study of Total Power* (New Haven: Yale University Press, 1957), Chapter 9.
5. Emil Ludwig, *Stalin* (New York: G. P. Putnam's Sons, 1942), p. 26.
6. Quoted in Bertram D. Wolfe, *Three Who Made a Revolution* (Boston: Beacon Press, 1955), p. 453.
7. J. V. Stalin, *Sochineniia* (Collected Works), (Moscow: State Publishing House, 1946-48), Vol. VI, p. 54. This and all further quotations have been translated by the present writer.
8. *Ibid.*, Vol. II.
9. The best account of this extraordinary episode is in Wolfe, *op. cit.*, pp. 535-57.
10. Milovan Djilas, *Conversations with Stalin* (New York: Frederick A. Praeger, 1962).

CHAPTER 3

See J. V. Stalin, *Sochineniia* (Collected Works), Moscow: State Publishing House, 1946-48; Edward Hallett Carr, *The Bolshevik Revolution, 1917-29*, New York: Macmillan Co. (Six volumes have appeared since 1950); William Henry Chamberlin, *The Russian Revolution*, New York: Macmillan, 1935, two volumes; Leonard Schapiro, *The Communist Party of the Soviet Union*, New York: Random House, 1960; Boris Souvarine, *Stalin: a Critical Survey of*

Bolshevism, New York: Alliance Book Corp., 1939; Isaac Deutscher, *Stalin, a Political Biography,* New York: Oxford University Press, 1949; also Deutscher, *The Prophet Armed,* New York: Oxford University Press, 1954; and Deutscher, *The Prophet Unarmed,* New York: Oxford University Press, 1959.

1. The most thorough account and analysis of the decisive phase of the struggle between Stalin and Trotsky is to be found in the middle chapters of Isaac Deutscher, *The Prophet Unarmed* (New York: Oxford University Press, 1957).
2. This "breaking" of mirrors in the presence of corpses was continued at the lyings-in-state of various important persons throughout Stalin's reign. It was practiced, apparently for the last time, at his own obsequies. Mirrors were often "broken" before pictures of the dead man displayed during the mourning period. The photograph of Stalin in the reception room of the Soviet Mission to the United Nations in New York was protected, when Stalin died, by "breaking" all the mirrors in the room. Stalin may have believed in this superstition, in a region of his mind. If so, it was the only superstition we know of from which his Marxist-Leninist ideology did not free him.
3. *Pravda,* January 30, 1924, pp. 1-2.
4. Stalin, *Sochineniia,* Vol. VI, p. 46.
5. *Loc. cit.*
6. *Loc. cit.*
7. *Ibid.,* p. 47.
8. *Loc. cit.*
9. *Ibid.,* p. 48.
10. *Loc. cit.*
11. *Ibid.,* p. 49.
12. *Loc. cit.*
13. *Ibid.,* p. 50.
14. *Ibid.,* p. 51.
15. Stalin, *Sochineniia,* Vol. VII. The authorized translation into English is *Problems of Leninism* (Moscow: Foreign Languages Publishing House, 1945).

CHAPTER 4

1. *Finskii Vestnik,* December 17, 1928, p. 10. *Finskii Vestnik* was a journal edited and published by Russian revolutionaries in Helsinki from 1891 to 1944, save in periods of police suppression and war chaos. Originally *narodnik,* its shifting editorial staff veered toward Bolshevism in the crisis of 1917. Throughout the 1920's, its line could have been described as "fellow-traveling." After 1930 its editors became increasingly critical of Stalin's regime, although they did

not break with it formally until the USSR attacked Finland in 1939. On an unspecified date in early December, 1928, an unnamed correspondent for *Finskii Vestnik* secured a long and rather fruitful interview with Stalin, which is not widely known in the English speaking world. It is translated from the Russian by the present writer.

2. *Loc. cit.*
3. *Ibid.*, pp. 10-11.
4. *Ibid.*, p. 11.
5. Many of these scientific opinion of Stalin's were expressed to the correspondent of *Finskii Vestnik*, and published on December 17, 1928, pp. 16-25. The opinions about the Bohr atom, the Heisenberg uncertainty principles, and some other atomic matters are taken from a shorter, more indirect, and less fruitful interview with Stalin published by *Finskii Vestnik* on December 16, 1938, pp. 1-14.
6. *Pravda*, February 14, 1949, p. 3.
7. *Finskii Vestnik*, December 17, 1928, pp. 21-24.
8. E.g., Stalin, *Sochineniia*, Vol. VII, p. 121.
9. *Finskii Vestnik*, December 17, 1928, pp. 16-17.
10. These experiments and this strain of Communist ideology are excellently illustrated in the version of the twenty-minute film, *A Day at the Moscow Zoo*, that was released in 1950. The contrast to Walt Disney's roughly contemporary, grim, bloody, Darwinian *African Lion* could hardly be sharper or more illuminating.
11. *Pravda*, September 11, 1948, p. 1.
12. All of these names were mentioned to the correspondent of *Finskii Vestnik*, December 17, 1928, pp. 36-39.
13. *Ibid.*, December 16, 1938, p. 6.
14. *Ibid.*, December 17, 1928, p. 29.
15. E.g., *ibid.*, p. 14.
16. *Ibid.*, p. 42.
17. E.g., *Pravda*, May 1, 1946, p. 1.
18. *Finskii Vestnik*, December 17, 1928, pp. 27-28.
19. See *loc. cit.* for many of these sentiments.
20. *Ibid.*, pp. 29-30.
21. For many years in the 1930's and 1940's a mother of five might receive a Medal of Soviet Motherhood, while a mother of ten might receive a Medal of Heroic Soviet Motherhood. Both might bear the title, Heroine Mother.
22. Djilas, *Conversations with Stalin*, pp. 180-81.
23. Stalin, *Sochineniia*, Vol. VII, pp. 199-200.
24. *Finskii Vestnik*, December 17, 1928, pp. 33-34.
25. *Ibid.*, pp. 6-8.
26. *Ibid.*, pp. 42-45.

27. *Ibid.*, p. 4.
28. *Ibid.*, p. 7.
29. *Ibid.*, pp. 8-9.
30. For the following discussion of Stalin's views of the ideal future, the author draws much material and analysis from Geroid Tanquary Robinson, "Stalin's Vision of Utopia; the Future Communist Society," *Proceedings of the American Philosophical Society*, Vol. 99, No. 1 (January 27, 1955), pp. 11-21.
31. A controversy raged in the early 1950's as to the correct translation of the Russian word *okruzhenie*. It was usually translated as "encirclement" in such phrases as "the capitalist encirclement of the USSR," and this was certainly the correct translation of the word in its diplomatic context. On the other hand, "surroundings" or "environment" seems a far better translation for sentences such as, "The individual will be brought up in a socialist *okruzhenie*." The dispute concerned the meaning of the word in such phrases as were quoted in the text. If *okruzhenie* meant "encirclement," Stalin's demands were perhaps modest; he might have wanted only the end of hostile alliances against the USSR. But if *okruzhenie* meant "environment," Stalin was striving for the annihilation of the capitalist powers themselves. The author believes the latter was the case.
32. *Finskii Vestnik*, December 17, 1928, p. 35.
33. In the late 1940's a Russian scientist named Alexander Bargomolets claimed that Soviet science might soon find a way to extend the average man's life to 150 years. This was hailed by Stalin as only the first step.
34. *Ibid.*, p. 41. Stalin quoted without acknowledgment one of Trotsky's more famous epigrams.

Chapter 5

See Julian Towster, *Political Power in the USSR*, New York: Oxford University Press, 1948; Merle Fainsod, *How Russia is Ruled*, Cambridge: Harvard University Press, 1953; Leonard Schapiro, *The Communist Party of the Soviet Union*, New York: Random House, 1960; Barrington Moore, *Soviet Politics—the Dilemma of Power*, Cambridge: Harvard University Press, 1950; Walt Whitman Rostow, *The Dynamics of Soviet Society*, New York: W. W. Norton, 1952; Harold J. Berman, *Justice in Russia*, Cambridge: Harvard University Press, 1950; John N. Hazard, *Law and Change in the USSR*, London: Stevens, Ltd., 1953; Alex Inkeles, *Public Opinion in the USSR: a Study in Mass Persuasion*, Cambridge: Harvard University Press, 1950; Rudolf Schlesinger, *Changing Attitudes in the Soviet Union: the Family*, London: Routledge and Kegan Paul, 1949; George S. Counts and Nucia Lodge, *The Country of the Blind*, Boston: Houghton Mifflin Co., 1949; George S. Counts, *The Challenge of Soviet Education*, New York: Macmillan Co., 1957.

1. *Pravda*, December 2, 1936, p. 1.
2. *Loc. cit.*
3. Membership figures are taken from Merle Fainsod, *How Russia is Ruled*, Table 2, p. 249.
4. *Finskii Vestnik*, December 17, 1928, p. 39.
5. Membership figures and estimates of the proportions of the various social classes, nationalities, and sexes in the Party are taken from Fainsod, *op. cit.*, Chapter 8.
6. When asked the number of apparatus men by the correspondent of *Finskii Vestnik* in December, 1938, Stalin merely replied that it was quality, not quantity, that mattered.
7. See Leonard Schapiro, *The Communist Party of the Soviet Union*, pp. 547-590.
8. Related to the author by the historian concerned, Sidney Monas of the University of Rochester.
9. *Pravda*, March 1, 1956, p. 1.
10. *Loc. cit.*
11. *Bol'shaia Sovetskaia Entsiklopediia* (Great Soviet Encyclopedia), article on *Shkoly* (Schools).
12. *Pravda*, August 20, 1940, p. 4.
13. All older school children in reasonable physical condition were compelled to practice parachute jumping, even though deaths mounted into thousands.
14. *Neue Züricher Zeitung*, April 17, 1956, p. 6.

Chapter 6

See Julian Towster, *Political Power in the USSR*, New York: Oxford University Press, 1948; Merle Fainsod, *How Russia is Ruled*, Cambridge: Harvard University Press, 1953; Leonard Schapiro, *The Communist Party of the Soviet Union*, New York: Random House, 1960; Barrington Moore, *Terror and Progress—USSR*, Cambridge: Harvard University Press, 1954; Walt Whitman Rostow, *The Dynamics of Soviet Society*, New York: W. W. Norton, 1952; D. Fedotoff-White, *The Growth of the Red Army*, Princeton: Princeton University Press, 1944; Raymond J. Garthoff, *Soviet Military Doctrine*, New York: The Free Press, 1953; B. H. Liddell Hart, ed., *The Red Army*, New York: Harcourt, Brace, 1956; Zbigniew K. Brzezinski, *The Permanent Purge*, Cambridge: Harvard University Press, 1956; David J. Dallin and Boris I. Nicolaevsky, *Forced Labor in Soviet Russia*, New Haven: Yale University Press, 1947; F. Beck and W. Godin, *Russian Purge and Extraction of Confession*, New York: Viking Press, 1951; Nathan Leites and Elsa Bernaut, *Ritual of Liquidation: the Case of the Moscow Trials*, New York: The Free Press, 1954; Simon Wolin and Robert M. Slusser, eds., *The Soviet Secret Police*, New York: Frederick A. Praeger, 1957.

NOTES TO CHAPTER 7   301

1. Louis Fischer, *The Life and Death of Stalin* (New York: Harper & Brothers, 1952), p. 154.
2. *The London Observer*, September 26, 1954, p. 2.
3. *Pravda*, October 29, 1961, p. 1.
4. Fainsod, *How Russia is Ruled*, p. 414.
5. When Malenkov was asked about the fate of Poskrebyshev by a French Socialist senator in 1954, he pretended not to recognize the name (*Le Monde*, July 25, 1954, p. 4).
6. The correspondent of *Finskii Vestnik* asked Stalin what he thought of these reactions by foreign leftists. Stalin replied that no such reactions had come to his attention, and that anyone who minded acknowledgment of his mistakes more than a prison term was a fool who was fully welcome to a prison term. (December 17, 1928, p. 18.)
7. But San Marino was not really a Communist regime. In spite of San Marino's nominal independence its Communist rulers would have been kept from murdering masses of their people by the Italian police, just as would the leaders of any other Communist municipal government in Italy.
8. Fainsod, *op. cit.*, p. 435.
9. *Pravda*, August 4, 1956, p. 2.
10. Zbigniew Brzezinski, *The Permanent Purge*, Cambridge: Harvard University Press, 1956, pp. 65-115.
11. Vladimir Zenzinov, *Les stalinistes* (Paris: Groubowski Frères, 1939), p. 76-81.

Chapter 7

See George B. Cressey, *The Basis of Soviet Strength*, New York: McGraw-Hill, 1945; Theodore Shabad, *The Geography of the USSR*, New York: Frederick A. Praeger, 1958; Maurice Dobb, *Soviet Economic Development Since 1917*, London: Routledge and Kegan Paul, 1948; Alexander Baykov, *The Development of the Soviet Economic System*, Cambridge: Harvard University Press, 1946; Harry Schwartz, *Russia's Soviet Economy*, New York: Prentice-Hall, 1954; Naum Jasny, *The Socialized Agriculture of the USSR*, Stanford: Stanford University Press, 1949; Lazar Volin, *A Survey of Soviet Russian Agriculture*, Washington: U.S. Government Printing Office, 1951; G. Bienstock, S. M. Schwarz, and A. Yugow, *Management in Soviet Industry and Agriculture*, New York: Oxford University Press, 1944; Alexander Erlich, *The Soviet Industrialization Debate, 1924-1928*, Cambridge: Harvard University Press, 1960.

1. This and other ideas of Stalin's about the peasantry, summarized in the next few paragraphs, were clearly expressed in *Finskii Vestnik*, December 17, 1928, pp. 11-13.

2. Potatoes and other root crops reproduce by budding, not by sexual fertilization. Russians and other Christians of Europe consequently accused the potato of hermaphroditism and masturbation, sometimes burned potatoes at the stake after formal trials, and often resisted growing them. Stalin thought this was typical of Christianity and the peasants and he was much amused, e.g., in *Finskii Vestnik*, December 17, 1928, p. 13.

3. According to this distinction between "left" and "right" Stalin usually pursued left strategies when they did not seem too risky, and was at heart a leftist. But Communists had drawn a different distinction between "left" and "right" from 1917 to 1921. In those years "leftist" was the label applied to a Party member who wished to push on immediately to free, egalitarian, collectivist, democratic institutions, while a "rightist" prudently recommended coercive controls, differential rewards in the interest of production, a compromise with private property such as the N.E.P., one man rule in factories, etc. In this usage of the terms, Stalin was generally a rightist.

4. Bukharin thus teased and outraged the Party by quoting "enrich yourselves" from the French Prime Minister before the Revolution of 1848, F. P. G. Guizot, whose dictum and regime had been belabored by Marx for their bourgeois crassness.

5. Bukharin's contributions to this great debate have been analyzed in Alexander Erlich, *The Soviet Industrialization Debate, 1924-1928* (Cambridge: Harvard University Press, 1960), Chapters I and IV.

6. Cf. Erlich, *op. cit.*, Chapter II. The name "Preobrazhensky" means, ironically, "Transfigurational."

7. Like Bukharin, Preobrazhensky outraged much Party opinion by thus playing with Marx's terms. Some of Preobrazhensky's ideas were similar to those of the French physiocrats of the eighteenth century, who also lived in a society in which it was tempting to think of squeezing the peasants to build up manufactures.

8. The remarkable but ultimately disappointing experiences of the Soviet communes were discussed thoroughly for the first time in Robert G. Wesson, *Soviet Communes* (New Brunswick: Rutgers University Press, 1963).

9. Erlich, *op. cit.*, p. 91. Erlich finds that Stalin's contributions to this great debate displayed considerable mental shoddiness.

10. Schapiro, *op. cit.*, pp. 361 ff.

11. As late as December, 1928, Stalin praised the state farm in a way that suggested he hoped to extend it over most of the USSR —at an unspecified rate, but without transitional steps through other institutions.

12. These losses of animals were finally confirmed by the regime

itself after Stalin's death, in Khrushchëv's first sensational speech against Stalin's policies in September, 1953.

13. Winston Churchill, *The Second World War* (Boston: Houghton Mifflin Co., 1950), Vol. IV, p. 315.

14. This consolidation, carried out under Khrushchëv's direction, and apparently with some enthusiasm on his part, was announced as part of a "second socialist revolution in agriculture." The most dramatic feature of this revolution was supposed to be the construction of *agrogorody* (cities in the fields) to house the populations of the new consolidated collectives. Peasants, however, resisted the planned concomitant loss of their garden plots, and Stalin proved unwilling to allocate the resources to build the necessary new housing in the *agrogorody* for over half the Soviet population.

CHAPTER 8

See George B. Cressey, *The Basis of Soviet Strength*, New York: McGraw-Hill, 1945; Theodore Shabad, *The Geography of the USSR*, New York: Frederick A. Praeger, 1958; Maurice Dobb, *Soviet Economic Development Since 1917*, London: Routledge and Kegan Paul, 1948; Alexander Baykov, *The Development of the Soviet Economic System*, Cambridge: Harvard University Press, 1946; Harry Schwartz, *Russia's Soviet Economy*, New York: Prentice-Hall, 1954; Abram Bergson, *The Real National Income of Soviet Russia Since 1928*, Cambridge: Harvard University Press, 1961; Warren Nutter, *The Growth of Industrial Production in the Soviet Union*, Princeton: Princeton University Press, 1962; Alec Nove, *The Soviet Economy: an Introduction*, New York: Frederick A. Praeger, 1961; Solomon M. Schwarz, *Labor in the Soviet Union*, New York: Frederick A. Praeger, 1952; Isaac Deutscher, *Soviet Trade Unions: Their Place in Soviet Labor Policy*, London: Royal Institute of International Affairs, 1950; Timothy Sosnovy, *Housing in the Soviet Union*, New York: Frederick A. Praeger, 1958; Franklyn D. Holzman, *Soviet Taxation*, Cambridge: Harvard University Press, 1955.

1. George B. Cressey, *The Basis of Soviet Strength* (New York: McGraw-Hill Book Co., 1945), p. 242.

2. Both Adam Smith and Marx had, in fact, discussed the problem of economic development at some length. Part of the recent effort to revive the intellectual respectability of Marx as an economist (e.g., by Joan Robinson of the University of London) is based on the belief that Marx was seriously concerned with the development of an industrial system, and not simply in the workings of one that had already been constructed.

3. In fact, Marx had written, but had not published, some papers attempting to apply mathematics to economic theory. In the 1920's these manuscripts belonged to the German Socialist Party. In 1933

the German Socialists had to take their archives abroad to keep them out of Hitler's hands. Some of the more scholarly material, including Marx's mathematical manuscripts, was offered for sale to the Soviet government, but Stalin was stingy about spending foreign exchange and he did not want to relieve the financial embarrassment of the hated German Socialists. These manuscripts, still unpublished, are now chiefly at the International Institute for Social History (German Section) in Amsterdam.

4. Material on Kondratiev's suggestions was kindly made available to the author by Leon Smolinski of Boston College.

5. Robert W. Campbell, "The Mechanization of Accounting in the Soviet Union," *American Slavic and East European Review*, Vol. XVII, No. 1 (February, 1958), pp. 59-80.

6. *Pravda*, September 10, 1956, p. 2.

7. Warren Nutter, *The Growth of Industrial Production in the Soviet Union* (Princeton: Princeton University Press, 1962).

8. In the years before World War I, investment in the Russian Empire sometimes reached the crucial figure of 12 per cent of gross national product, at which it becomes much easier for a nation to enter upon a period of self-sustaining industrial growth.

9. Japan never received any great amount of foreign investment in its industry during the crucial period of its growth before World War I. Communists attribute much of Japanese growth to the imperialist exploitation of its colonies. A more intractable problem for Communist analysis is Mexico, where the decisive industrial advance of the 1940's took place without major foreign investment, without an empire, and without coercive socialism.

10. Except possibly Cuba.

11. Except Ireland.

12. Paul H. Avrich, "The Bolshevik Revolution and Workers Control in Russian Industry," *Slavic Review*, Vol. XXII, No. 1 (March, 1963), pp. 47-63.

13. Henry W. Morton, *Soviet Sport* (New York: Collier Books, 1963), especially Chapters 4 and 6.

14. Edward Crankshaw, *Russia Without Stalin* (New York: Viking Press, 1956), Chapters 5 and 6.

15. *Pravda*, May 30, 1931, p. 1.

16. *Pravda*, August 12, 1954, p. 3.

17. This was the basic thesis of Trotsky's *The Revolution Betrayed* (London: Routledge and Kegan Paul, 1937).

18. Milovan Djilas, *The New Class* (New York: Frederick A. Praeger, 1957).

19. Karl Wittfogel, *Oriental Despotism: A Comparative Study of Total Power* (New Haven: Yale University Press, 1957).
20. Crankshaw, *op. cit.*, Chapters 5 and 6.
21. *Pravda*, December 27, 1953, p. 1.
22. A fully employed American factory worker may well make $6,500 a year after taxes. Very few American factory managers make as much as $110,000 a year after taxes.

CHAPTER 9

See Richard Pipes, *The Formation of the Soviet Union: Communism and Nationalism*, Cambridge: Harvard University Press, 1948; Walter Kolarz, *Russia and Her Colonies*, London: George Philip & Son, 1952; Frederick C. Barghoorn, *Soviet Russian Nationalism*, New York: Oxford University Press, 1956; Basil Dmytryshyn, *Moscow and the Ukraine, 1918-1953*, New York: Bookman Associates, 1956; Clarence A. Manning, *The Ukraine under the Soviets*, New York: Bookman Associates, 1953; Solomon M. Schwarz, *The Jews in the Soviet Union*, Syracuse: Syracuse University Press, 1951; Salo Baron, *The Jews of Russia and the Soviet Union*, New York: Columbia University Press, 1964; Alexander Park, *Bolshevism in Turkestan, 1917-1927*, New York: Columbia University Press, 1957; Charles Warren Hostler, *Turkism and the Soviets*, New York: Frederick A. Praeger, 1957; Serge Zenkovsky, *Pan-Turkism and Islam in Russia*, Cambridge: Harvard University Press, 1960.

1. J. V. Stalin, *Marksizm i voprosy iazykoznaniia* (Marxism and Questions of Linguistics) (Moscow: State Publishing House, 1950).
2. *Pravda*, January 16, 1949, p. 1.
3. Some confusion has been generated by Stalin's use of the words "nation" and "nationalism," and by a few of his later statements. He normally used "nation" and "people" to mean groups (and their states, if any) such as the French, the Ukrainians, and the Yakuts, who met his definition in detail. Their "nationalism" might be progressive or reactionary, depending on the historical situation. The USSR, according to such usages, was a union of "nations" or (more often) "peoples." The USSR was sometimes itself referred to as a "nation," usually in a diplomatic context, e.g., as a member of the United Nations. Far more often, the USSR was referred to as the "fatherland," or more neutrally as a "country" *(stran)*. Sentiment in favor of the USSR by its citizens was usually termed "patriotism," and only rarely "nationalism." But the phrase "Soviet people" was used at least as often as "peoples of the USSR" to indicate the fusion of the various nationalities into one unified whole—without implying that they had given up or should give up their languages or other permissible separate traits. A few late statements of Stalin's suggested that in the ideal future *all* national differences in the USSR and

even in the world at large might disappear. Possibly Stalin looked on his nationalities compromise as fitted only for the present stage of history. But this was contrary to the great bulk of his discourse on the subject, which implied by its use of words rather than by explicit statement that there would always be separate nationalities: slogans of the type, "The friendship of the Great Russian and the Georgian peoples will last forever."

4. "More than 175" was the official phrase, for 175 nationalities had legal standing by 1941. A few really minute sub-groups were listed as possessing their own languages, and were in fact encouraged to preserve them, even while they were allotted to a related or neighboring language-group for legal and practical purposes. After the deportation of six nationalities during World War II, the official phrase was sometimes amended to "more than 169," but not usually.

5. The necessity for Russians living in Yakut areas (say) to learn Yakut in the schools, for detribalized Yakuts to learn Yakut all over again, and for all Yakuts to learn the dialect of Yakut chosen by the regime's linguistics experts, made Yakut (and the other minor languages) unpopular with many groups as it never had been when it was a despised and persecuted language. The consequent reaction toward Great Russian was perhaps anticipated and welcomed by Stalin.

6. Walter Kolarz, *Russia and Her Colonies* (London: George Philip and Son, 1952), Chapters III and VII.

7. Trotsky, however, was in no sense a believer in national Communism. Since he was a Jew from the Ukraine, he had little sympathy for any Ukrainian nationalist movement.

8. This slogan was not only politically disruptive, in Stalin's estimation, but also ideologically insulting. The phrase had clearly been taken from Bismarck's anti-Catholic war cry of the 1870's, "Away from Rome!" Stalin always took comparisons between Communism and Roman Catholicism badly.

9. The Soviet regime has never admitted such a figure. As with most figures for mass deaths under Stalin, the number can only be estimated by studying the next census, in this case the census of 1939.

10. Bandera survived Stalin but was murdered in Munich by a Soviet agent sent by Khrushchëv, and armed with a science-fiction-like poison gas fountain pen.

11. Even after World War II, popular anti-Semitism and anti-Semitism on the part of petty government officials has been strongest in the Ukraine.

12. During the power struggle of the 1920's, Stalin was upbraided for the anti-Semitism of some of his phrases, including these. His

response was to deny that there was any anti-Semitic content to these forms of popular speech, when used by true Bolsheviks. *Cf.* the disputes over the morality of saying, "a nigger in the woodpile," etc., in America at the present time.

13. A Soviet diplomat explained to the author—with every evidence of sincerity—that the word "anti-Semitism" means in Russian only the killing, beating, jailing, and ghettoization of Jews, not the milder forms of public and private discrimination and contempt that the word now includes in English. Therefore, he insisted, there is no anti-Semitism in the USSR. He was probably right about most current usage of the word, but he forgot, or never knew, that in Lenin's lifetime the Party had higher standards of conduct toward Jews.

14. E.g., *Finskii Vestnik*, December 17, 1928, pp. 38-39.

15. The rationale for this selectivity was simple: Jews, because of their cosmopolitanism, would be least willing to praise Hitler, and therefore they should be given the most practice to overcome this disability of their parental environment.

16. These figures are taken from Gerald Reitlinger, *The Final Solution* (New York: Perpetua Books, 1961), Chapters 8 and 9, and Appendix I. Reitlinger's authoritative researches have led him to deflate, sometimes drastically, the death figures which in some cases have passed into proverb. For the total number of Jews killed by Hitler, Reitlinger suggests a figure between 4.2 and 4.6 million, preferring the lower range—not the conventional six million. Far higher estimates of the number of Soviet Jews killed are found in Solomon Schwarz, *The Jews of the Soviet Union* (Syracuse: Syracuse University Press, 1951). Schwarz's figures are normally quoted by specialists in Russian affairs, and by serious journalists. In the author's opinion, Reitlinger's reduction of the figures presented by Schwarz and others is convincing.

17. The buildup of the Karaganda Coal Basin during the early Five Year Plans, the evacuation of war industry and war refugees to Kazakhstan, the post-war progress of industry, and Khrushchëv's virgin lands program, have all led millions of European Russians to migrate to Kazakhstan, swamping the Turkish population.

CHAPTER 10

See Gleb Struve, *Soviet Russian Literature, 1917-1950*, Norman: University of Oklahoma Press, 1951; Marc Slonim, *Modern Russian Literature from Chekhov to the Present*, New York: Oxford University Press, 1953; B. V. Varneke, *History of the Soviet Theatre*, New York: Macmillan Co., 1951; Jay Leyda, *Kino: A History of the Russian and Soviet Film*, New York: Macmillan Co., 1960; Walter Kolarz, *Religion in the Soviet Union*, New York: Macmillan Co., 1961.

1. *Finskii Vestnik*, December 17, 1928, pp. 17-18.
2. *Ibid.*, pp. 24-25.
3. *Ibid.*, December 16, 1938, pp. 15-16.
4. *Ibid.*, December 17, 1928, pp. 23-24.
5. *Ibid.*, December 16, 1938, p. 16.
6. The religious, Slavophile components of the works of these writers and artists were played down by the Communists. Of the major cultural figures of the nineteenth century, only Chernyshevsky and Nekrasov impressed Stalin as having been as fully revolutionary as one well could be without the light of Marx and Lenin.
7. An illuminating discussion of this point occurs in Maurice Friedberg, "Socialist Realism Twenty-Five Years Afterwards," *American Slavic and East European Review*, Vol. XVIII, No. 2 (April, 1959), pp. 257-68.
8. Alexander Gerasimov, *Stalin and Voroshilov on the Kremlin Wall*, 1938. This painting was displayed for the rest of Stalin's reign in a place of honor in the State Tret'iakov Gallery of Russian Art in Moscow. Gerasimov became the equivalent of a court painter for Stalin. After the Twentieth Party Congress in 1956, Gerasimov was criticized for having encouraged Stalin's "cult of personality." His paintings were withdrawn from the Tret'iakov Gallery.
9. The widely circulated story about a sculpture contest in honor of Pushkin, and how it was won by an entry portraying Stalin reading a volume of Pushkin, is unfortunately without foundation. There were a number of statues of Stalin reading or holding books, but these did not usually show the title of the book.
10. Shostakovich on at least one occasion denied that this movement had any such program, but he was overruled by Stalin, Zhdanov, and the Soviet people.
11. *Pravda*, October 22, 1946, p. 4.
12. E.g., *The Stone Man*, released in 1950. Here a youth of twelve or so, although frightened of enemies and of a mysterious stone man with Medusa-like powers, eventually triumphs over brigands who are trying to prevent his father from building a solid stone house. The youth grows in the struggle, like Popeye under similar circumstances, not because he eats spinach but because he is shown how to work and fight by the stone man (a good power after all), who appears at the height of the fight to turn the brigands into stone. One need have no hesitation about identifying the youth as the positive hero, the stone man as Stalin, etc.
13. These and many other changes between the original text and

the 1953 edition were culled by David H. Stewart, "The Textual Evolution of *The Silent Don,*" *American Slavic and East European Review,* Vol. XVIII, No. 2 (April, 1959), pp. 226-37.

14. These limitations were almost transcended at times in a few novels, such as Vera Panova, *The Train,* most of which takes place at the disastrous beginning of the war. They were definitely not transcended in the Soviet war book that proved most popular in America, Konstantin Simonov's *Days and Nights,* an account of the Battle of Stalingrad.

15. One of the most extraordinary of the "cubist" statue bases lies under an ordinary statue of Lenin at the main entrance to the Gorky Park of Culture and Rest, in Tashkent

16. This was the occasion of the famous exchange between Bogoliubov and the chess correspondent of *Pravda,* who asked him, "In your opinion, is it a decisive advantage to play the white pieces?" Bogoliubov replied, "When I am white, I win because I am white; when I am black, I win because I am Bogoliubov."

17. A suggestion in the early 1950's to rename the red pieces "proletarians," etc., found no favor on high.

18. In a less dramatic version, "Perhaps they will fight for Mother Russia."

CHAPTER 11

See Louis Fischer, *The Soviets in World Affairs, 1917-1927,* 2nd ed., Princeton: Princeton University Press, 1951, two vols.; Max Beloff, *The Foreign Policy of Soviet Russia, 1929-1941,* New York: Oxford University Press, Vol. I: 1947, Vol. II: 1949; Franz Borkenau, *World Communism: a History of the Communist International,* New York: W. W. Norton, 1939; *Istoriia velikoi otechestvenoi voiny Sovetskaia Soiuza* (History of the Great Patriotic War of the Soviet Union), Moscow: State Publishing House, six volumes, 1960-64; Alexander Werth, *Russia at War, 1941-1945,* New York: E. P. Dutton, 1964; Alexander Dallin, *German Rule in Russia, 1941-1945,* London: Macmillan Co., 1957.

1. This was precisely Stalin's answer to this question when it was asked by the correspondent of *Finskii Vestnik,* December 17, 1928, p. 3.

2. *Ibid.,* pp. 3-4.

3. Georgi Dimitrov, *Reports to the Seventh Congress of the Communist International in Moscow, July-August, 1935* (Moscow: Foreign Languages Publishing House, 1935), pp. 78-81.

4. There were two exceptions to this general policy of helping Hitler. The Soviet government eventually refused to deliver its raw materials to the Germans until the latter came through with their

promised deliveries of manufactured goods, which were falling into serious arrears due to pressure on German production. And the Yugoslav Communists adopted a resistance line against the German conquerors of their country even before the Germans invaded the USSR—presumably not on Stalin's orders.

5. Churchill, *The Grand Alliance* (Boston: Houghton Mifflin Co., 1950), pp. 320-323.

6. Alexander Werth, *Russia at War, 1941-1945* (New York: E. P. Dutton, 1964), pp. 122-123.

7. Churchill, *op. cit.*, p. 333.

8. The author follows to some degree the arguments of Michael Cherniavsky, "Corporal Hitler, General Winter, and the Russian Peasant," *Yale Review*, Spring, 1962, pp. 86-108.

9. This charge was said to have drawn a particular gasp of horror from Khrushchëv's audience when he presented it during his secret speech at the Twentieth Party Congress in 1956.

10. Djilas, *Conversations with Stalin*, p. 60.

11. This is the leading distortion in the otherwise vastly informative official Soviet history of World War II published under Khrushchëv, *Istoriia velikoi otechestvenoi voiny Sovetskaia Soiuza* (History of the Great Patriotic War of the Soviet Union) (Moscow: State Publishing House, six volumes, 1960-64.

12. *Vide* Heinz Guderian, *Panzer Leader* (London: Routledge & Kegan Paul, 1952), and Walter Goerlitz, *Der Zweite Weltkrieg* (Stuttgart, 1951, two volumes).

13. Cherniavsky, *op. cit.*, p. 102.

14. The Russians claim that only 175,000 troops surrendered in the trap. Khrushchëv claimed that he urged the army to withdraw in time, but that Stalin insisted on a rigid defense, producing disaster.

CHAPTER 12

1. We still cannot be certain whether Stalin died of a series of apoplectic strokes, as announced, or whether he was done in by some of his own henchmen to save their necks from his next purge. With no confirming evidence of foul play after all these years, it is highly probable that Stalin *did* die a natural death. Mikoyan has sometimes regaled pompous foreign visitors with a story about how Beria danced for joy around the body of Stalin, until Stalin rallied briefly, opened a baleful eye, transfixed Beria with a stare, and reduced him to whimpering for forgiveness on his hands and knees. Those who are tempted to believe such things should study the similar scene in Eisenstein's film, *Ivan the Terrible, Part I* (1942).

BIBLIOGRAPHY

1. LIVES OF STALIN

Barbusse, Henri: *Stalin, a New World Seen Through One Man*, New York: Macmillan Co., 1935. The most nearly attractive Communist biography of Stalin.

Deutscher, Isaac: *Stalin, a Political Biography*, New York: Oxford University Press, 1949. The only major life of Stalin to carry the story through World War II, and consequently the most widely read. Exceedingly useful, in spite of its semi-Hegelian theory of history and its "moderate" judgments that now seem rather too pro-Stalin.

Levine, Isaac Don: *Stalin*, New York: Cosmopolitan Book Corp., 1931. This was the earliest useful life of Stalin, covering his first fifty years through his rise to power.

Souvarine, Boris: *Stalin: a Critical Survey of Bolshevism*, New York: Alliance Book Corp., 1939. This Franco-Russian former Communist broke with Stalin to write the most massively documented and effectively condemning biography that has yet appeared.

Trotsky, Leon: *Stalin, an Appraisal of the Man and His Influence*, New York: Harper & Brothers, 1941. Left incomplete when Trotsky was murdered, this book is naturally very hostile to Stalin. It combines Trotsky's thesis that Stalin was the instrument of the bureaucratic degeneration of the Party with a large number of unflattering personal anecdotes and details.

Wolfe, Bertram D.: *Three Who Made a Revolution*, New York: Dial Press, 1948; Chapters XXIII-XXXVI. The most thorough presentation of Stalin's life up to 1914, and of Stalin's rewriting of it.

2. WORKS OF STALIN

Sochineniia (Collected Works), Moscow: State Publishing House, 1946-48, thirteen volumes. The series ends with material from January, 1934. It is neither complete nor accurate up to that year, having been edited and censored during the worst period of rewriting history after World War II. *Works* (English translation), issued 1953-1955.

Many, but by no means all, of Stalin's later speeches and writings can be found in *Pravda* and *Izvestiia*, and in the Communist theoretical magazine *Bolshevik*. A number of Stalin's war speeches were reprinted in *O velikoi otechestvennoi voine Sovetskogo Soiuza* (On the Great Patriotic War of the Soviet Union), Moscow: State Publishing House, 5th edition, 1945. Available in English are Stalin's last two major writings, *Marxism and Questions of Linguistics*, Moscow: Foreign Languages Publishing House, 1950; and *Economic Problems of Communism*, Moscow: Foreign Languages Publishing House, 1952.

3. STALIN'S RISE TO POWER

In addition to some of the biographies listed above, see:

Carr, Edward Hallet: *A History of Soviet Russia, 1917-1929*, New York: Macmillan Co. (six volumes have appeared since 1950). The most ambitious and thorough non-Communist work to appear on the period. Written chiefly from Bolshevik sources, and concerned chiefly with the Bolshevik Party and regime. Professor Carr seems to believe that Lenin was a truly great man, but he is determinedly dispassionate about Stalin and Trotsky.

Chamberlin, William Henry: *The Russian Revolution*, New York: Macmillan Co., 1935, two volumes. Probably the best over-all history of the Russian Revolution from 1917 to 1921, hostile to the Bolsheviks, of mixed judgments about the Whites.

Deutscher, Isaac: *The Prophet Armed* and *The Prophet Unarmed*, New York: Oxford University Press, 1954 and 1959. These are the first two volumes of the three-volume biography of Trotsky, and take him up to his exile from the USSR in 1929. They deal extensively with the struggle with Stalin.

Schapiro, Leonard: *The Communist Party of the Soviet Union*, New York: Random House, 1960. The best over-all history of the Communist Party, under Lenin as well as under Stalin, covering thoroughly the ideology, politics, organization, and sociology of the Party.

The two best biographies of Lenin are Shub, David: *Lenin*, Garden

City: Doubleday & Co., 1949; and Fischer, Louis, *The Life of Lenin*, New York: Harper & Row, 1964.

4. THE POLITICS, INSTITUTIONS, AND METHODS OF STALIN'S RULE

Bauer, R. A.: *The New Man in Soviet Psychology*, Cambridge: Harvard University Press, 1952. Deals with Communist ideology, education, propaganda, and other efforts to remake humanity.

Beck, F., and Godin, W.: *Russian Purge and the Extraction of Confession*, New York: Viking Press, 1951. Clears up most mysteries about Stalin's methods.

Berman, Harold J.: *Justice in Russia*, Cambridge: Harvard University Press, 1950; and Hazard, John N.: *Law and Change in the USSR*, London: Stevens, Ltd., 1953. The two most interesting and thorough discussions of the rough course of law and justice in Stalin's Russia.

Brzezinski, Zbigniew K.: *The Permanent Purge*, Cambridge: Harvard University Press, 1956. Informative and stimulating analysis, presenting the thesis that the purge is the central, essential, and permanent institution of the Communist system.

Counts, George S.: *The Challenge of Soviet Education*, New York: Macmillan Co., 1957. Probably the most comprehensive of the many books on the history and nature of Soviet education.

Dallin, David J., and Nicolaevsky, Boris I.: *Forced Labor in Soviet Russia*, New Haven: Yale University Press, 1947. The most fruitful investigation into an intractable subject.

Fainsod, Merle: *How Russia is Ruled*, Cambridge: Harvard University Press, 1953. The classic work on Stalin's system, covering all aspects of Stalin's rule, both historically and analytically. Presents the most convincing picture of Stalin's machine as a coherent *system* for safeguarding and extending power.

———: *Smolensk under Soviet Rule*, Cambridge: Harvard University Press, 1958. Illustration of Stalin's system based on the archives of the Smolensk provincial government, captured by the Germans in 1941 and by the Americans in 1945.

Fedotoff-White, D.: *The Growth of the Red Army*, Princeton: Princeton University Press, 1944; and Liddell Hart, B. H., ed.: *The Red Army*, New York: Harcourt, Brace, 1956. These probably contain the most material about the pre-war and war developments of the Soviet armed forces.

Inkeles, Alex: *Public Opinion in the USSR: a Study in Mass Persuasion*, Cambridge: Harvard University Press, 1950. Deals with the endless ramifications of Stalin's propaganda machine.

Moore, Barrington: *Soviet Politics—the Dilemma of Power*, and *Terror and Progress—USSR*, Cambridge: Harvard University Press, 1950 and 1954. Stimulating examinations of Stalin's system in the light of the "dilemma"—that too much security and terror impede modern industrial progress, and vice versa.

Rostow, Walt Whitman: *The Dynamics of Soviet Society*, New York: W. W. Norton, 1952. A controversial effort to find a system in Stalin's system.

Schapiro, Leonard: *The Communist Party of the Soviet Union*, Part III, New York: Random House, 1960.

Schlesinger, Rudolf: *Changing Attitudes in the Soviet Union: The Family*, London: Routledge and Kegan Paul, 1949. Records the great change from early Revolutionary freedom to Stalinism.

Towster, Julian: *Political Power in the USSR*, New York: Oxford University Press, 1948. Intelligent analysis of Stalin's system, written when Stalin and world conditions made such an enterprise difficult.

Wolin, Simon, and Slusser, Robert, eds.: *The Soviet Secret Police*, New York: Frederick A. Praeger, 1957. Valuable on Stalin's police and the changes immediately after him.

5. ECONOMIC DEVELOPMENT UNDER STALIN

Belov, Fëdor: *A History of a Soviet Collective Farm*, New York: Frederick A. Praeger, 1955. Written by a chairman of a *kolkhoz*, who later escaped to tell his story.

Bergson, Abram: *The Real National Income of Soviet Russia Since 1928*, Cambridge: Harvard University Press, 1961. The culmination of the most impressive series of technical studies of the Soviet economy.

Bienstock, G., Schwarz, S. M., and Yugow, A.: *Management in Soviet Industry and Agriculture*, New York: Oxford University Press, 1944; Granick, David: *The Red Executive*, New York: Doubleday, 1960; Berliner, Joseph S.: *Factory and Manager in the USSR*, Cambridge: Harvard University Press, 1957. The three standard works on Soviet economic elites. Granick is the most sociological and readable.

Cressey, George B.: *The Basis of Soviet Strength*, New York: McGraw-Hill, 1945; and Shabad, Theodore: *Geography of the USSR: a Regional Survey*, New York: Columbia University Press, 1951. Cressey is more analytic and cautious about Soviet potential. Shabad is more up to date.

Dobb, Maurice: *Soviet Economic Development Since 1917*, London: Routledge and Kegan Paul, 1948; Baykov, Alexander: *The Development of the Soviet Economic System*, Cambridge: Harvard University Press, 1946; Schwartz, Harry: *Russia's Soviet Economy*, New York:

Prentice-Hall, 1954. To date, the three standard histories of economic development under Lenin and Stalin. Dobb is Marxist, but often valuable nonetheless. Baykov tries to be objective, and succeeds. Schwartz gives full vent to skepticism and criticism. Schwartz's work has the advantage of covering Stalin's last decade, is broader in scope and awareness of the human consequences of economics, is soundest in its judgments, and is easily the best for the general reader.

Erlich, Alexander: *The Soviet Industrialization Debate, 1924-1928*, Cambridge: Harvard University Press, 1961. The classic analysis of the momentous politico-economic debate that led up to Stalin's forward plunge.

Jasny, Naum: *The Socialized Agriculture of the USSR*, Stanford: Stanford University Press, 1949. An enormous, vastly informative, but excessively skeptical work.

Schwarz, Solomon M.: *Labor in the Soviet Union*, New York: Frederick A. Praeger, 1952; Holzman, Franklin D.: *Soviet Taxation*, Cambridge: Harvard University Press, 1955; Sosnovy, Timothy: *The Housing Problem in the USSR*, New York: Research Program on the USSR, 1954. The best works on their respective subjects.

6. Minority Groups under Stalin

Barghoorn, Frederick C.: *Soviet Russian Nationalism*, New York: Oxford University Press, 1956. Studies attitudes and institutions as they developed under Stalin.

Hostler, Charles Warren: *Turkism and the Soviets*, New York: Frederick A. Praeger, 1957. Combines the history of the Soviet Turks with developments south of the Soviet border.

Kolarz, Walter: *Russia and Her Colonies*, London: George Philip & Son, 1952. Still the most comprehensive study of minority peoples under Stalin.

Manning, Clarence A.: *The Ukraine under the Soviets;* and Dmytryshyn, Basil: *Moscow and the Ukraine, 1918-1953*, New York: Bookman Associates, 1953 and 1956. Both tell the story, but somewhat tendentiously.

Pipes, Richard: *The Formation of the Soviet Union: Nationalism and Communism*, Cambridge: Harvard University Press, 1948. Excellent history of the subject up to Lenin's illness and Stalin's Constitution.

Schwarz, Solomon M.: *The Jews in the Soviet Union*, Syracuse: Syracuse University Press, 1951; and Baron, Salo: *The Russian Jew under Tsar and Soviet*, New York: Macmillan Co., 1964. Schwarz has more space to devote to the subject, Baron incorporates recent research.

Vakar, Nicholas: *Belorussia*, Cambridge: Harvard University Press, 1956. Informative but tendentious.

7. SOVIET CULTURE AND STALIN

Curtiss, John Shelton: *The Russian Church and the Soviet State, 1917-1950*, Boston: Little, Brown & Co., 1953; and Kolarz, Walter: *Religion in the Soviet Union*, New York: Macmillan Co., 1961. These are the two best and most thorough studies; Kolarz covers the non-Orthodox religions as well.

Morton, Henry W.: *Soviet Sport*, New York: Collier Books, 1963. The pioneering work in its field.

Struve, Gleb: *Soviet Russian Literature, 1917-1950*, Norman: University of Oklahoma Press, 1951; and Slonim, Marc: *Modern Russian Literature from Chekhov to the Present*, New York: Oxford University Press, 1953. Probably the two most comprehensive and sensitive works on the subject.

Varneke, B. V.: *History of the Soviet Theatre*, New York: Macmillan Co., 1951; and Leyda, Jay: *Kino: A History of the Russian and Soviet Film*, New York: Macmillan Co., 1960. Cover their respective fields. There are no sound and comprehensive histories of the visual or musical arts in the USSR.

8. STALIN'S FOREIGN POLICY AND WORLD WAR II

Beloff, Max: *The Foreign Policy of the Soviet Union, 1929-1941*, New York: Oxford University Press, Vol. I: 1947, Vol. II: 1949. A deliberate continuation of the Fischer work (below), perhaps more solid, but without Fischer's values or fire.

Borkenau, Franz: *World Communism: A History of the Communist International*, New York: W. W. Norton, 1939. A thorough study by an ex-Communist who knew the men and events he described.

Brzezinski, Zbigniew K.: *The Soviet Bloc: Unity and Conflict*, Cambridge: Harvard University Press, 1960. The best study of Soviet policies and troubles in Eastern Europe, from World War II to Khrushchëv.

Dallin, Alexander: *German Rule in Russia, 1941-1945*, London: Macmillan Co., 1957. The definitive work on the subject.

Fischer, Louis: *The Soviets in World Affairs, 1917-1929*, 2nd ed., Princeton: Princeton University Press, 1951, two volumes. Although Fischer was rather pro-Bolshevik in the late 1920's when this work was written, it has stood the test of time. The classic study of its subject, incorporating the fruits of friendship with most of the makers of early Soviet foreign policy.

Istoriia velikoi otechestvennoi voiny Sovetskogo Soiuza (History of the Great Patriotic War of the Soviet Union), Moscow: State Publishing House, six volumes, 1960-64. The official Khrushchëvist history of the war, which consequently exaggerates Khrushchëv's importance and right-mindedness throughout the war. Nevertheless, it contains a vast amount of apparently accurate material, including much very frank analysis of the disasters of 1941. It will always be an indispensable source book.

Seton-Watson, Hugh: *From Lenin to Malenkov* (reprinted as *From Lenin to Khrushchëv*), New York: Frederick A. Praeger, 1953. An intelligent but breakneck survey of all Communist movements in Russia and abroad.

Werth, Alexander: *Russia at War, 1941-1945*, New York: E. P. Dutton, 1964. The most comprehensive work on the Russo-German war, full of perceptive reportage from an unequaled eyewitness, less penetrating on military events, thorough on political and diplomatic events.

INDEX

abortions, 77
Afghanistan, 226, 231, 262
Africa, 71
agit-prop, see propaganda
agriculture, 144-70 *passim; see also* collectivization of agriculture; peasants
Akhmatova, Anna, 108
Albania, 288
alcoholism, 194-5
Alekhine (Alëkhin), Alexander, 255, 256
Alexander Nevsky (film by Eisenstein), 74
Allilueva, Nadezhda, 37
alphabetical revolutions, 230, 232
America, 92, 101, 171, 180, 269, 277, 281, 284, 287, 289, 291
animals, slaughter of during collectivization, 159-60, 231
anthropology, 71-2
anti-Semitism, 49, 104, 219-26; *see also* Jews
Antonov-Ovseenko, Vladimir, 245
apparatus of the Communist Party, 105-7, 128-9, 198
architecture, 242, 249-54
Armenia and Armenians, 104, 206, 209
army, *see* Red Army
art, 205, 236-9, 243; *see also* architecture

artel, 153, 156-7, 161, 165; *see also* collective farms
Asia, 17-9, 71
Central (Turkestan), 209, 229, 230, 231
"Asiatic mode of production," 18, 79, 196
assassination, Stalin's fears of, 121-4
astronomy, 68-9
Atatürk, Mustafa Kemal, 230, 232
atheism, 24-5, 64-6, 207, 257
atoms, atomic bomb, 66-7, 172, 269, 290
Austria, 289
Azerbaidzhan, 209, 230

Babeuf, Gracchus, 73, 82
Babi Yar, massacre at, 224
Bach, Johann Sebastian, 243
Baku, 32
Bakunin, Mikhail, 84
Balkarians, 213
Baltic States, 209, 271, 277
Balzac, Honoré de, 239
Bandera, Stepan, 218
Barcelona, 268
Basmachi risings, 230
Beethoven, Ludwig van, 73, 243
Belorussians, 206, 209
Bergson, Abram, 11
Beria, Lavrenti, 106, 129, 141

319

Berlin, 273, 274, 287
Bessarabia, 271, 280
biology, 69-71, 115
Birobidzhan, 223
Black Hats, 230
black markets, see crime and black marketeering
Blum, Léon, 266-7
Bogoliubov, Evfim, 255
Bohr, Niels, 67
Bolsheviks, see Communist Party
Borotba group, 215
Botvinnik, Mikhail, 256
Brest-Litovsk, Treaty of, 45
Budënny, Semën, 282
Bukharin, Nigolai, 62, 134, 135, 136, 147, 151, 154, 155
Bulgaria, 215, 288
bureaucracy, see apparatus of the Communist Party; Communist Party; middle class, new Soviet

Canada, 180, 289
capitalism, 79, 82, 83, 84, 87, 92, 99-100, 108, 221
capitulations to the police, 130
Caucasus region (Transcaucasia), 17, 25, 28, 30, 32, 33, 72, 206, 226, 227
cells of the Communist Party, 85, 105
censorship, 27, 107-9
Central Committee of the Communist Party, 33, 39, 59, 62, 128, 155
Chapaev, Vasili (1451), *Chapaev* (film by Vasiliev brothers), 74
Chechen-Ingush, 213
Cheka, 6, 129-30, 140; see also police
Chernov, Viktor, 6
Chernyshevsky, Nikolai, 67, 74, 240, 243
chess, 36, 254-6
Chiang Kai-shek, 14, 267, 288
children, 74-5, 112, 118, 189
China, Chinese Communist Party, 2, 87, 89, 163, 165, 262, 267, 285, 289-90
Christianity, 17, 82, 239, 256-8
Churchill, Winston, 3, 14, 90, 108, 163, 272, 273
Chuvash, 233
civil defense, 117
Civil War, Russian, 6, 37, 42, 44, 45, 56, 57, 86, 87, 126, 129, 207-8, 214, 215, 220
class struggle, 79-80
collective farms, 98, 152-3, 156-7, 160-1, 163-8
collectivization of agriculture, 147-63, 217, 231
Comintern (the Communist International), 48, 58, 211, 261-2, 265-6, 270
communes, 153, 161
Communism, see Communist Party, ideology; Lenin, Vladimir; Stalin, Joseph Vissarionovich
Communist Party
and Stalin, 1-6
before the Revolution, 25-36 *passim*
in the Revolution of 1917, 36-42
in the Civil War, 42-5
intra-Party struggles in as Stalin rises to power, 44-63 *passim*
ideology, 64-95 *passim*
membership and organization, 101-7, 217, 222
in Great Purges, 133-4
and Great Debate, 146-51
and peasants, 151-70

INDEX

and Five Year Plans, 155, 172-202
and workers, 183-195
and new Soviet middle class, 195-202
and national minorities, 203-33
and culture, 238, 239, 245, 258
and foreign affairs, 259-73
and World War II, 273-86
in Stalin's last years, 287-91
after Stalin's death, 291-2
computers, 175-6
Congresses of the Communist Party, 105
  6th in 1917, 40
  10th in 1921, 44
  12th in 1923, 48, 49, 216
  13th in 1924, 59
  15th in 1927, 148, 151, 177
  14th in 1925, 154
  19th in 1952, 291
Constitution of the USSR, 204
  of 1924, 57, 60, 99, 208, 209, 210
  of 1936, 98-9, 110, 136, 209-10
consumer goods, 181, 187-8, 291
contraceptives, 77
Copernicus, Nicholas, 82
cosmopolitanism, 221
counterrevolutionary threats, 97-101, 146, 155
Courbet, Gustave, 236, 239
crime and black marketeering, 109, 188-9, 198-9
Crimean Tatars, 213, 230, 232
Cuba, 89
cult of personality, 2, 20, 97
culture, 2, 234-58 *passim*, 291
currency "reform," 188
Czechoslovakia, 266, 287, 288

Daghestan, 216, 233
Darkness at Noon by Arthur Koestler, 135

Darwin, Charles, 69, 71, 73
Daumier, Honoré, 239
death toll, *see* killings; war losses
democracy, 62, 117, 209
democratic centralism, 105
Democritus, 73, 81
Depression of 1929-1939, 8-9, 180, 263
determinism and freedom, 4-8
dialectical materialism, 68, 82-3, 235
dictatorship of the proletariat, 55-6, 57
Dimitrov, Georgi, 265-6
Djilas, Milovan, 36, 78, 195-6
Djugashvili, *see* Stalin, Joseph Vissarionovich
Dnieprostroi Dam, 174, 177, 212
doctors' plot, 225
Dostoevsky, Fëdor, 78, 135
Dzerzhinsky, Felix, 140

"the East," 18-9, 212, 232
Eastern Europe, 92, 101, 163, 216, 225, 266, 285-9, 291
economic interpretations of history, 4-5, 78, 96-8
Economic Problems of Socialism in the USSR by Stalin, 291
education, 110-7, 201
Eisenhower, Dwight, 90
Eisenstein, Sergei, 74, 137, 244, 245
ends and means, 89-90
Engels, Friedrich, 67, 68, 83, 93
Enver Bey Pasha, 229
Epicurus, 82
evolution, 68, 71

Fainsod, Merle, 3, 127
family life, 20-3, 77, 116, 118, 119
famine of 1933, 160, 164, 217

Fascism, 263
feudalism, 81-2
films, 243-5
Finland and the Finns, 30, 40, 209, 212, 271, 280, 288
Five Year Plans, 174, 175, 176, 177-83, 197, 212, 219, 223, 248-9, 263, 264, 283-4
  First, 10, 77, 118, 119, 131, 155, 176-8
  Second, 178, 271
  Third, 178, 271, 282
folk culture, 215, 242
foreign policy, 259-73
Fourier, Charles, 82
France, French Communist Party, 228, 265, 266, 267, 270, 271, 288, 289
Franco, Francisco, 267-8
French Revolution, 26, 56, 82, 97, 239
Freud, Sigmund, and Freudian theories, 14, 21, 22, 23, 76, 137
Frunze, Mikhail 61-2

garden plots of peasants, 168
genetics, 69-71
genius, 2, 73-4, 116
geology, 68-9
Georgia and the Georgians, 15-8, 20, 21, 23, 26, 28, 32, 44, 45, 47, 57, 104, 122, 140, 141, 204, 205, 209, 211
Germans, Volga, 213
Germany and the Germans, 18, 40, 45, 60, 82, 100, 135, 137, 180, 218, 224-5, 262, 263, 270-83
  East Germany, 108, 288
  German Communist Party, 263-4
  German Socialist Party, 263-4
Goebbels, Joseph, 108
Goethe, Johann Wolfgang von, 73, 94

Gogol, Nikolai, 240
Gorer, Geoffrey, 16
Gori, 15, 17, 20, 24
Gorky, Maxim, 240
Gosplan (State Planning Commission), 173, 176, 177, 180
G.P.U., 130-2; *see also* police
Great Britain, 228, 271, 272, 275, 278, 284
Great Debate in the Communist Party, 87-8, 146-51
Great Purges, 6, 45, 76-7, 99, 101, 129, 133-41, 217, 224, 231, 284
Great Russians, 56-7, 104, 201, 203, 204, 207, 212, 214, 220, 223, 224
Greece
  ancient, 81-2, 239
  modern, 276, 278, 288
Guderian, Heinz, 276

head flattening, 17
Hebrew, 221-2
Hegel, Georg W. F., 82
Heisenberg, Werner, 67
Hiss, Alger, 269
history, writing of, 242
Hitler, Adolf, 2, 4, 7, 9, 14, 15, 20, 44, 101, 122, 139, 181, 182, 183, 224, 259, 263, 256, 268, 270-85 *passim*, 294
Hoover, Herbert, 10
hours of labor, 190
housing, 193-5, 200
Hrushevsky, Mikhail, 216
Hugo, Victor, 24, 26
human nature, 72-3, 78
Hungary, 165, 233, 262, 288

idealism, 64, 82
ideology, 5, 6
  definition of, 12-3
  Lenin's, 64-95

Stalin's, 64-95
  of power and terror, 96-101, 102, 107, 115-6, 124, 131-2, 137
  of collectivization and industrialization, 144-6, 153-8, 162, 164-5, 169-70, 172-6, 190-1
  of nationalities, 203-8, 220-1
  of culture, 235-43, 254, 256
  of foreign policy and war, 259-60, 270, 274, 285
  of Stalin's last years, 287, 290, 291, 292
illiteracy, 110-1
imperialism, Soviet, 201, 227-8
incentives to work, 166-8, 181, 187-8
India, 228, 291
Indonesia, 207
industrialization, 1, 5, 6, 8, 9, 82, 93, 146-52, 155, 171-202 passim, 211-2, 228, 231, 233, 293
inevitability of war, 259, 270
intelligentsia, 24, 25, 29
interest, 174
International Brigades, 267
Iran, 226, 262
Iremashvili, Joseph, 29
Iron Curtain, 108, 287, 291
Israel, 225
Italy, 288, 289
Iudenich, Nikolai, 42
Ivan the Terrible (film by Eisenstein), 244

Japan, 90, 180, 183, 223, 265, 267, 269, 270
Jews, 104, 119, 199, 206, 211, 214, 218, 219-26, 256, 258, 265

Kaganovich, 185, 216, 220
Kalinin, Mikhail, 223

Kalmyks, 206, 213
Kamenev, Lev, 48, 49, 50, 59, 60, 61, 62, 130, 133, 134, 220
Kaplan, Fania, 43
Karachai, 213
Kataev, Valentin, 248
Katyn forest, massacre of, 132
Kazakhs, 217, 231
Kerensky, Alexander, 6, 40
Khachaturian, Aram, 244
Khrushchëv, Nikita, 10, 11, 36, 91, 106, 122, 123, 124, 128, 133, 134, 137, 139, 167, 169, 182, 197, 217, 218, 219, 274, 275, 292
Khvylovy, Mykola, 217
Kiev, 216, 224
killings, 2, 8, 20, 44, 62, 70, 89-90, 125-141 *passim*, 162, 213, 217, 218, 224, 231, 268
Kirov, Sergei, 133
"Koba," pseudonym for Stalin, 33-4
Koestler, Arthur, 135
kolkhoz; see collective farms
Kollontai, Alexandra, 77, 104
Komsomol, 102-3, 114
Kondratiev, Nikolai, 175
Korea, 287, 288, 290
Kornilov, Lavr, 40-1
Kossior, Stanislav, 134, 217
Kremlin, 30, 50, 123, 132, 242, 275, 279
Krupskaia, Nadezhda, 31, 59, 104
Kuibyshev (city), 229
kulaks, 98, 99-100, 131, 144-59 *passim*
Kun, Bela, 262
Kursk, battle of, 276
Kuznets Basin, 177

labor camps, 10, 118, 291, *see also* Siberia

324   INDEX

labor discipline, 191-5
labor turnover, 191-2
language, 205-7, 211
Lavrov, Piotr, 84
League of Militant Atheists, 257
League of Nations, 261
left opposition, 61-2, 133, 162
left strategy, 146, 149
Lend-Lease, 281
Lenin, Vladimir, 6, 12, 14, 15, 18, 19, 20, 25
    ideology and activities, 12, 19, 34, 60, 62-3, 66, 67, 68, 73, 77, 83-7, 89, 93, 95, 97-8, 111, 129, 138-9, 145, 174, 185, 215, 219, 235, 254, 260, 270, 285, 290, 292
    career, 30, 31, 32, 33, 34, 39-43, 44, 46-51
    Testament, 47-8, 59
    funeral, 50-1, 58
    in "Stalin's Vow" speech, 52-9
    tomb, 58, 123, 249
Leningrad, 271-6; *see also* Petrograd; St. Petersburg
Leningrad Symphony by Shostakovich, 242
Leninism, *see* ideology; Lenin, Vladimir
Leonardo da Vinci, 82
Leontiev, Vasili, 175
linguistics, 205
literacy, 110-1
literature, 112, 236, 237, 238-41, 243
Little Octobrists, 102
Lomonosov, Mikhail, 73
Ludwig, Emil, 22
Luxemburg, Rosa, 86
Lysenko, Trofim, 70

Machine Tractor Stations, 166-7
Madrid, 267
Magnitogorsk, 174, 177, 194
Maiakovsky, Vladimir, 244
Makhno, Nestor, 214
Malenkov, Georgi, 106, 129, 197, 200
Malinowski, Roman, 35-6
Manchuria, 288, 290
Mao Tse-tung, 1, 44, 79, 163, 182, 289-90
Marr, Nikolai, 205
Marx, Karl, 6, 15, 23, 24, 44, 56, 66, 67, 68, 73, 82, 83, 86, 93, 221, 285
Marxism, Marxism-Leninism, *see* ideology; Lenin, Vladimir; Stalin, Joseph Vissarionovich
Marxism and the National Question by Stalin, 35, 204, 206-7
materialism, 64, 66-7, 68, 82, 235
mathematical economics, 175-6
Mead, Margaret, 16
membership of Communist Party, 59, 101-2, 133
Mendel, Gregor, 70
Mendeleev, Dmitri, 66
Mensheviks, 27, 32, 39, 45, 47, 102
Messame Dassy, 26-7
Mexico, 153
Meyerhold, Vsevolod, 241, 244
Michelangelo, 73, 94
Michurin, Ivan, 70
middle class, new Soviet, 103, 137, 195-202
Mikoyan, Anastas, 106, 124, 137
minorities, national, 203-33 *passim*; *see also* nationalities
Molotov, Viacheslav, 7, 39, 46, 122, 132, 176, 272, 289
monks, 24-6, 65-6, 257
Morelly, Abbé, 82
Morgan, Thomas Hunt, 70
Morozov, Pavlik, 75

Moscow, 42, 48, 51, 127, 140
  279, 280, 281
  battle of, 273, 274, 276, 277, 278,
  State University, 250-1, 253,
  Agricultural Exposition, 250
Mother by Gorky, 240
murders, *see* killings
music, 242, 243
Muslims, 17, 19, 193, 195, 226-33
Musorgsky, Modest, 239
Mussolini, Benito, 14, 90, 263

narodniks, *see* Socialist
  Revolutionaries and
  narodniks
National Communism, 215-6, 290
nationalism, 207-8, 210-1
nationalities, 34, 35, 40, 41-2, 44,
  56-7, 58, 79-80, 104, 203-33,
  257
NATO, 289
natural resources, 171-2
Nazis, *see* Hitler, Adolf
Nechaev, Sergei, 84
Negro, American, 206, 214
Nekrasov, Nikolai, 241-2
Nevsky, Alexander, 205
new countries, 6, 8, 178, 182-3
New Economic Policy (NEP), 44,
  97-8, 146, 151, 183
New Soviet Man, 72, 94, 110, 118
Newton, Isaac, 73
N.K.V.D., 132-5, 141, 268; *see also*
  Great Purges; police
novels, 10, 239-41, 246-9

October (film by Eisenstein), 245
officers of the Red Army, 125-7,
  199, 274-5, 282, 283
oil, 171-2, 178
*One Day in the Life of Ivan
  Denisovich* by Solzhenitsyn,
  135
On Guard for Peace (cantata by

Prokoviev), 242
Ordzhonikidze, Sergo, 122
Orgburo, 43, 46, 222
Orthodox Church, 257-8

painting, 242
Palestine, 221, 223
paranoia, Stalin's, 5, 30, 35-6, 62,
  99, 123-4, 138-42, 273, 286,
  287, 291, 293
Paris, 83
Partisans, 218, 276, 278, 288
Patriarchate, 258
Pauling, Linus, 67
Pavlov, Ivan, 136
peaceful coexistence, 292
peasants, 56, 57, 58, 97-9, 103-4,
  124-5, 131, 144-70 *passim*,
  192-4
personal secretariat, Stalin's, 107
Peter the Great, 286
Petrograd, 39-42, 48; *see also*
  Leningrad; St. Petersburg
physics, 66-7
Pioneers, 102, 114
Plato, 82
Plekhanov, Georgi, 219
poetry, 241-2, 243
Poland and the Poles, 44, 80, 132,
  165, 212, 229, 233, 270, 271,
  277, 288
police, 99, 101, 106, 109, 117, 119,
  127, 129-41 *passim*, 157, 212,
  217, 222, 229, 234, 268, 286,
  287, 291
Tsarist, 24, 25, 27-8, 30, 32, 33
Politburo, 41, 42, 43, 46, 48, 61,
  62, 128, 135
positive hero, 240
Poskrebyshëv, Alexander, 129
Pravda, 33, 51, 161
Preobrazhensky, Evgenii, 149-52,
  155, 162

prisoners of war, 276, 277, 280, 282
Problems of Leninism by Stalin, 60-1
Prokofiev, Sergei, 242, 243, 244
proletariat, 83, 97-9, 103, 172-95 *passim*; *see* workers
propaganda, 91-2, 107, 109-10, 164, 188, 195
prostitution, 77
psychology, 73-8
purges, *see* Great Purges; police
Pushkin, Alexander, 73, 239

The Quiet Don by Sholokhov, 247-8

Rabkhrin, 43, 47, 48
Radek, Karl, 46, 47, 130, 134, 135, 220
railroads, 174, 179
Rakovsky, Khristian, 215, 216
Razin, Stenka, 74, 145, 205
Red Army, 42, 43, 44, 49, 57, 60, 61, 62, 87-8, 92, 106, 157, 210, 268, 272-83, 288
religion, 206, 210, 256-8
Renaissance, 82, 239
Repin, Ilia, 236, 239
revisionism, 83, 292
revolutionaries, Russian, 14, 24, 25, 66, 81, 84, 109, 234, 235, 236, 250
Revolutions
  of 1905, 29, 30
  of 1917, 36-41, 45, 79
right deviation, 130
right strategy, 146-9, 163
Robinson, Geroid Tanquary, 12, 92*n*
Roosevelt, Franklin, 11, 14, 90, 95, 286
Rumania, 209, 271, 288

Russians, *see* Great Russians
Rykov, Aleksei, 62

St. Petersburg, 33, 35, 252; *see also* Leningrad; Petrograd
Schapiro, Leonard, 3
Schwartz, Harry, 3
science, 65, 66-71, 82, 112, 114-5, 172, 235
Secretary-General of the Communist Party, 46, 47, 48, 50, 55, 60
sex, 22-3, 75, 247, 248, 249
Shamil, 216
shock workers, 191
Sholokhov, Mikhail, 247-8
Shvernik, Nikolai, 185
Siberia, 28, 33, 35, 70, 72, 131, 134, 157, 158, 179, 190, 212, 218, 219, 225, 226
Skrypnik, Mykola, 215, 217
Smolensk
  government archive, 10
  battle of, 276, 280
socialism, *see* ideology
socialism in one country, 60, 88-9
Socialist Realism, 238-56
Socialist Revolutionaries and *narodniks*, 39, 43, 71, 73, 84, 144, 215, 239, 241
Solzhenitsyn, Alexander, 135
Sorge, Richard, 269
soviets, 41, 51
  Supreme Soviet, 123, 209, 210
sovkhoz, *see* state farms
Spanish Civil War, 261, 266, 267-8
Spartacus, 73
spies, 100, 268, 272
sports, 112, 119, 186
Stakhanov, Aleksei, and Stakhanovites, 191-2
Stalin, Joseph Vissarionovich

importance and reputation, 1-2, 286, 292, 294
problems concerning, 4-13
birth, 14
origins, family, and childhood, 14-23
education, 23-6
revolutionary career, 24-39
character, 26, 29, 31, 36-8
and Lenin, 30-51
paranoia, 30, 35-6, 62, 99, 123-4, 138-42, 273, 286, 287, 291, 293
rise to power, 41-62
ideology, 64-95
on power, 96-101
and Communist Party, 101-7
propaganda and educational system, 107-17
totalitarianism, 117-20
precautions against overthrow, 121-41
police, 129-141
on agriculture and collectivization, 144-63
on industrialization and the Five Year Plans, 171-83
nationalities policies, 203-33
cultural policies, 234-58
foreign policy to World War II, 259-73
World War II, 273-85
rule after World War II, 286-91
death, 291
"Stalin," pseudonym, 29, 33-4
Stalinallée (East Berlin), 253
Stalingrad (Tsaritsyn), 42, 274, 277
Stalin-Hitler Pact, 270-1
Stalinism, see ideology; Lenin, Vladimir; Stalin, Joseph Vissarionovich
Stalin's parents
father, 20-2
mother, 20-2
first wife, Ekaterina Svanidze, 29
first child, Iakov Djugashvili, 29, 37
second wife, Nadezhda Allilueva, 37
second child, Vasili Stalin, 37-8
third child, Svetlana Stalina, 37-8
"Stalin's Vow" speech, 51-9
standard of living, 169, 192-4, 199-200
Stanislavsky, Konstantin, 241
state farms, 152, 156, 157
statistics, 10-1, 177-80, 198
steel, 178, 179
stomach ulcers, 77
Stravinsky, Igor, 243
students, 112, 115
Sultan-Galiev, Mirza, 229, 230, 231
Svanidze, Ekaterina, 29
Sverdlov, Jacob, 41, 220
swaddling hypothesis, 16-7

Tadzhiks, 233
Tampere (Tammerfors) Conference of Bolsheviks, 30
Tashkent, 231
Tatar-Bashkir Autonomous Republic, 208, 229
taxation, 166-8
Tbilisi (Tiflis), 20, 24, 26, 27
terror, 121-43; see also Great Purges; police
Thaelmann, Ernst, 264
theatre, 241, 243
Time Forward by Valentin Kataev, 249, 254
Timiriazev, Kliment, 70
Tito, Joseph Broz, 216, 287, 289, 290
Titoists, 2, 225

Tkachev, Piotr, 84
Tolstoi, Leo, 236, 240, 246
Tomsky, Mikhail, 62, 185
totalitarianism, 117-8, 143, 169, 293
Toz, 153, 156, 161
trade unions, 185-7, 267
tragedy, 246-8
Transcaucasia, *see* Caucasus region
transmission belts to the masses, 117
Trotsky, Leon, 9, 11, 14, 15, 20, 40-62 *passim*, 106, 125, 126, 135, 196, 216, 220, 222, 262, 265
Trotskyites, 2, 54, 67, 104, 126, 130, 149, 151, 154, 162, 216, 222, 249, 262, 268
Tsarist régime, 14, 24, 28, 30, 36, 84, 85, 86, 252
Tukhachevsky, Mikhail, 126, 137
Turkey, 226, 230, 262, 289
Turks in the USSR, 206, 226-33

Ukraine and the Ukrainians, 47, 57, 104, 160, 206, 208, 209, 212, 213-9, 276, 279, 282
Union of Soviet Writers, 243
Union Republics, 208-9, 215
United Front, 265
United Nations, 287
unity of Communism, 54-5, 58, 59, 290
universities, 102, 114-5, 201
USSR, 60, 81, 88, 92, 98-9, 208, 209
 and foreign Communists, 260
 in World War II, 273-86
Uzbeks, 231

Vienna, 33
Vietnam, 89
Voroshilov, Klim 37, 42, 106, 242

wages, 187-8, 190-1
Walras, Leon, 175
War Communism, 44
war losses, 284-5
Warsaw, 44
weapons, 271, 275, 276, 278, 281-2, 283
What is to be Done? by Chernyshevsky, 240
What is to be Done? by Lenin, 84
winter, Russian, 277, 280
Winter Palace (St. Petersburg), 245
Wittfogel, Karl, 196
women, 76, 104, 112, 113, 189, 200, 254
workers, 56, 58, 80-1; *see also* proletariat
World Revolution, 88, 260, 270, 285, 290
World Wars
 II, 2, 7, 9, 67, 90, 118, 124, 125, 137, 178-83, 202, 212, 259-285, 286, 294
 III, 2, 269, 287, 290
 I, 36, 44, 86

Yagoda, Henryk, 131, 140
Yakuts, 226
Yenukidze, 122
Yezhov, Nikolai, and the *Yezhovshchina*, 141
Yiddish, 221-2, 225, 256
youth, 75, 102-3, 114-7
Yugoslavia, 165, 216, 233, 275, 276, 278, 288, 289

Zhdanov, Andrei, 219, 225, 244
Zinoviev, Grigori, 48, 49, 50, 58, 59, 60, 61, 62, 130, 133, 211, 220, 262
Zionism, 221
Zola, Emile, 236, 239, 240